EGALITARIAN CAPITALISM

EGALITARIAN CAPITALISM

JOBS, INCOMES, AND GROWTH IN AFFLUENT COUNTRIES

LANE KENWORTHY

A Volume in the American Sociological Association's
Rose Series in Sociology

Russell Sage Foundation • New York

Library of Congress Cataloging-in-Publication Data

Kenworthy, Lane.
   Egalitarian capitalism : jobs, incomes, and growth in affluent
countries / Lane Kenworthy.
      p. cm — (Rose series in sociology)
   A study of the differences among 16 countries: Australia, Austria,
Belgium, Canada, Denmark, Finland, France, Germany, Italy, Japan, the Netherlands,
Norway, Sweden, Switzerland, the United Kingdom, and the United States from the
mid-1970s through the 1990s.
   Includes bibliographical references and index.
   ISBN 0-87154-451-2
   1. Income distribution—Developed countries. 2. Developed
countries—Economic conditions. 3. Employment (Economic theory)
4. Economic development. 5. Capitalism—Developed countries.
6. Equality—Developed countries. I. Title: Jobs, incomes, and equality
in affluent countries. II. Title. III. Series.

HC79.I5K415 2004
331.13'3'09172209045—dc22

2004040969

Text design by Suzanne Nichols.

RUSSELL SAGE FOUNDATION
112 East 64th Street, New York, New York 10021
10   9   8   7   6   5   4   3   2   1

Previous Volumes in the Series

Forthcoming Titles

= The Rose Series = in Sociology

The American Sociological Association's Rose Series in Sociology publishes books that integrate knowledge and address controversies from a sociological perspective. Books in the Rose Series are at the forefront of sociological knowledge. They are lively and often involve timely and fundamental issues of significant social concern. The series is intended for broad dissemination throughout sociology, across social science and other professional communities, and to policy audiences. The series was established in 1967 by a bequest to ASA from Arnold and Caroline Rose to support innovations in scholarly publishing.

DOUGLAS L. ANDERTON
DAN CLAWSON
NAOMI GERSTEL
JOYA MISRA
RANDALL STOKES
ROBERT ZUSSMAN

EDITORS

For Kim

Contents

About the Author

Lane Kenworthy is assistant professor of sociology at Emory University.

═ Acknowledgments ═

Iowe thanks to many people who provided helpful comments on various parts of this book. I am particularly grateful to Gøsta Esping-Andersen, Alex Hicks, Bruce Western, and the Rose series editors, especially Joya Misra, who gave me pointed and insightful feedback on the full manuscript. Bernhard Kittel offered very useful advice on substantive and methodological matters relating to several of the chapters. Much of the argument in chapter 3 was developed jointly with Jonas Pontusson. Discussions with Torben Iversen were helpful in advancing my thinking about the issue addressed in chapter 5.

Other colleagues who offered valuable comments and suggestions include Pablo Beramendi, Anders Björklund, John Boli, Terry Boswell, David Brady, Irene Browne, Eero Carroll, Tom Cusack, Bernhard Ebbinghaus, Werner Eichhorst, Tommy Ferrarini, Richard Freeman, Steffen Ganghof, Markus Gangl, Janet Gornick, Karin Gottschall, Anke Hassel, Anton Hemerijck, Larry Kahn, Randi Kjeldstad, Tomas Korpi, Walter Korpi, Antje Kurdelbusch, Frank Lechner, Stephanie Moller, Jim Mosher, John Myles, Joakim Palme, David Rueda, Fritz Scharpf, Marc Schneiberg, Tim Smeeding, John Stephens, Wolfgang Streeck, Duane Swank, Sigurt Vitols, Michael Wallerstein, Christopher Way, Regina Werum, and Erik Wright. A number of graduate students in the sociology department at Emory University also gave me useful feedback: Rachel Askew, Franziska Bieri, Alison Faupel, Kevin Greene, Cindy Hinton, Shelley Matthews, Nital Patel, Velina Petrova, Diogo Pinheiro, Anna Rubtsova, Girija Sankaranarayanan, and Vaughn Schmutz. I apologize to any others whom I may inadvertently have left off this list.

Paul Alkemade, Caroline de Tombeur, Kati Foley, David Jesuit, Tim Smeeding, Dennis Sullivan, and Koen Vleminckx were instrumental in helping me learn how to use the Luxembourg Income Study (LIS) database.

Torben Iversen, Stephen Nickell, Duane Swank, and several analysts at the Organization for Economic Cooperation and Development (OECD) kindly allowed me to borrow unpublished data.

Large portions of the book were written while I was a visiting scholar at the Max Planck Institute for the Study of Societies (MPIfG) in Cologne, Germany. I am very grateful to the institute's directors, Wolfgang Streeck and Fritz Scharpf, for making it possible for me to take advantage of its superb research environment and facilities. I also thank the many colleagues at the institute who helped me to better understand particular details about the economies and societies of various European countries.

For excellent work on the book's editing and production, I thank Cindy Buck, Suzanne Nichols, and Genna Patacsil at Russell Sage.

Needless to say, none of the people I have mentioned should be held responsible for the book's shortcomings.

Most of all, I want to thank my wife and best friend, Kim, who makes it all worthwhile.

═ Chapter 1 ═

Introduction: Egalitarian Capitalism in the Late Twentieth Century

Must we give up on the vision of a dynamic and productive yet relatively egalitarian form of capitalism? This is the question I seek to address in this book.

Many people would prefer to live in a society that is not only affluent but also reasonably egalitarian. In 1999, for example, significant majorities of citizens polled by the International Social Survey Program (ISSP) said that income differences in their country were too large: 71 percent in Australia, 86 percent in Austria, 71 percent in Canada, 88 percent in France, 82 percent in Germany, 69 percent in Japan, 73 percent in Norway, 71 percent in Sweden, 82 percent in the United Kingdom, and 66 percent in the United States (ISSP 1999).

The principal argument for egalitarianism is that it is fair. Much of what determines people's earnings and income—intelligence, creativity, physical and social skills, motivation, persistence, confidence, inherited wealth—is a product of genetics, parents' assets and traits, and the quality of childhood neighborhoods and schools. These things are not chosen; they are a matter of luck. A nontrivial portion of earnings and income inequality is therefore undeserved, which makes institutions and policies that can reduce inequality attractive to many (Rawls 1971; Roemer 1997). Other arguments for equality focus on its consequences. Income inequality may contribute to higher crime rates, disproportionate political power wielded by the wealthy, lower levels of educational attainment, and perhaps even slower economic growth. Of course, few if any egalitarians favor perfect equality of outcomes. Complete equality would substantially reduce work incentives, undermining both economic growth and the principle of reciprocity (all who are able to contribute do so).

A sensible contemporary vision of an egalitarian capitalist society, in my view, would prioritize not only limited income inequality but

1

also high living standards—particularly for those at the bottom of the distribution—and a high employment rate. There are other reasonable aims, such as reducing wealth inequality, improving access to basic material needs, and increasing mobility (Boushey et al. 2001; Gottschalk and Danziger 1998; Leisering and Leibfried 1999; Mayer and Jencks 1989; Wolff 1995/2002). Although I discuss these aims briefly in chapters 6 and 7, for the most part I set them aside in this book. The book is mainly about differences across countries, and data limitations make it much more difficult to draw comparative conclusions about wealth, material hardship, and mobility than about jobs, incomes, and income inequality.

Suggesting that equality should not come at the expense of the living standards of the poor is unlikely to be controversial, but why is a high employment rate important? One argument in favor of employment has to do with its social nature. Heightened geographical mobility, later marriage, and increased divorce have loosened neighborhood and family ties, and as a result, work is an increasingly important site of social interaction. Work has other intrinsic benefits: it imposes regularity and discipline on people's lives. However, the chief argument in favor of high employment is that it is increasingly critical to the goal of limiting income inequality.

This is true in two respects. First, employment affects the distribution of earnings across households. Half a century ago it was normal for many working-age adults to not be in the labor force. They were mainly women, and their husbands were employed. The fact that some adults were employed and others were not had little impact on the distribution of earnings among households because inequality of employment occurred mainly within, rather than between, households. That is no longer the case. With women increasingly in paid work, inequality of employment occurs more and more between households. In other words, instead of having many households with one (usually male) earner and one (usually female) non-earner, a country with a low or moderate employment rate now is more likely to have many households with two earners and many with no earners (Gregg 1996; OECD 1998b). This increases inequality of earnings between households (Förster and Pearson 2002).

Second, employment is important for low inequality in its role in redistribution. Governments engage in redistribution in a variety of ways (Esping-Andersen 1990, 1999; Goodin et al. 1999). "Social democratic" welfare regimes in the Nordic countries provide benefits to most of the population, and those benefits tend to be relatively equal (flat-rate). This in itself alters the distribution of income—assuming taxes are not regressive, giving every household an equal lump sum reduces inequality (Rothstein 1998, 146–47). And redistribution is furthered through some targeting and inequality in benefit levels, as well as through taxing back part of the benefits paid to those who need them the least. (Social democratic welfare states also tend to offer extensive public provision of services, such as health care and child care. Though it does not alter the distribution of income, this too has an equalizing effect.) "Conservative" welfare regimes in the continental European countries rely disproportionately on social insurance programs in which benefit levels are determined by an individual's former labor market status and earnings level. This type of program is not particularly redistributive in design, but because of some targeting and a relatively high overall *level* of transfers, continental welfare states nevertheless do tend to achieve a significant amount of redistribution. In the Anglo (English-speaking) countries, "liberal" welfare regimes provide minimal benefits that are narrowly targeted to the most needy (means-tested). This is the most efficient redistributive strategy; it achieves the most redistribution per amount of income transferred. But in comparative terms the level of transfers in these nations tends to be low, so relatively little redistribution is effected (Korpi and Palme 1998).

Welfare states in all affluent countries currently face a number of threats, of which two are perhaps most critical. The first is a demographic crunch. Most public pension systems are financed on a "pay-as-you-go" basis; benefits for retirees come directly from current taxes. With low fertility rates, limited immigration, and lengthening life spans, the cost of public pensions becomes ever larger relative to the tax base from which they are funded. Since pensions typically are the largest category of social expenditure aside from health care, this puts a severe strain on the welfare state.

The other threat is capital mobility. With investors now able to easily shift resources outside their home country, governments face increased pressure to reduce tax rates. Predictions of an all-out "race to the bottom" thus far have not been borne out, but tax rates have indeed been lowered in most nations. Such reductions are usually accompanied by a broadening of the tax base in order to minimize the reduction in revenues (Ganghof 2000; Genschel 2001). Yet revenues nevertheless have tended to fall. In every affluent nation aside from Norway and the United States, tax revenues as a share of gross domestic product (GDP) are lower than at their peak (typically in the late 1980s or early 1990s).

With tax revenue squeezed at the same time that welfare state costs are rising, something has to give. One option is to adjust the pension system—for example, by raising the retirement age a bit, reducing benefit levels somewhat, or taxing back the benefits of well-to-do retirees at steeper rates. But these measures may not yield enough cost savings.

Another option is to increase immigration. But if many of the immigrants have limited skills, increasing immigration may end up adding to the cost of the welfare state, at least in the short or medium term. The best solution to the dilemma of the welfare state's rising costs and shrinking tax revenues is to increase the employment rate (Esping-Andersen 1999; Esping-Andersen et al. 2002; Ferrera, Hemerijck, and Rhodes 2000; Scharpf and Schmidt 2000). Doing so is doubly beneficial: higher employment yields an increase in tax revenues without an increase in tax rates, and to the extent that employment moves some recipients of government benefits into the workforce, welfare state costs are reduced.

Egalitarians thus should have three goals: low inequality, high living standards, and high employment. During the post–World War II "golden age" it was believed by many that these goals were not only compatible but mutually reinforcing. And through the mid-1970s a handful of countries—Sweden, Denmark, Germany, and a few others—succeeded in achieving all three. But the 1980s and 1990s are viewed by some as having called into question the extent to which low inequality remains an attainable goal and, more important, the extent to which low inequality is compatible with high and rising living standards and/or employment.

The End of Equality?

One concern is that egalitarianism itself may no longer be viable. In assessing this concern, it is helpful to think about inequality at three levels: earnings inequality among employed individuals (frequently referred to as "pay inequality" or "wage inequality"); earnings inequality among households; and income inequality among households when not just earnings but also investment income, taxes, and government transfers are included ("posttax-posttransfer income inequality" or "disposable income inequality").

Earnings compression among employed individuals has been threatened by an array of developments (Alderson and Nielsen 2002; Morris and Western 1999). Declining unionization levels and the decentralization of wage setting in many countries have weakened the major institutional force supporting wage compression. Growth in the supply of female and immigrant job-seekers has put downward pressure on wages at the low end of the labor market. The shift of employment from manufacturing to services has reduced the share of jobs in the sector where pay has traditionally been most compressed and increased it in the sector where it tends to be most dispersed. Heightened competition in various industries, a product of globalization and deregulation, has encouraged firms to become more cost-conscious and thus intent on reducing pay levels—particularly at the bottom levels where employees are more replaceable. Enhanced ability to move factories and offices abroad has provided employers with additional leverage in making such demands.

There is good reason to suspect that earnings disparities have widened across households as well (Burtless 1999; Nielsen and Alderson 2001). The degree of pay inequality among employed individuals is a key contributor to earnings inequality among households; thus, if the former has increased, we should expect the latter to also have increased. Because non-employment tends to be distributed unequally across households, declines in employment that have occurred in a number of nations are likely to have increased interhousehold earnings inequality. The same is true of part-time employment (as a share of total employment), single-adult households, and marital homogamy, each of which has grown in many countries.

Finally, capital mobility has increasingly constrained the tax capacities of national governments, presumably restricting their redistributive capabilities. In other words, at a time when economic developments seem likely to have increased the degree of market earnings inequality, governments have faced heightened pressure to cut back on programs designed to compensate for such inequality. Indeed, almost all affluent nations instituted welfare state cutbacks at some point during the 1980s and 1990s, in the form of stricter eligibility requirements, reduced benefit levels, and/or shorter benefit duration (Clayton and Pontusson 1998; Gilbert 2002; Hicks 1999; Huber and Stephens 2001; Pierson 2001; Ploug 1999; Swank 2002).

Given these developments, can the comparatively low levels of income inequality achieved by the Nordic and some of the continental European countries be sustained? Figure 1.1 shows levels of earnings inequality among employed individuals, earnings inequality among households, and posttax-posttransfer income inequality among households in 1979 (or the closest year for which data are available) and in 2000 for Sweden, Germany, and the United States. These three countries are commonly cited as representative of the Nordic, continental European, and Anglo groups of nations, respectively. The years 1979 and 2000 were the peaks of the 1970s and 1990s business cycles, so they are suitable for purposes of comparison. (For reasons I discuss in chapter 2, different measures of inequality are used in this figure, but in each case larger numbers indicate more inequality.) The figure suggests that, with one exception (individual earnings inequality in Germany), the level of inequality did increase on all three dimensions in each of the three countries. On the other hand, the differences between the three

Figure 1.1   Inequality, Economic Growth, Employment Growth, and Real Income Growth in Sweden, Germany, and the United States, 1980s and 1990s

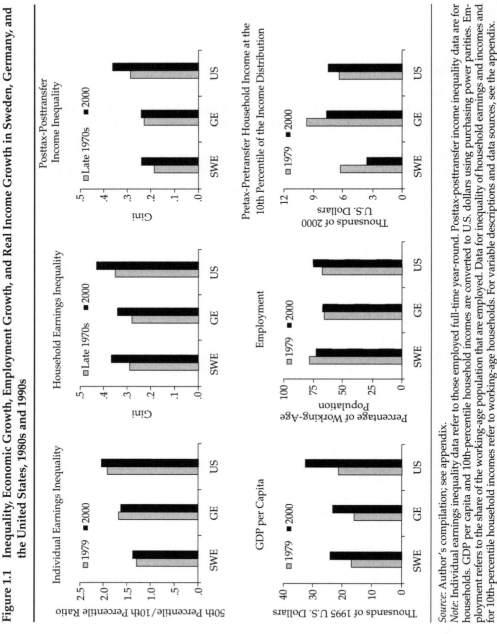

Source: Author's compilation; see appendix.
Note: Individual earnings inequality data refer to those employed full-time year-round. Posttax-posttransfer income inequality data are for households. GDP per capita and 10th-percentile household incomes are converted to U.S. dollars using purchasing power parities. Employment refers to the share of the working-age population that are employed. Data for inequality of household earnings and incomes and for 10th-percentile household incomes refer to working-age households. For variable descriptions and data sources, see the appendix.

countries did not diminish; Sweden and Germany remained considerably more egalitarian than the United States. In chapter 3 I explore this issue in greater depth across a larger number of affluent nations.

Potential Trade-offs

A second concern is that, even if egalitarianism remains viable, it may no longer be compatible with high and rising living standards. Hardcore advocates of free markets have long argued against "excessive" pursuit of equality (Friedman 1962; Hayek 1960). But in recent years even scholars with egalitarian sympathies have expressed some skepticism about the degree to which countries can effectively combine low inequality with a strong economy (Blau and Kahn 2002a; Boix 1998; Esping-Andersen 1999; Hemerijck and Schludi 2000; Iversen 1999; Pfaller, Gough, and Therborn 1991; Scharpf and Schmidt 2000; Streeck 2001). The chief concern has to do with potential adverse effects of pay compression (low earnings inequality among employed individuals) and generous social welfare programs on growth of economic output (GDP), employment, and real incomes.

An Equality-Growth Trade-off?

Debate about whether low inequality is compatible with a dynamic, productive economy has a long history. It has most commonly focused on the relationship between inequality and economic growth. The traditional view of this relationship, outlined famously in Arthur Okun's 1975 book *Equality and Efficiency: The Big Trade-off*, holds that inequality is beneficial for growth. The mechanisms underlying this presumed effect are relatively straightforward. Investment, work effort, and skills are key sources of growth. The wealthy are the principal source of savings and investment in a capitalist economy, so the smaller their income share, the less investment there is expected to be. And absent the prospect of sizable financial gain, individuals may limit their work effort and skill development.

Others have suggested reasons why income inequality may instead be bad for growth (Birdsall, Ross, and Sabot 1995; Bowles and Gintis 1995; Kenworthy 1995, ch. 3; Perotti 1996). Since the wealthy tend to save a higher share of their income than do the poor, greater inequality may weaken consumer demand, which can be as debilitating for growth as low investment. High levels of inequality may be viewed by those at the middle and lower ranges of the income distribution as excessively unfair, thereby reducing worker motivation and workplace cooperation. High levels of inequality also may reduce the share of the population that can afford to invest in postsecondary education. In addition, the financial constraints and frustration generated by high levels of inequality may reduce trust, cooperation, civic engagement, and other growth-enhancing forms of social capital.

In the 1990s the traditional view was challenged on empirical grounds as a slew of analyses discovered that countries with more inequality tend to have slower rates of economic growth (see, for example, Birdsall, Ross, and Sabot 1995; Clarke 1995; Perotti 1996; Persson and Tabellini 1994). However, less-developed countries account for the bulk of the cases in these studies, so the findings may offer little insight into processes in affluent economies. Recently, several studies of rich countries have found evidence for a growth-enhancing effect of inequality, consistent with the traditional view (Barro 2000; Brandolini and Rossi 1998; Forbes 2000). The lower-left chart in figure 1.1 shows levels of per capita GDP in 1979 and 2000. At both time points the level in the United States was substantially higher than in Sweden or Germany, and the gap widened a bit in the 1980s and 1990s.

Is the traditional view correct, then? Is income inequality beneficial for economic growth once nations reach a certain level of affluence? I explore this question in chapter 4.

An Equality-Jobs Trade-off?

As suggested earlier, there is good reason to consider a high employment rate to be an integral component of the egalitarian vision, because high employment is increasingly likely to be a prerequisite for a generous welfare state. But might equality in fact constitute an impediment to high employment?

In many affluent nations the fastest-growing job sector, and the likely locus of much future employment growth, is private-sector consumer-related services—restaurants, hotels, retail trade, cleaning, child care, and the like. Because of productivity increases and low-wage competition from developing countries, manufacturing is unlikely to provide a major source of new job opportunities, and many new labor force entrants are unlikely to be qualified for high-skilled service positions. In most consumer service jobs, productivity levels are relatively low and difficult to increase. Firms therefore can pay high wages only by passing the cost on to customers. But if the market is reasonably competitive, customers will refuse to pay a higher price. Hence, many of the new consumer service jobs will pay relatively low wages. This in turn means that earnings inequality among the employed will rise. Alternatively, such employment could be created in the public sector. Government jobs are shielded from market competition, thereby permitting above-market wages. But this increases the cost burden on the state, which is difficult to sustain in an age of capital mobility. Thus, for the Nordic and continental European countries, high employment may hinge on allowing lower wages at the bottom of the distribution, which implies greater pay inequality (Esping-Andersen 1999; Ferrera, Hemerijck, and Rhodes 2000; Iversen 1999; Scharpf and Schmidt 2000).

Indeed, a commonplace view holds that affluent countries face a trade-off between pay equality and jobs (Becker 1996; Blanchard and Wolfers 2000; Blau and Kahn 2002a; *The Economist* 1997; Iversen and Wren 1998; Krugman 1996; OECD 1994, 1996b; Siebert 1997). In the "U.S. model," wages for those at or near the bottom of the labor market are relatively low. This makes it attractive for companies to hire such workers. The American labor market is thus characterized by low earnings for those at the bottom, but also by extensive job creation and high employment. In the "European model," high relative wages at the low end of the distribution encourage companies to employ fewer workers. Countries in Europe therefore feature relatively high earnings for those at the bottom but little job creation and low employment. The lower-middle chart in figure 1.1 shows employment rates in Sweden, Germany, and the United States. At the beginning of the 1980s Sweden had the highest employment rate among the three countries, with Germany and the United States roughly even. But in the 1980s and 1990s employment declined in Sweden, was stagnant in Germany, and increased in the United States. By 2000 the United States had the highest rate among the three countries.

But allowing greater pay differentials hardly seems an ideal solution. Not only is a larger degree of pay inequality objectionable in and of itself; it also carries over to the distribution of household income. From an egalitarian perspective, a U.S.-style labor market, which features a high employment rate but a large number of low-paying jobs and consequently high inequality and poverty, is far from optimal. The question is: Can high employment be achieved with a low or moderate level of pay inequality? Is there a route to high employment that does not rely on extensive earnings and/or income disparities? I examine this issue in chapter 5.

An Equality-Incomes Trade-off?

If equality does impede the growth of economic output and/or employment, it may result in stagnant or falling real living standards for those at the low end of the income distribution. This, in my view, is the most important concern about potential incompatibilities between equality and other aims. There are good reasons to worry about the degree of separation between the rich and the rest of society, but the chief reason why most egalitarians favor limited inequality is because they presume that those at the bottom will be better off.

The well-being of individuals and households at the bottom of the distribution is most commonly studied by analyzing poverty. The central debate has concerned the impact of redistribution on poverty. To most supporters of the welfare state, one of its chief benefits is poverty reduction (Goodin et al. 1999). By redistributing income from the well-off to the poor, social welfare programs help to raise the incomes of households with low earnings. In contrast, many welfare state critics and even some supporters contend that, over time, generous social welfare programs reduce the growth of economic output and/or employment (Arrow 1979; Friedman and Friedman 1979; Lindbeck 1995; Murray 1984). As a result, the welfare state may increase poverty rather than reduce it.

To a large extent, proponents of these two views talk past one another. Welfare state supporters typically focus on *relative* poverty. A relative measure of poverty sets the poverty line for each country at a certain percentage (usually 50 percent) of the median income within that country. The poverty line thus differs across countries. Welfare state critics, on the other hand, focus principally on *absolute* poverty. An absolute measure of poverty uses the same poverty line (in converted currency units) for all nations. Across affluent countries, welfare state generosity is very strongly associated with low relative poverty (Brady 2001; Moller et al. 2003; OECD 2001e; Smeeding, Rainwater, and Burtless 2001). But there has been very little cross-country research addressing the possibility that redistribution may harm the poor in an absolute sense.

The lower-right chart in figure 1.1 shows real pretax-pretransfer household income levels (per equivalent person; see chapter 2) at the 10th percentile of the distribution in Sweden, Germany, and the United States. The 10th percentile is commonly used in studying the low end of the distribution (hence the frequent use of 90th percentile/10th percentile and 50th percentile/10th percentile ratios), since data for lower levels are more likely to suffer from measurement error. Consistent with the critics' argument, during the 1980s and 1990s the real income level at the 10th percentile fell in Sweden and Germany while it increased in the United States. Of course, what ultimately matters to people is income after taxes and government transfers are counted, and these three countries are not necessarily representative of all affluent nations. Still, these figures suggest a potential incompatibility between equality and real income growth for the poor. I explore this issue in chapter 6.

My Analytical Approach

For those who favor an egalitarian version of capitalism as well as those who do not, the issues and questions I have outlined here are significant. This book examines them from a comparative perspective. I focus on the world's richest nations, excluding a few with very small populations (such as Iceland and Luxembourg) and some others for which adequate data are lacking (Greece, Ireland, Israel, New Zealand, Portugal, and Spain). The countries included are Australia, Austria, Belgium, Canada, Denmark, Finland, France, Germany, Italy, Japan, the Netherlands, Norway, Sweden, Switzerland, the United Kingdom, and the United States. At various points in the book I refer to these sixteen countries as members of the three groups mentioned earlier: Nordic (Denmark, Finland, Norway, and Sweden), continental European (Austria, Belgium, France, Germany, Italy, the Netherlands, and Switzerland), and Anglo (Australia, Canada, the United Kingdom, and the United States). This draws on the typologies of political economies outlined by Jonas Pontusson (forthcoming) and Fritz Scharpf (2000), of welfare states by Gøsta Esping-Andersen (1990, 1999), and of families of nations by Francis Castles, Manfred Schmidt, and Göran Therborn (Castles 1993). I use this grouping simply as a heuristic device, to facilitate the exposition. Economic institutions and policies in Japan are such that it does not fit well into any of these groups; because of data limitations, Japan plays a limited role in the book in any case.

I examine the post–golden age period beginning in the mid-1970s, with an emphasis on the 1980s and 1990s. Much of the research on cross-country variation in inequality and poverty has focused on levels. My focus, by contrast, is chiefly on cross-country variation in *changes over time*. The 1980s and 1990s are viewed by many as a new and qualitatively distinct epoch for affluent economies. For some this distinctiveness is due to globalization, while others attribute it to heightened domestic competition, changes in policy orientations, demographic shifts, or some combination of these. Because economic institutions, policies, and performance patterns tend to change slowly, current cross-country variation in levels may be largely a product of determinants from an earlier era. Thus, in analyzing developments in the 1980s and 1990s, it is most useful to focus on cross-country differences in change during this period. For instance, differing levels of unionization may have had a sizable influence on cross-country differences in pay inequality in the 1950s, 1960s, and 1970s. As a result, unionization may continue to be an important explanatory factor in accounting for current cross-country variation in levels of pay inequality. But cross-country differences in changes in pay inequality in the 1980s and 1990s—

and thus potentially in future decades—may be a product mainly of other factors.

The analyses in the book are largely quantitative. Yet for the most part they are relatively "low-tech." I make extensive use of scatter-plot graphs and very simple regressions, owing in part to limitations imposed by the available data and in part to my interest in long-term processes and in separating analyses of levels from analyses of change over time (see chapter 2). This low-tech approach has the additional advantage of making the analyses accessible to those not well versed in sophisticated econometric techniques.

In chapter 7, I shift from comparative statistical analyses to country case studies in order to shed further light on the feasibility of egalitarian capitalism in the modern world economy. And in the book's final chapter, I offer a set of suggestions for how affluent societies might most effectively reconcile equality, high living standards, and high employment.

═ Chapter 2 ═

Method and Data

This book explores trends in inequality, incomes, and employment across the world's richest nations in the 1980s and 1990s. There are a variety of ways to approach the task of analyzing national-level institutions, policies, and/or performance outcomes. One approach is in-depth country case studies (see, for example, Danziger and Gottschalk 1995). A second is intensive comparison of a small number of countries (Kautto et al. 1999). A third involves using structured synthesis of the findings of case studies and/or country comparisons to draw conclusions about patterns across a larger group of nations (Scharpf 2000). A fourth approach is statistical analysis of quantitative data for some or all of the countries of interest. Of course, it is possible to combine two or more of these approaches (Huber and Stephens 2001).

I pursue mainly the fourth approach here, though I rely on the second in chapter 6 and on the third in chapter 7. I make no claim that statistical analysis is the most accurate or informative of the various approaches—merely that it is one approach that is likely to offer some insight into the questions at hand. My view is that answers to questions about comparative patterns of inequality and related socioeconomic phenomena can be generated only through a combination of analytical strategies. By itself, statistical analysis can never give us full and complete answers. But it can help.

In this chapter, I briefly discuss some key issues related to the method and data I use throughout the book.

Method

Five methodological issues that are central to the analyses in the book are worth addressing explicitly at the outset.

Small N's and Omitted Variables

Perhaps the most important challenge facing quantitative analyses of affluent nations is the "small-N problem." The number of cases (countries) is too small to permit multivariate analyses that include all of the potentially relevant explanatory factors. Analyses therefore run the risk of omitted-variable bias. If a variable that is correlated with both the independent variable of interest and the dependent variable is not included in the regression, the coefficient for the independent variable may overestimate its true effect.

In recent years most quantitative comparative research on rich countries has utilized pooled time-series cross-section (TSCS) regression analysis with annual data. The country-year becomes the unit of analysis, significantly increasing the number of observations. With fifteen or so countries and data for, say, twenty years, the number of observations totals three hundred. This allows for more fully specified models. However, this type of analysis is problematic for assessing relatively long-term causal processes. Estimates of long-run effects that are based on single-year data run the risk of overwhelming the signal with noise. Furthermore, some of the most interesting and potentially important explanatory factors in analyses of distributive and other economic outcomes are relatively inert institutions and policies. Since they do not change from year to year, there is little rationale for estimating their effect on year-to-year outcomes.

In any case, the Luxembourg Income Study—my main source of data for inequality—has data for each country only at five-year intervals. This obviously prohibits a pooled TSCS analysis with annual data. If data are available over a large number of years, pooled TSCS analysis can be based on periods, such as business cycles or decades, rather than single years (Barro 2000; Hicks and Kenworthy 1998). Several recent studies using LIS data have pursued this strategy (Bradley et al. 2003; Brady 2001; Moller et al. 2003). If all of the LIS datasets for all fifteen affluent countries (there are no LIS datasets for Japan) are pooled, the N increases to around seventy-five, which is an improvement in terms of the number of independent variables that can be included in a regression model. But there is a cost: five-year intervals provide a fairly short time frame for assessing relatively long-term effects; they are better than a single year but still very likely too brief. Another concern is that the number of years covered varies significantly across the countries, from seven for the United States to just two for Switzerland. Some countries therefore influence the estimated coefficients to a much greater extent than others.

My approach here is to rely on single-period cross-country regressions that cover as long a period of time as possible. (Other recent comparative studies of economic institutions and performance that make use of single-period cross-sectional regressions include Traxler, Blaschke, and Kittel [2001] and Western [1997, ch. 6].) This means there is only a single observation for each country, producing an N of just fifteen or so. In some instances there are only a small number of relevant explanatory variables, so I proceed in a typical fashion by testing all of the variables together and then in various combinations. In other instances in which there are a large number of potentially relevant explanatory factors, I proceed by testing all possible combinations of three or fewer variables. The explanatory variable(s) of interest are thus included in a variety of regressions with each control variable, though never in a single regression with all of the control variables together. If a variable turns out to be empirically irrelevant in these regressions and theoretical considerations do not suggest that it *must* be included in the model, I discard it. Often this strategy leads to a "best" regression model with a relatively small number of explanatory variables. This approach helps to reduce the danger of omitted-variable bias, though it does not fully avoid it. It also provides a useful test of the sensitivity of the results to model specification (Leamer 1983, 1985).

Determinants of Levels Versus Determinants of Change over Time

Another advantage of pooled time-series cross-section analysis is that it allows the researcher to combine information about variation in levels with information about variation over time rather than be compelled to focus on one or the other. However, this is not necessarily a good thing. Cross-country variation in levels may be caused by factors different from those that cause cross-country variation in change over time (see, for example, Western and Healy 1999). Over a long enough period, causal effects should be similar. But there is no reason to presume that the chief determinants of levels of inequality in 2000, for example, have also been the principal determinants of changes in inequality over the preceding ten or twenty years. Differences in the causes of variation in levels versus variation over time are often hidden in pooled TSCS regressions (Kittel 1999). I use separate analyses to examine cross-country variation in levels and cross-country variation in over-time trends. As noted in chapter 1, my principal interest is in the latter.

Unobserved Heterogeneity Bias

Single-period cross-country regressions such as those I rely on are vulnerable to bias stemming from "unobserved heterogeneity" ("country fixed effects"). Each nation has peculiarities, such as its culture, which may have an impact on outcomes such as inequality and economic growth. To the extent that such unmeasured country-specific differences are correlated with a particular independent variable in a regression, the estimated effect of that variable is biased upward. This is usually dealt with in pooled time-series cross-section regressions by including country dummy variables, though that introduces other potential problems (Beck and Katz 2001; Plümper, Troeger, and Manow, forthcoming). Unobserved heterogeneity bias tends to be more of a problem in analyses of variation in levels than in analyses of change. Since most of the analyses in this book focus on the latter, the problem may be of limited relevance. Nevertheless, my inability to control for country fixed effects may somewhat inflate the estimated effects of the variables included in the regressions.

Statistical Significance and Substantive Significance

Inference plays a key role in statistical analysis. If a regression analysis using data from a sample suggests an association between two variables, we usually want to know the likelihood that this association exists in the larger population from which the sample is drawn. However, social scientists sometimes fetishize statistical significance, ignoring the question of whether an association is substantively significant—that is, of substantial strength or importance (Bollen 1995; McCloskey and Ziliak 1996). I attempt throughout the book to emphasize the magnitude and relevance of estimated effects. One way I do this is by focusing on standardized regression coefficients. Standardized coefficients indicate the number of standard deviations of change in the dependent variable estimated to result from an increase of one standard deviation in the independent variable. They vary around zero, typically within a range of minus one to plus one, which facilitates comparison of the magnitude of the effects of independent variables.

A more basic issue is whether tests of statistical significance apply at all. The countries on which I focus are not a sample drawn at random from a population. They are not at all representative—economically, politically, or socially—of the full population of countries in the world. Nor is it accurate to view them as a sample of affluent nations drawn from a population that consists of affluent nations in multiple time periods. All of the data I analyze are from the same period: the 1980s and 1990s. Instead, these countries constitute the population, or rather most of the population, of affluent democratic nations in the years 1980 to 2000. Standard inferential concerns therefore are not applicable (Berk, Western, and Weiss 1995).[1]

At the same time, the standard error, on which the test of statistical significance for a regression coefficient is based, does convey information about the precision of the coefficient estimate (Traxler, Blaschke, and Kittel 2001, 30). A t-statistic, calculated as the regression coefficient divided by its standard error, provides an indicator of the size of the estimated effect in relation to the amount of variability in the estimate. This is helpful in determining whether an association indeed exists and, if so, how strong it is. In conjunction with other information, I make use of the information provided by the t-statistic in reaching a judgment about the existence and strength of an association between an explanatory variable and an outcome variable. Specifically, I consider: the consistency of the explanatory variable's coefficient sign in regressions that include various combinations of control variables; the absolute size of the coefficient; and the size of the coefficient in relation to its variability, as expressed in the t-statistic.

Theoretical Indeterminacy and Social "Laws"

Much of what scientists attempt to do is to test theories. A theory is a statement about the causal relationship between two variables. For example: if two people are identical in every other relevant respect, the one with more education is likely to have higher earnings. There are compelling reasons to think that the purported positive effect of educational attainment on earnings is genuinely causal: more education is likely to increase a person's productivity on the job, and employers are likely to suspect that this is the case and so pay better-educated employees more even if those employees are not actually more productive. In addition, there is no particular reason to suspect that more education has the effect of reducing earnings. Thus, if empirical evidence is consistent with this theory, social scientists are likely to conclude that educational attainment increases earnings. Most will think of this as something akin to a social "law."

Other theories are based on less compelling accounts of the causal linkage between variables. One of the theories I explore in this book, for example, holds that income inequality is beneficial for economic growth. This theory is based in part on the notion that people's propensity to save rises with income, that private savings is the chief source of investment in a capitalist economy, and that investment is key to economic growth. Reducing inequality is therefore expected to reduce savings, investment, and hence the rate of growth. However, consumption is also critical to growth. Since the poor tend to consume a larger portion of their incomes, raising those incomes (by, for instance, redistributing money from the well-to-do) may increase consumption and therefore increase the growth rate. Since both of these theoretical claims have some plausibility, an empirical finding that, say, inequality is bad for growth should not, in my view, be considered a general "law," even if we feel confident that the analysis has yielded true results (there are no important omitted variables, no significant measurement error, and so on). In other words, we should not, based on these results, conclude that inequality is bad for growth. Instead, we should conclude that it was bad for growth among the particular countries during the particular period examined. This is so even if a large number of studies for various groups of countries and during various time periods yield similar results.

This type of theoretical indeterminacy is common in studying economic and political processes in affluent countries. Thus, in most instances throughout this book I use language such as "X was positively related to Y for such-and-such countries during the 1980s and 1990s," rather than "X is positively related to Y." That does not mean the empirical findings are irrelevant. They are the best evidence we have regarding how things worked in rich democratic nations in recent decades. But in most cases it would be unreasonable to conclude that they tell us more than that.

Data

Descriptions and data sources for all of the variables I use are listed in the appendix. For those interested, the data themselves are available on my web page, the address for which also is listed in the appendix.

I use two sources of data on the distributions of earnings and income in affluent countries. For earnings among employed individuals, I rely on a dataset compiled by the Organization for Economic Cooperation and Development (OECD). The data are for earnings among individuals employed full-time year-round, at the 10th, 50th, 90th, and other percentiles of the earnings distribution. This enables calculation of "percentile ratio" measures of earnings inequality, such as 90th percentile/10th percentile and 50th percentile/10th percentile ratios (the latter are used in figure 1.1). The data are somewhat sparse for a few countries in terms of years and percentiles, but they are sufficient to facilitate analysis of a reasonably large number of nations over the 1980s and 1990s.

For earnings and incomes among households, I use the Luxembourg Income Study (LIS). This is the most reliable source for comparable cross-country data on household earnings and incomes in affluent countries (Atkinson and Brandolini 2001). The LIS data come from surveys or tax records collected in the individual countries, but considerable effort is made to harmonize the datasets so that they are truly comparable across nations. (Extensive documentation of these efforts is available on the LIS website at www.lisproject.org.) The LIS data are available in waves: for each country, there is an observation around 1985, 1990, and 1995; for most, there is one around 1980; for a handful of countries, there also are (as of this writing) observations around 1975 or 2000.

A great advantage of the LIS database is that it consists of individual-level data for each country. This makes it possible to calculate inequality and poverty measures using specifications designed by the researcher.

The LIS datasets have three household-level variables that are particularly useful for measuring earnings, income before taxes and transfers, and income after taxes and transfers: earnings (EARNING), market income (MI), and disposable personal income (DPI), respectively. For expositional convenience, throughout the book I use the terms "pretax-pretransfer," "pre," and "market" as synonyms; the same is true for "posttax-posttransfer," "post," and "disposable." Terms such as "market inequality" and "redistribution" also are used here simply for convenience. Collective actors such as unions and politically constructed institutions such as centralized wage bargaining and public employment play an important role in the process that determines the distribution of earnings (Rueda and Pontusson 2000; Wallerstein 1999). And social-welfare programs may have significant effects on the earnings distribution by altering the economic behavior of individuals (Beramendi 2001). I do not mean to imply, in other words, that the distribution of pretax-pretransfer income is simply an outcome of "market forces" or that the effects of redistributive policies come into play only after the earnings distribution has been established.

Sources of market income in the LIS datasets include earnings, property income (interest, rent, dividends), and private pensions. Disposable income adds government transfers and net tax payments. Government transfers include cash benefits and "near-cash" transfers (such as food stamps in the United States and housing assistance in the United Kingdom and Sweden), but not services such as education, medical care, child care, and most housing subsidies. Taxes include personal income and employee payroll taxes, but not sales or value-added taxes.

The LIS data thus include two major components of income excluded from the standard Census Bureau data in the United States: near-cash transfers and (most) taxes. The chief deficiency of the LIS data is that they do not include the value of services such as health care and child care.

Several measurement and coding issues are particularly worthy of note.

Adjusting Household Incomes for Household Size

The measurement unit I use for calculating income levels and income inequality is the household (Canberra Group 2001). This makes sense as earnings and other sources of income are generally pooled among household members (albeit not necessarily equally). But households with differing numbers of persons presumably have different income needs. It is therefore standard practice to adjust household income figures for household size. I do so using a conventional "equivalence scale": household income is divided by the square root of the number of persons in the household (Atkinson, Rainwater, and Smeeding 1995; Canberra Group 2001). This presumes that larger households enjoy economies of scale in their use of income, so that, for instance, a household of four needs only twice as much income as a household of one rather than four times as much. Income figures reported throughout the book therefore represent household income per "equivalent person."

Top- and Bottom-Coding of Incomes

Respondents to surveys may overestimate or underestimate their earnings or income. To minimize the effect of this, it is standard practice in analyses using the LIS data to top-code and bottom-code the country datasets in calculating income levels and income inequality. That is, upper and lower limits for earnings and incomes are set based on some multiple and fraction of the median or mean. Any reported incomes above or below these figures are recoded as the limit figures. I follow the official LIS practice (see www.lisproject.org) of top-coding at ten times the unequivalized median and bottom-coding at 1 percent of the equivalized mean. In other words, extremely high earnings and incomes are recoded as ten times the median prior to adjustment for household size, and extremely low (including negative and zero) earnings and incomes are recoded as 1 percent of the mean after adjustment for household size. Households reporting a posttax-posttransfer income of zero are dropped.

Accounting Period

In the LIS datasets income is measured over a period of one year. This is standard in studies of income levels and income inequality, but it is worth noting that it is not ideal. Income for a given household may fluctuate from year to year for any of a number of reasons—temporary joblessness, sickness, extra overtime work, a profit-sharing bonus, an investment income windfall, and so on. For purposes of accurately measuring income levels and income inequality, it is therefore preferable to average income over a period of five or ten years or even longer. On the other hand, it is not clear that a one-year measure is likely to introduce much bias in comparing across countries or over time.

Inequality Measures

Researchers use more than a dozen different measures of inequality. The most commonly used measure, and the one on which I mainly rely, is the Gini coefficient (or Gini index). The Gini is attractive because it represents the overall degree of inequality with a single number. It ranges from zero to one, with larger numbers indicating greater inequality.

Another common measure is a ratio of incomes at selected percentiles. Typically, researchers focus on the incomes of the persons or households at the 10th percentile, the 50th (median) percentile, and the 90th percentile. The 10th and 90th are chosen because they are near the bottom and top but less likely than those at the very bottom and top to be biased by measurement error or extreme values. Then 90th percentile/10th percentile, 90th percentile/50th percentile, and/or 50th percentile/10th percentile ratios are calculated. I use percentile ratios primarily in circumstances where data limitations make it impossible to calculate a Gini coefficient—mainly when I use the OECD data on earnings among individuals employed full-time year-round.

German Unification

Prior to 1990 figures for "Germany" refer to West Germany. From 1990 forward they refer to unified Germany. I discuss in the individual chapters instances where this might affect findings.

= Chapter 3 =

The End of Equality?

A market economy tends to generate sizable income disparities across individuals and households. In a context of free exchange, differences in initial assets, ability, power, and luck are bound to produce differences in earnings and incomes. In democratic societies, however, labor unions and political parties have traditionally mitigated the inequality generated by the market. Unions reduce pay inequality among employed individuals, and political parties implement government tax and transfer programs that redistribute income from households with high earnings to ones with low earnings.

Among affluent capitalist nations, there is considerable variation in the degree of inequality produced by markets, unions, governments, and other forces. Using LIS data (see chapter 2), figure 3.1 shows levels of pretax-pretransfer and posttax-posttransfer income inequality among working-age households in thirteen countries as of the mid-1990s. The former is influenced by market processes, institutions such as unions and collective wage bargaining, and demographic factors such as household size and composition. The latter is a product of these plus redistribution achieved through government taxes and transfers. The difference between the two bars for each country indicates the degree of redistribution. In most nations the distribution of "market" (pretax-pretransfer) household income was the chief determinant of the distribution of disposable income. Indeed, in some countries, such as the United States, Italy, and Switzerland, redistribution reduced the degree of inequality only slightly. In other nations redistribution played a major role. In Sweden, for example, the degree of posttax-posttransfer inequality was half that of pretax-pretransfer inequality, indicating an extensive alteration by the welfare state of the market distribution of household income.

Among scholars and policymakers, there is growing skepticism that the success of unions, welfare states, and other institutions at reducing inequality can be sustained. The chief threats to institutional efforts to reduce inequality, in this view, are globalization, the shift of employment from manufacturing to services, and labor fragmentation. As in-

Figure 3.1   Pretax-Pretransfer and Posttax-Posttransfer Household Income Inequality in Thirteen Countries, Mid-1990s

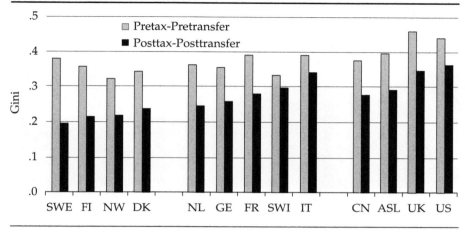

Source: Author's compilation; see appendix.

vestors and firms have become increasingly able to shift assets across national borders, governments face pressure to reduce taxes, which constrains their ability to redistribute income. Because of heightened competition resulting in part from globalization, firms have become more aggressive in opposing union efforts to limit pay differentials. As employment in manufacturing has shrunk and been replaced by service-sector jobs, a larger share of the workforce is employed in a sector with wider pay differentials. In addition, segmentation among workers—particularly between high- and low-skilled and private- and public-sector employees—has reduced the unity and hence the strength of unions.

It is perhaps not surprising, then, that several recent studies report an upward trend in inequality in many affluent countries. David Rueda and Jonas Pontusson (2000), for instance, find that earnings inequality among employed individuals increased in eleven of sixteen countries in the period from 1973 to 1995. And Arthur Alderson and François Nielsen (2002) find an increase in income inequality in ten of sixteen countries between the late 1960s and the early 1990s.

Figure 3.2 shows trends in income inequality in the 1980s and 1990s in the affluent countries for which comparable data are available. The data are for posttax-posttransfer income inequality among households. Inequality increased in all but two countries during this period. This should perhaps be cause for concern among those who prefer a less un-

Figure 3.2   Posttax-Posttransfer Household Income Inequality in Thirteen Countries, Mid-1980s and Mid-1990s

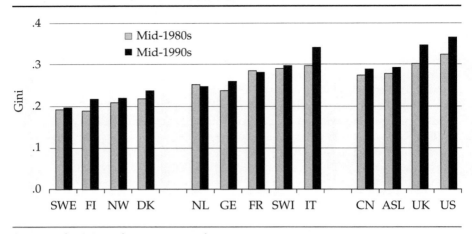

Source: Author's compilation; see appendix.

equal distribution of income. On the other hand, the increase was largest in less-egalitarian nations—such as the United States, the United Kingdom, and Italy. Aside from Finland and Denmark, countries that began the period with lower levels of inequality tended to experience a smaller increase. This suggests that low levels of income inequality may in fact be sustainable.

My aim in this chapter, which draws heavily on joint research with Jonas Pontusson (Kenworthy and Pontusson 2004), is to unpack these trends. Was rising income inequality due mainly to increases in earnings inequality? To decreases in government redistribution? To both? Perhaps household earnings inequality increased substantially, but this was partially offset by increases in redistribution. Did changes in household earnings inequality and in redistribution contribute in varying degrees in different countries? Answers to these questions have implications for the present and future of egalitarianism in affluent nations.

Posttax-posttransfer income inequality among households can be decomposed into: inequality of earnings among households, inequality of investment income among households, and government redistribution. It turns out that, for purposes of cross-national analysis of rich countries, the second of these three components can be ignored. There is little difference between household earnings inequality and household pretax-pretransfer ("market") income inequality. In other words, adding investment income does not affect the patterns of cross-country variation.[1] In analyzing posttax-posttransfer income inequality, I therefore concentrate solely on household earnings and redistribution.

I examine not only trends in household earnings inequality and in redistribution but also the determinants of those trends. A number of recent studies have explored causes of earnings inequality among employed individuals (Acemoglu 2002; Burtless 1998; Danziger and Gottschalk 1995; Levy 1998; Morris and Western 1999; Mosher 2002; Rueda and Pontusson 2000; Wallerstein 1999). But very few have analyzed the determinants of earnings inequality among households (Bradley et al. 2003; Kenworthy and Pontusson 2004). There is a vast literature on the determinants of government redistributive effort (Bradley et al. 2003; Esping-Andersen 1990; Garrett 1998; Hicks 1999; Huber and Stephens 2001; Iversen and Cusack 2000; Kittel and Obinger 2001; Olsen 2002; Pierson 2001; Swank 2002), but in almost all of these studies redistribution is measured using a proxy such as government social expenditures or transfers as a share of GDP. I instead use a measure of *actual* redistribution, calculated as the difference between pretax-pretransfer inequality and posttax-posttransfer inequality. (A similar measure has been used in other contexts; see Bradley et al. 2003; Hicks and Kenworthy 2003; Hicks and Swank 1984; Kenworthy and Pontusson 2004; Mitchell 1991; Sainsbury and Morissens 2002.)

Data and Measures

Most of the existing comparative research has focused on cross-country variation in levels of inequality (Alderson and Nielsen 2002; Bradley et al. 2003; Gustafsson and Johansson 1999; Hewitt 1977; Katz, Mahler, and Franz 1983; Muller 1989; Stephens 1979; van Arnhem and Schotsman 1982).[2] As I noted in chapter 1, my interest is instead in cross-country variation in *over-time trends*. For each country in the Luxembourg Income Study database there is an observation around 1985, 1990, and 1995. For most there is one around 1980. For a few countries there also are observations around 1970, 1975, and/or 2000. To maximize the number of countries, I focus on change over time between the mid-1980s and the mid-1990s. Although ten years is a short time span to use in assessing longitudinal developments, this is the most sensible choice given the available data. The middle years of these two decades represent comparable points in the business cycle for most OECD countries, which would not be the case were I to opt for a slightly longer period by comparing the *early* 1980s with the mid-1990s. Also, for four of the countries I include there is no early 1980s observation.

I include the thirteen countries shown in figures 3.1 and 3.2: Aus-

Table 3.1   Countries and Years Included in the Analyses

	Mid-1980s	Mid-1990s
Nordic		
Denmark	1987	1997
Finland	1987	1995
Norway	1986	1995
Sweden	1987	1995
Continental		
France	1984	1994
Germany	1984	1994
Italy	1986	1995
Netherlands	1983	1994
Switzerland	1982	1992
Anglo		
Australia	1985	1994
Canada	1987	1997
United Kingdom	1986	1995
United States	1986	1997

Source: Author's compilation; see appendix.

tralia, Canada, Denmark, Finland, France, Germany, Italy, the Netherlands, Norway, Sweden, Switzerland, the United Kingdom, and the United States. Austria, Belgium, and Japan cannot be included owing to lack of sufficient LIS data.[3] Table 3.1 shows the specific years to which the data for each of the thirteen countries apply.

I measure change as an absolute difference rather than as a percentage difference (see also Chevan and Stokes 2000). That is, change in earnings inequality and in government redistribution is calculated as the mid-1990s value minus the mid-1980s value rather than as this difference divided by the mid-1980s value. I do this mainly for substantive reasons. What matters to real people is the amount of absolute change, not the amount of change relative to the prior level. As a practical matter, however, this choice has little significance; the patterns are similar regardless of which type of change measure is used.

Descriptions and data sources for all of the variables I use are listed in the appendix. All are measured in the LIS years shown in table 3.1. The main inequality measure I use is the Gini coefficient, which ranges in value between zero and one, with larger numbers indicating greater inequality. The measure of redistribution is calculated as the Gini for household earnings minus the Gini for posttax-posttransfer income— that is, the reduction in inequality achieved by taxes and transfers. As noted earlier, this differs from levels of social spending or transfers, the measure typically deployed in studies of welfare state effort. Because one of my chief interests is in the nexus between labor market dynamics and welfare state dynamics, I focus on the working-age population: I examine only households with a "head" age twenty-five to fifty-nine, thus excluding those most likely to be students or retirees. Following convention, I adjust the household earnings and income figures for household size, using an "equivalence scale" of the square root of household size (see chapter 2 for more detail).

Changes in Household Earnings Inequality

Figure 3.3 shows levels of household earnings inequality in the mid-1980s and mid-1990s. Inequality increased in all but one country (the Netherlands), and it did so most sharply in the comparatively egalitarian Nordic countries.

What explains the cross-country variation in changes in household earnings inequality? Much of the recent literature appears to assume, explicitly or implicitly, that the increase in earnings inequality among households has been driven largely by a rise in earnings inequality among employed individuals. Indeed, there is a fairly strong correlation across countries between levels of pay inequality and levels of household earnings inequality: for the thirteen nations examined here, $r = .65$ as of the mid-1990s. The degree of pay inequality is itself influenced by a host of factors, including: the degree of education and skill

Figure 3.3   Household Earnings Inequality in Thirteen Countries, Mid-1980s and Mid-1990s

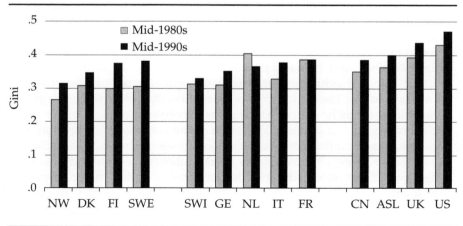

Source: Author's compilation; see appendix.

inequality among the workforce; the female and immigrant shares in the workforce; the extent of globalization and competition in the economy; the level of unemployment; the distribution of employment in manufacturing versus services and in the private versus public sectors; the level of unionization; the degree of extension of union pay agreements to non-union employees; the centralization or coordination of pay setting; and the existence and level of a statutory or collectively bargained minimum wage (Alderson and Nielsen 2002; Galbraith 1998; Morris and Western 1999; Rueda and Pontusson 2000; Wallerstein 1999).

In cross-country studies, pay inequality is typically measured using a 90th percentile/10th percentile ratio, which is the ratio of the annual earnings of a worker at the 90th percentile of the distribution to that of a worker at the 10th percentile.[4] As of the mid-1990s the 90th percentile/10th percentile ratio ranged from a low of 2.0 in Norway to a high of 4.6 in the United States. In other words, a worker at the 90th percentile of the pay distribution in Norway earned twice as much as a worker at the 10th percentile, while in the United States she or he earned about four and a half times as much.

Certainly we would expect household earnings inequality to be in part a function of individual-level earnings inequality. But there are other factors that may matter too. One is employment. Controlling for earnings inequality among the employed, a lower employment rate may contribute to higher earnings inequality among households. A country could have a low degree of earnings dispersion among individuals who have jobs but many individuals who are without jobs—who either are not in the labor force or are unemployed—and therefore greater earnings inequality across households. Among the thirteen countries included in the analyses here, employment rates as of the mid-1990s ranged from a low of 53 percent in Italy to around 65 percent in several other continental countries, to more than 75 percent in Denmark, Norway, and Switzerland.

Part-time and temporary employment might also have an influence. If we control for the overall employment rate, countries with a larger share of part-time or temporary workers may have greater earnings inequality across households. The lower annual earnings of part-time and temporary employees—owing to lower pay per hour, fewer hours worked per week, or fewer weeks worked per year—may pull down the earnings of households in the lower part of the distribution, yielding greater inequality. Unfortunately, reliable comparative data on temporary employees are not available. Part-time employment in the mid-1990s varied from about 10 percent of total employment in Finland and Italy to 25 to 30 percent in Australia and the Netherlands.

A fourth potentially influential factor is the number of earners in households. Particularly relevant here is the share of households with only a single earner. Such households are more likely to have low overall earnings. Thus, a country with a larger proportion of single-earner households may have greater earnings inequality across households. But isn't the effect of single-earner households captured by the employment rate? Not necessarily. For any given pair of adults, even if both are employed, they may be in the same (dual-earner) household or in two separate (single-earner) households. As of the mid-1990s single-earner households accounted for approximately one-quarter of households with at least one earner in Norway and Finland, versus almost half in Italy, the Netherlands, and Switzerland.

A fifth factor is the prevalence of marital homogamy—the extent to which high earners tend to be married to (or to cohabitate with) other high earners and low earners with other low earners. The larger the correlation between spouses' earnings, the greater we can expect earnings inequality across households to be. Marital homogamy has received limited attention in the literature, but according to Gary Burtless (1999), it accounts for 13 percent of the rise in household income inequality in the United States between 1979 and 1997. Interspousal earnings correlations among dual-earner couples in the mid-1990s ranged from −.11 in Switzerland and .01 in the Netherlands up to .33 in France and .34 in Italy.

Table 3.2 shows the results of regressions of change in household earnings inequality on various combinations of change in earnings inequality among full-time employed individuals, change in the employment rate, change in single-earner households, and change in marital homogamy. All of these variables are measured as mid-1990s value minus mid-1980s value. I do not include change in part-time employment in the regressions because data for several countries are not available for the mid-1980s and because, across the countries for which data are available, this variable is highly correlated with change in the total employment rate ($r = .70$). As I explained in chapter 2, since the number of observations is very small (thirteen), I estimate a series of regressions that include all possible combinations of three or fewer of the independent variables. The table reports the minimum, median, and maximum standardized coefficients for each variable in these regressions. It also reports the results of a regression that includes all four of the variables ("full model") and of the regression that yields the largest adjusted R-squared ("best model").

Change in inequality among employed individuals has the expected positive association with change in household earnings inequality. In the full and best models, it has moderate-sized standardized coeffi-

Table 3.2   Regression Results: Determinants of Change in Household Earnings Inequality, Mid-1980s to Mid-1990s

	Full Model	Best Model	All Possible Models		
			Minimum	Median	Maximum
Change in earnings inequality among full-time year-round employed individuals	.31 (2.50)	.34 (2.28)	−.13 (.57)	.15 (.61)	.35 (2.54)
Change in employment	−.69 (4.31)	−.75 (4.95)	−.87 (3.64)	−.64 (5.80)	−.52 (2.49)
Change in single-earner households	.09 (.40)		.11 (.49)	.51 (2.54)	.69 (2.33)
Change in marital homogamy	.34 (1.71)	.35 (2.37)	.26 (1.16)	.36 (1.82)	.65 (2.20)

Source: Author's analysis; see appendix.
Notes: Standardized coefficients, with absolute t-ratios (based on heteroskedasticity-robust standard errors) in parentheses. OLS regressions. Results for "all possible models" are low, median, and high coefficient for each variable from regressions using all possible combinations of the independent variables (four variables, fifteen regressions). "Best model" regression is the one with the largest adjusted R-squared. All variables are measured as mid-1990s value minus mid-1980s value. Minimum and maximum R-squared: .02, .75. N = 13.

cients of around .35 and relatively large t-statistics. Change in single-earner households consistently has the expected positive sign, but its coefficients and t-statistics are not always large; when all of the other variables are included (full model), it appears to be irrelevant. Change in marital homogamy is positively associated with change in household earnings inequality.

The change in employment variable dominates these regressions. It yields standardized coefficients ranging from −.52 to −.87, with consistently large t-statistics. In the full and best models, its standardized coefficients are twice as large as those for any of the other variables. Figure 3.4 provides a graphic depiction of the association across countries between change in the employment rate and change in household earnings inequality. The relationship is negative and quite strong, with a relatively close fit (r = −.79). In countries with declining employment rates—most notably Finland and Sweden, but also Norway, Denmark, and Italy—we observe relatively large increases in household earnings inequality. By contrast, in nations with rising employment—particularly the Netherlands and Switzerland—we see a decrease or a more modest increase in household inequality.

Is there reverse causality here? That is, might increases in household

**Figure 3.4   Change in Household Earnings Inequality by Change in
Employment, Thirteen Countries, Mid-1980s to Mid-1990s**

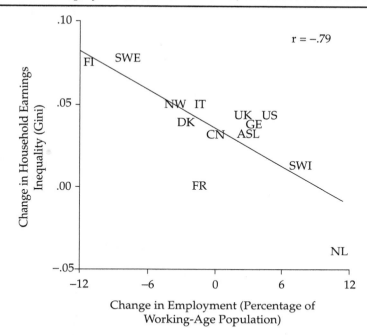

Source: Author's compilation; see appendix.

earnings inequality have caused declines in employment, rather than
the other way around? I cannot think of a reason why this would be the
case, whereas there is a simple mechanism that would account for why
a decline in employment would cause an increase in household earnings inequality: more households have fewer earners. It appears that
low-earning households were disproportionately hurt by employment
contraction, in terms of their job prospects and earnings, and disproportionately helped by employment growth (see also Blank and Blinder
1986).

In the absence of panel data that track the employment and earnings
of a group of households over time, it is difficult to document this interpretation of the causal pattern. But it is quite consistent with several
pieces of available evidence. First, if the key development is the way in
which employment trends affect low-earning households, there should
be an even stronger association between change in employment and
change in household earnings inequality among households with earnings below the median. That is indeed the case: $r = -.94$.[5] Second, as fig-

ure 3.4 indicates, household earnings inequality increased most sharply in Sweden and Finland, and it decreased only in the Netherlands. The changes in these three countries were due almost entirely to changes in the bottom half of the distribution. The 50th percentile/10th percentile earnings ratio among households increased from 2.9 to 23.8 in Sweden and from 2.7 to 7.5 in Finland, while in the Netherlands it dropped from 90.9 to 45.5. Third, consider the share of households in the bottom earnings quartile that had no employed person. In Sweden the share increased by seventeen percentage points between the mid-1980s and the mid-1990s, and in Finland it increased by ten percentage points. In the Netherlands, by contrast, the share dropped by twenty-three percentage points (my calculations from LIS data). Finally, during the 1990s employment in Sweden declined much more rapidly among those with the least education and manual workers than among better-educated and salaried employees (Åberg 2003, 210; Palme et al. 2002, 37).

Several caveats should be made here. First, the importance of employment trends might be specific to the particular period I analyze— the mid-1980s to the mid-1990s. Certainly developments in some of the countries have shifted in more recent years. This is true most notably for Sweden and Finland, the two nations with the worst employment performance during the years analyzed here. The employment rate in Sweden increased from 72 percent in 1995 to 75 percent in 2002. In Finland it jumped from 61 percent in 1995 to 68 percent in 2002. The question, however, is not whether the positioning or performance of particular countries is specific to the mid-1980s to mid-1990s period. Instead, the question is whether the strong association between employment trends and household earnings inequality trends applies exclusively to this period. There are LIS data for the mid-1970s for five countries: Canada, Germany, Sweden, the United Kingdom, and the United States. Over the decade from the mid-1970s to the mid-1980s, change in employment is negatively correlated with changes in household earnings inequality across these five countries: $r = -.58$. This is consistent with the pattern for the mid-1980s to the mid-1990s, but with only five countries we should not put too much stock in this correlation. We will not know if the association continued past the mid-1990s until the next wave of LIS datasets is fully available.

Second, employment was not the main determinant of over-time developments in household earnings inequality in every country. For example, as figure 3.4 shows, five nations—the United States, the United Kingdom, Australia, Germany, and Switzerland—experienced increases in employment yet also increases in household earnings inequality. In addition, several countries—most notably the United States and Sweden, but also Italy, the United Kingdom, and Australia—experienced increases in both earnings inequality among employed individuals and earnings inequality among households, suggesting that the former may have contributed to the latter. Indeed, if we focus only on the eight countries bunched together in the middle of figure 3.4—Norway, Denmark, Italy, Canada, the United Kingdom, the United States, Australia, and Germany—the cross-country variation in changes in household earnings inequality owes as much to changes in individual-level earnings inequality as to changes in employment. A regression with just these eight countries yields a standardized coefficient of −.73 for change in employment and .72 for change in earnings inequality among employed individuals.

The U.S. case is a particularly noteworthy exception. Household earnings inequality increased in the United States during this period, and it did so to a greater extent than in many other affluent countries (figure 3.4). But that was not because low-earning households suffered employment declines. The share of U.S. households with earnings in the bottom quartile that had no employed person *decreased* by five percentage points between the mid-1980s and the mid-1990s. Figure 3.5 plots change in household earnings inequality by change in employ-

Figure 3.5   Change in Household Earnings Inequality by Change in Employment, U.S. States, Mid-1980s to Mid-1990s

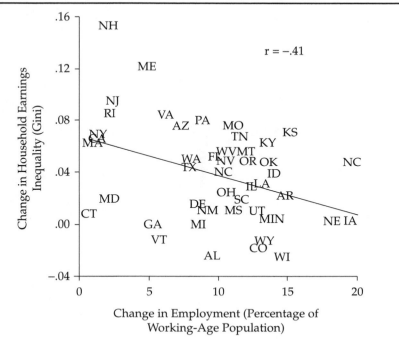

Source: Author's compilation; see appendix.

ment from the mid-1980s to the mid-1990s for the forty-eight contiguous U.S. states. Although the relationship is a negative one, like that in figure 3.4, the association is noticeably weaker. And despite the fact that the employment rate increased in every state, earnings inequality rose in most of them. This too suggests that employment has not been the key determinant of trends in household earnings inequality in the United States. Instead, the chief culprits in the U.S. case appear to have been increased earnings inequality among employed individuals, a growing prevalence of single-adult households, and increased marital homogamy (Burtless 1999; Gottschalk and Danziger 2003).

A third caveat is that the *level* of earnings inequality among employed individuals may have affected changes in household earnings inequality through an effect on employment growth. A compressed earnings distribution among the full-time employed may be an impediment to the creation of private-sector consumer services jobs and thereby to aggregate employment growth (Esping-Andersen 1999; Iversen and Wren 1998). I examine this possibility in chapter 5. I find that a low level of earnings inequality may have indeed slowed employment growth during the 1980s and 1990s, but that the association is relatively weak. The main determinant of cross-country differences in employment growth instead seems to have been tax rates. Employment regulations, outward direct foreign investment, and economic growth also appear to have mattered.

Figure 3.6   Change in Total Employment and in Female Employment in Thirteen Countries, Mid-1980s to Mid-1990s

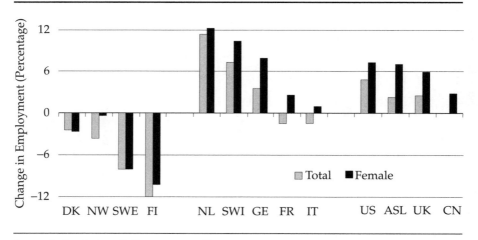

Source: Author's compilation; see appendix.

Finally, it is worth noting that patterns of employment change were heavily gendered. Figure 3.6 shows changes in female employment next to changes in total employment. If the bars are of equal height, employment developments for women were similar to those for the entire working-age population—that is, they were about the same as those for men. That is the case for most of the Nordic countries. The employment declines in those four countries were gender-neutral, except in Norway, where they affected men more than women. By contrast, almost all of the continental and Anglo nations experienced employment increases, and in every case the increase occurred disproportionately among women. This has implications for strategies to raise employment, an issue I address in chapters 5 and 8.

Changes in Redistribution

Figure 3.7 shows levels of redistribution as of the mid-1980s and mid-1990s. As noted earlier, this is a measure of *actual* redistribution—the reduction in inequality achieved by taxes and government transfers. Contrary to the recent emphasis on declining redistributiveness of welfare states (Clayton and Pontusson 1998; Pierson 2001), the figure shows an increase in redistribution in eleven of the thirteen countries. The rise was substantial in the Nordic countries and more moderate in the continental and Anglo nations.

Figure 3.7   Redistribution in Thirteen Countries, Mid-1980s and Mid-1990s

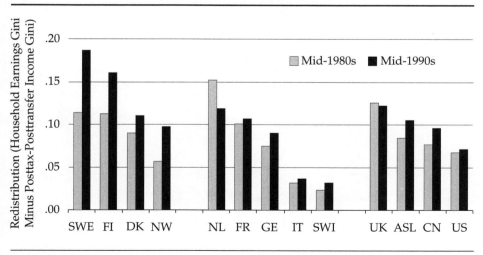

Source: Author's compilation; see appendix.

What accounts for the cross-country variation in changes in redistribution during this period? It appears that here too the key determinant was employment developments (Kenworthy and Pontusson 2004). Figure 3.8 shows this clearly. In countries with large employment declines, such as Sweden and Finland, redistribution increased substantially. In countries with smaller employment losses, it increased to a lesser extent. In the Netherlands, which enjoyed a sharp rise in employment, redistribution decreased noticeably. In analyses not shown here, I regress change in redistribution on change in a host of causal variables prominent in recent cross-country research: left government, Christian Democratic government, voter turnout, union participation in economic policymaking, wage-bargaining centralization, unionization, industry-specific skills, GDP per capita, deindustrialization, trade, and female labor force participation. The regressions include all possible combinations of three or fewer of the variables. The change in employment

Figure 3.8   Change in Redistribution by Change in Employment, Thirteen Countries, Mid-1980s to Mid-1990s

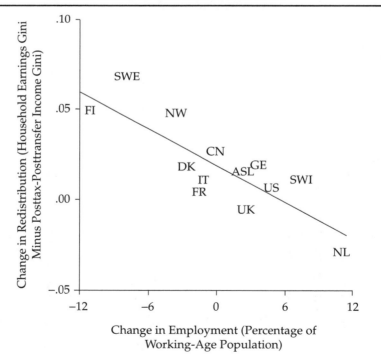

Change in Employment (Percentage of Working-Age Population)

Source: Author's compilation; see appendix.

variable is consistently negatively signed and has by far the largest standardized coefficients and t-values among the variables.

For many of these countries, the period between the mid-1980s and the mid-1990s was one of welfare state retrenchment—a scaling back of *intended* redistribution (Clayton and Pontusson 1998; Gilbert 2002; Hicks 1999; Huber and Stephens 2001; Kuhnle 2000; Pierson 2001; Ploug 1999; Swank 2002). Eligibility rules were tightened, replacement rates reduced, and stricter time limits imposed for unemployment, sickness, disability, and other benefits. Yet *actual* redistribution nevertheless increased in almost all countries (figure 3.7). The principal reason is that rising unemployment and labor force withdrawal, along with the consequent lower incomes for many households, increased the share of the working-age population eligible for government transfers.[6] In both Sweden and Finland the number of unemployment benefit recipients jumped more than fivefold between the mid-1980s and the mid-1990s, and the number of social assistance recipients nearly doubled (Ploug 1999, 83, 95; see also Marklund and Nordlund 1999, 29). The share of working-age households receiving unemployment compensation jumped from 12 percent to 25 percent in Sweden and from 10 percent to 32 percent in Finland (my calculations from LIS data). For the most part, in other words, the increase in redistribution was the product of an "expansionary compensation effect" (Garrett 1995; Rhodes 1996). It was not the result of a redistribution-enhancing shift in the characteristics of such programs, but rather an automatic, built-in response by existing social-welfare programs to falling employment (Kenworthy and Pontusson 2004).

But might the causality instead run in the other direction? Generous social-welfare programs may create substantial work disincentives. Thus, perhaps the strong inverse association between changes in employment and changes in redistribution in figure 3.8 emerges because increases in redistribution caused declines in employment, rather than because declines in employment caused increases in redistribution. However, this seems improbable. As just noted, between the mid-1980s and the mid-1990s most affluent countries implemented (moderate) cutbacks in social-welfare programs—tightening eligibility criteria, reducing replacement rates, and shortening the duration of benefits. It seems unlikely that this triggered a *decrease* in the share of working-age adults choosing to work. Since these cutbacks heightened the incentive to work, any effect on the employment rate should have instead been in the direction of causing a *rise* in employment. The association between changes in employment and changes in redistribution would therefore appear to be due to the former causing the latter, rather than the other way around. Exogenously produced job losses and labor force withdrawal increased the share of the working-age population eligible for benefits (in spite of tighter eligibility restrictions), triggering an automatic increase in redistributive transfers.[7]

What about welfare state generosity (what I have referred to here as intended redistribution)? Did it matter? There is good reason to expect that it should. A decline in employment should generate a larger increase in redistribution in a country with a more generous welfare state. This can be assessed through a regression of mid-1980s to mid-1990s change in redistribution on three variables: change in employment, the generosity of social-welfare programs, and a multiplicative interaction term. The interaction term tests whether the effect of changes in employment on changes in redistribution varies according to the degree of welfare state generosity. To measure welfare state generosity I use the average gross unemployment benefit replacement rate over the mid-1980s to the mid-1990s.[8] The regression equation is as follows:

$$\Delta \text{ redistribution} = .004519$$
$$+ .001775 \ \Delta \text{ employment}$$
$$+ .000274 \text{ replacement rate}$$
$$- .000081 \text{ interaction: } \Delta \text{ employment} \times \text{replacement rate}$$

Since an interaction term is included, the coefficients (and t-statistics) for the other variables do not have their usual interpretation. What is important is the interaction term itself. Because standardized coefficients are not interpretable for interaction variables, I show the unstandardized coefficients here. The coefficient for the interaction term is negative, as expected, and it has a large t-statistic of 3.47. This suggests that a decline in employment did tend to generate a larger increase in actual redistribution in countries where the replacement rate was higher. This regression yields an R-squared of .81, accounting for most of the cross-country variation in changes in redistribution.

Figure 3.9 shows the degree to which changes in employment are estimated to have altered redistribution, conditional on the level of welfare state generosity. For employment declines, the lines slope up to the right, indicating that a given decline in employment led to a larger increase in redistribution where the unemployment benefit replacement rate was higher. Sweden, Finland, and Denmark are illustrative cases. The replacement rates in Denmark and Finland were virtually identical (at around 60 percent). Redistribution increased more in Finland because there was a larger decrease in employment. Sweden experienced a slightly less severe employment decline than Finland, but redistribu-

Figure 3.9   Estimated Impact of Changes in Employment on Changes in Redistribution, Depending on the Level of Welfare State Generosity, Mid-1980s to Mid-1990s

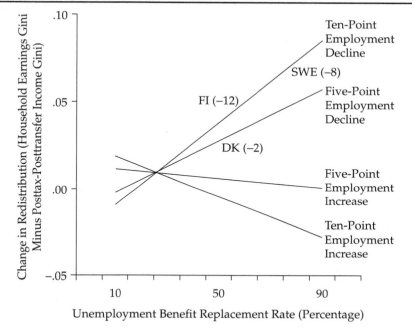

Source: Author's analysis.
Note: Numbers in parentheses indicate change in employment.

tion nevertheless increased more in Sweden because its replacement rate was considerably higher (around 85 percent).

The lines representing an increase in employment slope down to the right. This indicates that a rise in employment tended to cause a larger decline (or smaller rise) in redistribution where the replacement rate was higher. Households that formerly had one or more adults out of work—who had therefore received unemployment (or sickness or disability) benefits—no longer got those benefits once those adults moved into the workforce. Actual redistribution therefore decreased, and it did so to a greater extent in countries where the benefits were more generous than where they were less generous.

Actual redistribution—the degree to which taxes and transfers alter the market distribution of income—is a function of intended redistribution and of "need." For working-age households, need is a function chiefly of the degree of non-employment and of low earnings among the employed. The findings here suggest that during the period from the mid-1980s to the mid-1990s cross-country differences in changes in actual redistribution were determined largely by changes in employment (need), in conjunction with the level of welfare state generosity (intended redistribution).[9]

The Net Effect of Employment Changes

Employment developments appear to have played a central role in both aspects of over-time changes in inequality among working-age households. In particular, employment declines are strongly associated with both rising household earnings inequality and rising redistribution. What, then, is their net effect? If a decrease in employment produces an increase in market inequality but also an increase in redistribution, there may be little net change in posttax-posttransfer household income inequality. By the same token, an employment increase may cause a decline in market inequality but also a reduction in redistribution, again yielding little or no net alteration of posttax-posttransfer inequality.

The experiences of Sweden and the Netherlands are illustrative. As of the mid-1980s Sweden had a lower level of household earnings inequality among working-age households than the Netherlands (figure 3.3). Because of contrasting employment trends, however, between the mid-1980s and the mid-1990s household earnings inequality decreased in the Netherlands and increased substantially in Sweden. This is shown in figure 3.10. By the mid-1990s the level of household earnings inequality was higher in Sweden than in the Netherlands (figure 3.3). Both countries implemented some moderate welfare state cutbacks in the late 1980s and early 1990s. Yet because of declining employment, in Sweden a growing number of individuals and households became eligible for unemployment compensation or social assistance benefits, resulting in an increase in redistribution (figure 3.8). In the Netherlands the opposite occurred: rising employment produced a decrease in redistribution. Consequently, there was little change in posttax-posttransfer income inequality in either of these two nations: a very marginal increase in Sweden and a very marginal decrease in the Netherlands (figure 3.10).

Because changes in employment have these offsetting effects, in the short run sizable increases in posttax-posttransfer inequality are more likely to result from increases in earnings inequality among employed individuals, single-earner households, or marital homogamy than from declines in employment. This is illustrated by the contrasting develop-

Figure 3.10   Change in Household Earnings Inequality and Change in Posttax-Posttransfer Household Income Inequality in Thirteen Countries, Mid-1980s to Mid-1990s

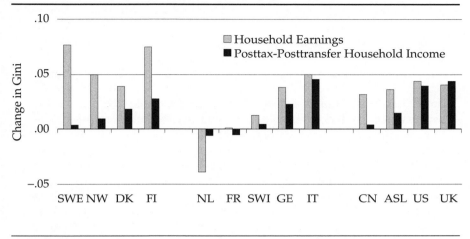

Source: Author's compilation; see appendix.

ments in Sweden, Norway, and Finland on the one hand, and in the United States, the United Kingdom, and Italy on the other. Household earnings inequality rose in all six of these countries between the mid-1980s and the mid-1990s (figure 3.10). In the three Nordic nations this was almost entirely a product of employment declines, but that was not the case in the United States and the United Kingdom, and it was true only to a limited extent in Italy (figure 3.4). Because of this difference in the source of rising household earnings inequality, as well as a difference in welfare state generosity, there was much less of an increase in compensatory redistribution in the latter three countries (figure 3.8). Despite a more modest rise in earnings inequality, these three nations therefore ended up with a more pronounced increase in inequality of posttax-posttransfer income than did Sweden, Norway, and Finland (figure 3.10).

In the long run, however, employment could conceivably turn out to be more important in influencing developments in posttax-posttransfer inequality. As just noted, part of the reason why redistribution increased relatively little in the United States, the United Kingdom, and Italy is that existing social-welfare programs in those countries are less generous than in Sweden, Norway, and Finland. A fall in employment generates a larger increase in redistribution, and therefore a smaller rise in posttax-posttransfer income inequality, in a country with a more generous welfare state (figure 3.9). Differences in welfare state generosity are a product of voter preferences ("tastes for equality") and political-economic actors and institutions, such as organized labor movements, leftist parties, corporatist arrangements, and government structures (Hicks 1999; Huber and Stephens 2001). Yet a long-term decline in employment could pose a threat to the generosity of welfare states even in countries with relatively egalitarian preferences and institutions. The redistributive burden—the tax burden necessary to sustain generous transfer programs—in a country with continuously declining employment might eventually become unsustainable, at least in the public mind, which could lead to significant cutbacks in such programs. This in turn could cause such a country to shift to a higher "equilibrium" level of posttax-posttransfer income inequality.

Although this scenario is not outside the realm of possibility, it has not happened thus far in any of the Nordic or continental countries. Between the mid-1980s and mid-1990s the only affluent country that experienced a sharp drop in employment and implemented a nontrivial reduction in its replacement rate for unemployment benefits was Sweden. The Swedish employment rate dropped from 81 percent in 1990 to 70 percent in 1996. Partly because of growing sentiment that an overly generous welfare state had contributed to the employment decline, the replacement rate for a worker who became unemployed was cut from 90 percent of former earnings to 80 percent. Yet at 80 percent Sweden's replacement rate remained the highest among affluent nations.

Since the mid-1990s employment rates in the more egalitarian countries have increased, in a few cases substantially. Between the mid-1990s and 2002 the employment rate rose by six percentage points in Finland, by four percentage points in Norway, by three percentage points in Sweden, and by two percentage points in Denmark. These increases should have helped to reduce the perceived need for welfare state cutbacks.

Conclusion

What are the implications of these findings for the viability of egalitarian capitalism? On the one hand, a number of the countries that experienced the worst employment performance and therefore suffered the sharpest increases in household earnings inequality are relatively egalitarian nations—particularly Sweden and Finland, but also Norway and Denmark. This suggests that there might be something about the institutions and/or policies that promote equality in these countries that contributes, in the current economic environment, to poor employment performance. I explore this issue in chapters 5 and 6.

On the other hand, the findings offer clear evidence of the importance of social-welfare programs in contributing to low disposable income inequality. In every country that suffered an employment decline (except the United Kingdom), the welfare state helped to partially offset the rise in household earnings inequality. And as figure 3.9 makes clear, the more generous the welfare state, the greater the degree of compensatory redistribution.

Because increases in household earnings inequality that resulted from employment declines tended to be offset by compensatory government redistribution, the rise in posttax–posttransfer income inequality was modest in relatively egalitarian countries such as Sweden, Finland, Norway, and Denmark (figure 3.10). By contrast, the rise in income inequality was generally larger in less egalitarian countries, such as the United States and the United Kingdom, where household earnings inequality increased mainly for reasons other than employment decline and where welfare states are less generous. Thus, the more egalitarian countries appear to have weathered the employment crises of the early to mid-1990s fairly successfully—that is, without suffering major increases in income inequality. And employment levels have increased since the mid-1990s in all of these nations, suggesting that there is reason for optimism about the continued viability of relatively low levels of inequality.

= Chapter 4 =

An Equality-Growth Trade-off?

Egalitarianism may still be viable, but is it counterproductive? That is, can low inequality be achieved only at the expense of other desirable goals? In this chapter I examine the oldest of these concerns: that equality impedes economic growth.

There are two opposing views about the effect of income inequality on economic growth. One holds that inequality is beneficial for growth. Arthur Okun's 1975 book *Equality and Efficiency: The Big Trade-off* offers the classic expression of this perspective: "Any insistence on carving the pie into equal slices would shrink the size of the pie. That fact poses the trade-off between economic equality and efficiency." Okun professes that "equality in the distribution of incomes . . . would be my ethical preference. Abstracting from the costs and consequences, I would prefer more equality of income to less." But he concludes that given the existence of a trade-off between equality and growth, society ought to forgo reduction of inequality in favor of a healthy economy (Okun 1975, 47–48).

The mechanisms underlying this presumed effect are relatively straightforward (Aghion, Caroli, and García-Peñalosa 1999, 1620; Arrow 1979; Browning and Johnson 1984; Kaldor 1956, 1957; Letwin 1983; Mirrlees 1971; Okun 1975; Stiglitz 1969; Welch 1999). Investment, work effort, and skills are key sources of growth. First, those with higher incomes tend to save a larger share of their income than do those with moderate or low incomes; by necessity, the latter tend to spend most of their income. The wealthy thus are the principal source of investment in a capitalist economy. Consequently, the smaller the income share of the rich—that is, the less inequality—the less investment there will be. Second, compressed earnings distributions and the high tax rates used to fund redistributive programs reduce the financial gain from hard work and skill development. This may cause people to reduce their work effort and investment in skills. And those with limited labor market prospects may be tempted to live off government benefits rather than work.

Few dispute that a perfectly equal distribution of income would indeed have deleterious economic consequences. Complete distributive equality would virtually eliminate monetary incentives, which surely would substantially reduce work effort and investment. Skeptics have pointed out, however, that there is reason to question these hypothesized processes at actually existing levels of inequality (Alesina and Rodrik 1994; Bénabou 1996; Birdsall, Ross, and Sabot 1995; Bowles and Gintis 1995; Clarke 1995; Gomez and Meltz 2001; Kenworthy 1995, ch. 3; Osberg 1984, ch. 12; Perotti 1996; Persson and Tabellini 1994; Slemrod 2003; Thurow 1981).

First, the savings-investment channel presumes a closed economy. If capital is available from foreign sources, as is increasingly the case, investment is less dependent on the domestic savings rate. In addition, since the wealthy tend to save a higher share of their income than do the poor, greater inequality may yield weaker consumer demand. Demand can be just as important as investment in sustaining economic growth. Moreover, low demand may in turn lead to less investment, rather than more, owing to a lower profit rate and less capacity utilization.

Second, individuals' response to higher tax rates is theoretically ambiguous. Some may reduce their work effort or skill development because the payoff is low, whereas others may increase them because doing so is necessary to attain the desired income.

In addition, high levels of inequality may be viewed by those at the middle and bottom of the income distribution as excessively unfair, thereby reducing worker motivation and workplace cooperation. Equity theory in social psychology posits that workers who perceive themselves as unfairly paid lower their work effort (Adams 1965). Theoretical work by economists builds on this notion to suggest, for example, that "equality is desirable on efficiency grounds. The compression of wages suppresses unwanted uncooperative behavior" (Lazear 1989, 563; see also Akerlof and Yellen 1990; Levine 1991; Schmid 1993; Solow 1990). A variety of empirical studies have found that when workers perceive their pay as unfair relative to that of others, they tend to be resentful and may reduce their work effort or cooperation (see Akerlof and Yellen 1990; Cook and Hegtvedt 1983). Similarly, experiments indicate that people tend to care about being treated fairly and are willing to resist perceived unfairness even if doing so is costly to them (Kahneman, Knetsch, and Thaler 1991). Of course, fairness norms vary somewhat across countries (Kelley and Evans 1993). A particular degree of income inequality may be viewed as less objectionable by workers in the United States than by their counterparts in Sweden. But if norms regarding fair income distribution differ less across countries than do actual levels of inequality, which seems quite possible, then differing levels of inequality could result in differing degrees of work effort and workplace cooperation.

Third, higher levels of inequality may increase the share of the population that finds it difficult to invest in college education. This is particularly likely to be true in the United States. Even with substantial funds available for financial aid, many students from lower-income households are forced to pay a relatively large amount to attend college. A study by the U.S. Census Bureau (Boggess and Ryan 2002, table 6a) found that among students from families with incomes below $25,000, the average yearly cost of attending college as of 1996 was $6,000. The average amount covered by financial aid was $3,000, leaving the remaining $3,000 to be paid by the students or their parents. Thomas Kane (2001) reports that in 1980, 55 percent of children from families in the top income quartile attended a four-year college compared to 29 percent of those from families in the bottom quartile. By 1992, as income inequality increased, the difference had widened to 66 percent versus 28 percent. These quartile differences are smaller but still sizable when parents' education, student test scores, and student high school rank are controlled for (Kane 2001).

Several additional reasons have been suggested for why inequality may be bad for growth. One is that the financial constraints and frustration generated by high levels of inequality may reduce trust, cooperation, civic engagement, and other growth-enhancing forms of social capital. Similarly, it may spur a greater amount of crime, leading to heightened expenditure on nonproductive "guard labor."

Another suggestion is that higher levels of market inequality may generate popular demand for increased government spending, particularly on transfers, which may reduce growth. However, this effect does not appear to occur in affluent nations. In such nations higher levels of market inequality are not associated with higher levels of government transfers. Instead, more unequal countries tend to have less generous welfare states; for the mid-1990s, pretax-pretransfer income inequality and government transfers as a share of GDP correlate at −.51 across the fifteen affluent countries for which data are available.

And finally, it has been suggested that income polarization may foster extralegal demands for economic or political reform. Rebellions, revolutions, and other forms of violent collective action may adversely affect growth by diminishing political stability. However, this causal channel too seems unlikely to apply to affluent countries. Political stability in rich nations has not in recent decades been disrupted by violent collective action stemming from excessive inequality.

In the 1990s the then-conventional Okun view was called into question on empirical grounds as a slew of analyses discovered that countries with more inequality tend to have slower rates of economic growth (see, for example, Birdsall, Ross, and Sabot 1995; Clarke 1995; Perotti 1996; Persson and Tabellini 1994). However, less-developed countries account for the bulk of the cases in all of these studies. The findings may therefore offer little insight into processes in affluent economies.

Interestingly, several recent studies of rich countries have found evidence for a growth-enhancing effect of inequality (Barro 2000; Brandolini and Rossi 1998; Forbes 2000). Is the Okun view correct, then? Is income inequality beneficial for economic growth once nations reach a certain level of affluence?

This chapter offers a reassessment of this issue. Theoretical expectations are indeterminate, so the question can only be answered empirically. I conduct three sets of analyses. I begin by examining the effect of inequality on growth across fifteen rich countries in the 1980s and 1990s. I then conduct a similar analysis for the U.S. states. Finally, I explore longitudinal trends in the United States since World War II. In each case I examine both the aggregate relationship between inequality and growth and the hypothesized causal mechanisms.

Four of the six mechanisms through which inequality is hypothesized to reduce growth may apply with greater force to poverty. If a large share of the population have very low incomes, this may be particularly likely to undercut consumer demand, reduce motivation to work, limit opportunities for education, and breed frustration and social disharmony. In the final section of the chapter, I therefore reexamine the cross-country, cross-state, and over-time U.S. analyses to see whether a focus on poverty rather than inequality alters the findings.

Research on inequality's effect on growth has presumed that the growth of economic output is of considerable importance for societal well-being. Yet a reasonable argument can be made that the growth of *incomes*—as indicated by the median income or by the income level at lower points in the distribution—is a much more relevant concern. Although I am quite sympathetic to this view, the level of economic output does establish the upper limits for incomes. It is therefore likely to have considerable bearing on real income levels. Indeed, among the affluent countries I examine here there is a very strong association between mid-1990s levels of gross domestic product (GDP) per capita and median posttax-posttransfer household income (adjusted for household size): $r = .89$. I therefore bracket this issue and follow the lead of prior researchers who have focused on output growth as the outcome of interest.

Cross-Country Patterns

Findings suggesting that less egalitarian countries grow more rapidly are consistent with the tenor of much recent commentary about the European and U.S. economic models. During the 1990s concern grew among researchers, policymakers, and citizens about the seemingly excessive generosity of European welfare states and the apparent rigidities of European labor markets (see Esping-Andersen and Regini 2000; Pierson 2001). The less regulated and less egalitarian U.S. economy was increasingly viewed as better suited to achieving rapid economic growth.

In this section, I examine the effect of income inequality on growth across fifteen rich OECD countries in the 1980s and 1990s. I use the Luxembourg Income Study database as the source of data on income inequality. The three recent studies that find a growth-enhancing effect of inequality in affluent countries rely on data from the Deininger and Squire (1996, n.d.) dataset, which includes more observations, but at the expense of cross-country comparability (Atkinson and Brandolini 2001). The LIS database includes data for years prior to the 1980s for only a few countries. Thus, my analysis is confined to the period 1980 to 2000. I include fifteen nations for which LIS income inequality data are available circa 1980: Australia, Austria, Belgium, Canada, Denmark, Finland, France, Germany, Italy, the Netherlands, Norway, Sweden, Switzerland, the United Kingdom, and the United States. I use the Gini coefficient for posttax-posttransfer income to measure inequality. As noted in chapter 2, Gini coefficients range from zero to one, with larger numbers indicating greater inequality. Economic growth is measured as the average annual rate of change in real GDP per capita. Definitions and data sources for all variables are listed in the appendix.

My approach to analyzing the effect of income inequality on growth is similar in a number of respects to that of Robert Barro (2000) and many of the other recent growth analyses by economists. First, whatever impact income inequality may have on economic growth, it is almost certain to be primarily a long-run effect rather than a short-run one. The hypothesized causal mechanisms described earlier probably take a while to play out. For instance, suppose a lower level of inequality boosts educational attainment. This may lead to faster growth, but only after at least a decade or more. Two of the recent cross-national studies that find a positive effect of inequality on growth analyze relatively short-run effects: Andrea Brandolini and Nicola Rossi (1998) find such an effect using annual data, and Kristin Forbes (2000) does so using five-year periods. These time periods are so short as to cast doubt on the plausibility of the apparent relationship. When Forbes extends her analysis to ten-year periods, the inequality variable is no longer statistically significant. I examine the effect of inequality on growth over a twenty-year period covering the 1980s and 1990s.

Second, most of the variation in income inequality is across countries rather than over time. The coefficient of variation for posttax-posttransfer Ginis across the fifteen countries circa 1980 is .14, while the average coefficient of variation for Ginis within each country during the 1980s and 1990s is only .05. Thus, analyses with a cross-sectional focus are more likely to yield informative estimates of causal effects than are analyses with a longitudinal emphasis (Jackman 1985, 173ff.). In addition, cross-sectional analyses are appropriate for analyzing long-run effects (Firebaugh and Beck 1994, 636).

Third, the specified relationship is between levels of inequality and growth of real output per capita. Reverse causality is a potential concern: a variety of studies suggest a possible effect of economic growth on the level of inequality (see, for example, Alderson and Nielsen 2002; Barro 2000; Kuznets 1955). To avoid this problem I measure inequality around 1980, since growth during the 1980s and 1990s cannot have caused the level of inequality at the beginning of this period. This would be problematic if inequality changed a substantial amount over time and there was significant cross-country variation in the degree of change. But although there was indeed an increase in inequality in many of these nations (see figure 3.2), that did not alter the cross-country variation in levels very much. The correlation across the fifteen countries between posttax-posttransfer income inequality circa 1980 and circa 1995 is .85.[1]

Fourth, when comparing growth performance it is critical to take into account each country's initial level of per capita GDP. Among the affluent OECD nations, a strong "catch-up" process has operated since World War II: poorer nations grow faster than richer ones because the former are able to benefit from technological developments and larger markets in the latter (Baumol, Nelson, and Wolff 1994; Hicks and Kenworthy 1998). In a regression of 1980 to 2000 growth rates on 1979 levels of per capita GDP, the initial per capita GDP variable has a standardized coefficient of −.56 and an absolute t-statistic larger than 2.00. I use the residuals from this regression as the dependent variable in the analyses here. They represent growth rates adjusted for catch-up effects.

Figure 4.1 plots 1980 to 2000 catch-up-adjusted growth rates by 1980 levels of income inequality. The pattern suggests a possible negative effect of inequality on growth, but it is a very weak effect at best. The most heavily populated portion of the chart is the lower-right corner, which corresponds to higher inequality and lower growth. But to the extent that there is a pattern of inverse association between the two variables, it is substantially weakened by the strong growth perfor-

Figure 4.1   Catch-Up-Adjusted Economic Growth by Income Inequality Circa 1980, Fifteen Countries, 1980 to 2000

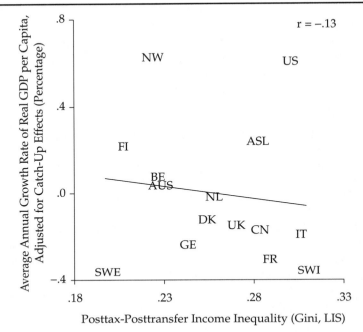

Source: Author's compilation; see appendix.

mance of the high-inequality United States and the poor growth performance of low-inequality Sweden.

What happens when we turn to multivariate analysis? I include a variety of variables that have been found relevant in prior cross-country growth studies (Barro 2000; Garrett 1998, ch. 5; Gemmell 1996; Hall and Gingerich 2001; Hicks and Kenworthy 1998; Levine and Renelt 1992; Olson 1982; Sala-i-Martin 1997). These variables (with the expected direction of effect in parentheses) are: nonworking-age (under fifteen or over sixty-four) share of the population (–); real long-term interest rates (–); government tax revenues as a share of GDP (–); left government (+); inflation (–); trade (±); terms of trade, measured as the ratio of export prices to import prices (+); union concentration (+); institutional coherence (+); and firm-level economic cooperation (+). Several other potential controls—change in terms of trade, unionization, change in unionization, and business concentration—are not included because they are too highly correlated with income inequality (r > ±.65). Four additional variables are added separately because they represent possible channels through which inequality may affect growth: investment as a share of GDP (+); labor force participation as a share of the working-age population (+); educational attainment, measured as the share of persons age twenty-five to sixty-four with a tertiary education (+); and social capital, measured using survey data on the degree of trust (+). All of the control variables are measured as stocks (levels), using a period average. For those for which there is a theoretical rationale and available data, I also include a flow (change) measure.

Table 4.1 shows the regression results. Economic growth adjusted for catch-up effects is the dependent variable. Because of the small number of cases (fifteen) relative to the number of explanatory factors, I estimate a series of regressions that include all possible combinations of three or fewer of the independent variables. The table shows the minimum, median, and maximum standardized coefficients for the inequality variable and for the control variables that are consistently signed and have t-ratios larger than 1.00 (in absolute value) in at least half of the regressions in which they are included. I then estimate models that include various combinations of the surviving variables and report the models that explain the largest share of the cross-country variation in economic growth.

The inequality coefficient is negatively signed in almost all of the regressions, suggesting an adverse effect of inequality on growth. And in the best overall and three-variable regressions (fourth and fifth columns), the standardized coefficient is fairly large. In many of the models, however, the t-statistic for the inequality coefficient is smaller than 1.00, suggesting a great deal of variability in the estimated effect. More important, the consistent negative signs for the inequality coefficients are sensitive to the inclusion or exclusion of Norway. Norway had one of the lowest levels of inequality among the fifteen countries, along with one of the fastest catch-up-adjusted growth rates. But Norway's strong growth performance arguably was much more a product of its oil resources than of its low inequality. When Norway is omitted from the regressions, the sign for the inequality coefficient turns positive in some of the specifications and its t-statistic is always very small (not shown). This suggests that inequality probably had no effect on the cross-country variation in growth in the 1980s and 1990s.

These analyses are vulnerable to unobserved heterogeneity bias (see chapter 2). That is, there may be unmeasured country-specific features, such as culture, that are correlated with the level of income inequality and have an impact on growth. The coefficient for the inequality variable could be picking up what actually are the effects of some such features. However, it is difficult to say which direction such bias might work in. If the unmeasured traits of low-inequality countries such as

Table 4.1   Regression Results: Effect of Income Inequality and Other Variables on Catch-Up-Adjusted Economic Growth, Fifteen Countries, 1980 to 2000

	All Possible Models of Three or Fewer Variables			Best Models	
	Minimum	Median	Maximum	1	2
Income inequality (posttax-post-transfer), circa 1980	−.57 (1.84)	−.22 (.78)	.01 (.11)	−.44 (2.14)	−.47 (2.30)
Other variables					
Government tax revenues	−.71 (2.30)	−.67 (2.25)	−.39 (1.44)	−.38 (1.58)	−.39 (1.79)
Terms of trade	.17 (.65)	.52 (1.95)	.59 (2.24)	.13 (.56)	
Educational attainment	.55 (2.46)	.68 (3.00)	.70 (3.08)	.48 (1.67)	.55 (2.44)
Inequality coefficient when investment is added	−.50 (1.56)	−.13 (.51)	.03 (.10)		
Inequality coefficient when change in investment is added	−.43 (1.43)	−.07 (.25)	.05 (.15)		
Inequality coefficient when labor force participation is added	−.56 (1.73)	−.14 (.41)	−.04 (.14)		
Inequality coefficient when change in labor force participation is added	−.58 (1.73)	−.30 (.99)	−.17 (.67)		
Inequality coefficient when educational attainment is added	−.47 (2.30)	−.24 (.98)	−.16 (.65)		
Inequality coefficient when social capital is added	−.39 (1.21)	−.01 (.04)	.05 (.19)		

Source: Author's analysis; see appendix.
Notes: Standardized coefficients, with absolute t-ratios (based on heteroskedasticity-robust standard errors) in parentheses. OLS regressions. Results in columns 1, 2, and 3 are from regressions using all possible combinations of three or fewer of the independent variables (12 variables, 296 regressions). Variables included in the regressions but not reported here owing to inconsistent signs and lack of absolute t-ratios greater than 1.00 in at least half of the regressions are: nonworking-age share of the population, change in nonworking-age share of the population, real long-term interest rates, left government, inflation, trade, change in trade, union concentration, institutional coherence, and firm-level economic cooperation. "Best models" regressions are those with the largest adjusted R-squared. The results in the lower portion of the table are from regressions with income inequality, the variable listed for the particular row of the table (for example, investment), and each of the other eleven control variables (eleven regressions). Aside from income inequality, all levels variables are measured as period averages. Change variables are measured as the average annual rate of change. Minimum and maximum R-squared: .02, .55. N = 15.

Sweden and Finland are good for growth whereas those of high-inequality countries such as the United States and Switzerland are bad for growth, then the inequality coefficient is biased in favor of finding a negative effect of inequality on growth. If the reverse is true, then the inequality coefficient is biased in favor of finding a positive effect of inequality on growth. I do not think there are strong a priori reasons to favor one or the other of these two possibilities. I therefore suspect that any bias resulting from unmeasured country-specific traits is likely to be relatively small.

The results shown in the lower portion of the table test the purported causal channels through which inequality might affect growth. (Data on tertiary education are not available over a long enough period of time to create a measure of change in educational attainment. The same is true for social capital.) If inequality had an effect on growth, adding a variable that represents a true causal channel should reduce the size of the coefficient for the inequality variable. However, because there is no robust impact of inequality in the regressions reported in the top portion of the table, these tests are superfluous. As it turns out, the coefficient for the inequality variable is not affected at all by the addition of investment, labor force participation, or social capital. Nor are these variables themselves related to growth. Educational attainment, by contrast, appears to have a strong positive association with growth. However, it is only weakly correlated with inequality and in the "wrong" direction $(r = .18)$. Moreover, when educational attainment is added to the regression, the coefficient for the inequality variable gets larger—the opposite of what we would expect if educational attainment were a mechanism through which inequality reduces growth. The lack of evidence for a causal mechanism reinforces the conclusion that inequality had no effect on economic growth across the fifteen countries.

On the other hand, one of the variables that *is* consistently related to growth performance in these regressions is government tax revenues. This variable is negatively signed, suggesting that a larger tax share reduces economic growth. And the standardized coefficients are relatively large. Since high tax levels are a prerequisite for extensive redistribution, which is one of the principal means of achieving low inequality, perhaps this provides indirect evidence of a growth-enhancing effect of inequality. In other words, perhaps low inequality itself did not impede growth, but the chief strategy for generating low inequality did. This, however, turns out not to be the case. The strong growth-reducing results for the tax revenues variable are a function of (1) multicollinearity, as it is relatively closely correlated with income inequality $(r = -.59)$, and (2) the influence of the United States. When the inequality variable is dropped from the regressions, the tax revenues variable sometimes turns positive and has consistently small t-statistics. The same is true if the United States, whose growth performance was on par with Norway's, is omitted. Did the United States have strong growth performance *because* of its low taxes? Possibly, but the United States also had comparatively low taxes in the several decades preceding the 1980s and 1990s, and its growth performance then was among the weakest in this group of countries (Kenworthy 1995, ch. 4).

Cross-State Patterns

Brandolini and Rossi's (1998) recent study reporting a positive effect of inequality on growth in affluent countries finds this effect to exist only among the Anglo nations. This suggests that it may be worthwhile to examine the relationship in this more limited subset of countries. It seems plausible to suspect that, if inequality does have a growth-enhancing effect, the effect is most likely to hold in countries with more individualistic cultures. The problem, for purposes of analysis, is that there are only a few Anglo countries. Brandolini and Rossi deal with this limitation by conducting a pooled time-series analysis with annual observations. As suggested earlier, this is far too short a period for an informative exploration of inequality's effect on growth.

A useful way to get around the problem of too few Anglo nations is to examine the U.S. states. Of course, the states differ notably from affluent countries in that state boundaries are highly porous with regard to the movement of capital, labor, and technology. Shifts of plants across state borders were already common by the late 1800s, when textile mills began moving from New England to the South. Financing can easily be obtained from outside state borders. Labor mobility across states is sufficiently unimpeded that the country's labor market was characterized as truly "national" in scope by the 1960s (Wright 1987). And there are no major barriers to the flow of technology between states. This degree of economic integration calls into question the relevance of state-level features as determinants of state growth rates. National boundaries, although they have been eroded somewhat by globalization over the past two decades, remain less porous in this respect (Helliwell 1998).

However, despite the potential for such integration to eliminate state differences in economic conditions and thus in performance outcomes, the states do differ a great deal in their economic structures, policy choices, and performance patterns (Kenworthy 1999b). Most relevant for my purposes here, the states continue to vary considerably in their rates of economic growth, and prior studies (for example, Brace 1993; Gray and Lowery 1988) have found a statistically and substantively significant impact of state-level factors on that variation. The states thus seem a suitable unit of analysis for assessing the growth effects of factors such as income inequality.

For consistency with the country-level analysis, I again focus on the 1980s and 1990s. Like most state-level analyses of economic performance, I exclude Alaska and Hawaii. Growth is measured as the average annual rate of change in real gross state product (GSP) per capita. Here too I adjust the growth rates for catch-up effects. A regression of 1980 to 2000 growth on 1979 levels of real per capita GSP yields a standardized coefficient of −.38 with a t-statistic larger than 2.00. I use the residuals from this regression as the dependent variable in the analyses. I utilize income inequality data for 1979 from the U.S. Census Bureau. Unlike the LIS data, those available from the Census Bureau do not include capital gains, the value of near-cash transfers such as food stamps, or taxes. A Gini coefficient for each state can be calculated from the LIS data, but there is no state identifier in the 1979 LIS U.S. dataset. The earliest LIS year for which state Ginis can be computed is 1986. These Ginis for posttax-posttransfer income correlate at .65 with the 1979 Census Bureau Ginis. Because this correlation is only moderately strong, I tried substituting the LIS data in the analyses. Doing so did not substantively alter the results.

Figure 4.2 plots catch-up-adjusted growth over 1980 to 2000 by 1979 levels of income inequality in the U.S. states. The pattern is similar to that for affluent countries (figure 4.1). It suggests a possible growth-reducing effect of inequality, but again the effect is at best a relatively weak one.

As with the cross-country analyses, the next step is to introduce a set of control variables that are likely to be related to both inequality and growth to see whether they alter the estimate of inequality's effect. Interest rates, inflation, trade, and terms of trade cannot be included because no state-level data exist for these variables. I include the following variables that were used in the cross-country analyses: non-working-age share of the population (−); government tax revenues as a share of GSP (−); left government, measured as the proportion of the period in which the Democratic Party controlled both houses of the state legislature and the governorship simultaneously (+); unionization (−); union concentration (+); and business concentration (+). I also include several additional variables. One is a dummy variable for "sunbelt" states (+), since firms and workers may have a greater proclivity to start up in or move to warmer climates. The second is a measure of economic development policies (sometimes called "industrial policies"), such as technology transfer, support for research and development or for employee training, facilitation of cooperation among firms, export assis-

Figure 4.2   Catch-Up-Adjusted Economic Growth by Income Inequality Circa 1980, U.S. States, 1980 to 2000

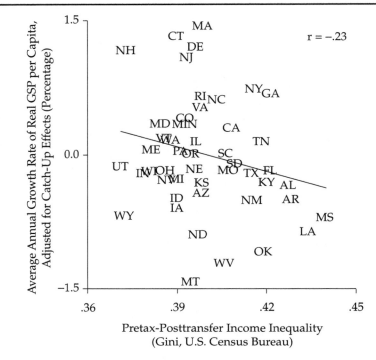

Source: Author's compilation; see appendix.

tance, and the like (+). The third is federal military contracts and payroll expenditures as a share of GSP (+); these are allocated variably across the states and may help to boost growth. Once again, some of the control variables are measured only as stocks, using a period average, while others are measured as both stocks and flows.

As with the cross-country analysis, it is possible that these findings are biased by unmeasured state-specific characteristics. Here too, though, it is not clear in which direction such a bias might work.

To test the causal mechanisms I again include variables representing the labor force participation rate (+), educational attainment (+), and social capital (+). Educational attainment is measured here as the share of persons age twenty-five and over with a four-year college degree. Social capital is measured with an index based on fourteen indicators such as trust, participation in groups and community activities,

and voter participation, among others. There are no state-level investment data. The savings-investment channel is unlikely to hold in the
state context in any case: investment flows so freely across state borders that the savings rate within a particular state is not likely to have
a strong impact on investment within that state. The same is true for
the consumption-investment channel: when a reasonably large share
of the goods and services produced in a state are sold outside the
state, as is certainly the case in the contemporary American economy,
there is little reason to suspect that the level of investment within a
state is determined to any noteworthy degree by consumption within
that state.

Table 4.2 reports the regression results. With a state-level analysis the
number of cases increases to forty-eight, so it is possible to follow the
more traditional procedure of starting with a large number of independent variables and removing those that are statistically irrelevant. I begin with a regression that includes inequality and all of the control variables. Stepwise deletion of variables with the smallest absolute t-value
results in the equation reported in column 1. In these regressions and a
variety of others that include various combinations of the controls, the
income inequality coefficient always has a negative sign and reasonably large t-statistics, suggesting an adverse impact on growth. This result is not fully robust, however. Utah is among the states with the lowest levels of inequality. If it is removed, the inequality coefficient drops
to just −.08 and the t-statistic falls to .63 (in absolute value). Still, the coefficient does remain negatively signed, suggesting a possible negative
impact—albeit a very weak one.

Income inequality is inversely correlated with levels of labor force
participation, educational attainment, and social capital ($r = -.66, -.39,$
$-.55$), which is consistent with the hypothesis of a negative effect of inequality on growth. Columns 2, 4, and 6 of the table show the results
when each of these variables, respectively, is added to the regression.
Adding the social capital variable has only a minor impact on the inequality coefficient, but the addition of labor force participation and educational attainment causes the coefficient to drop to almost zero. The
labor force participation variable itself is positively signed, but it is
fairly small, both in absolute size and in relation to its standard error.
Nor does it improve when other combinations of the control variables
are tried. Educational attainment, by contrast, is strongly related to
growth, and this relationship holds up in a variety of alternative model
specifications. This suggests that inequality may have contributed to
slower growth across the U.S. states by reducing college-level educational attainment.

Perhaps, however, the apparent link between college completion

Table 4.2   Regression Results: Effect of Income Inequality and Other Variables on Catch-Up-Adjusted Economic Growth, U.S. States, 1980 to 2000

	1	2	3	4	5	6
Income inequality (pretax-posttransfer), 1979	−.18 (1.56)	−.04 (.26)	−.17 (1.39)	−.03 (.20)	−.22 (1.85)	−.21 (1.37)
Other variables						
Nonworking-age population	−.45 (3.65)	−.45 (3.65)	−.51 (3.28)	−.38 (3.12)	−.47 (3.81)	−.43 (2.87)
Government tax revenues	−.18 (1.55)	−.12 (1.01)	−.17 (1.46)	−.12 (1.04)	−.14 (1.22)	−.18 (1.55)
Business concentration	.14 (1.41)	.09 (.79)	.13 (1.16)	.05 (.42)	.13 (1.21)	.15 (1.20)
Economic develop-ment policies	.14 (1.85)	.24 (2.03)	.19 (1.54)	.12 (1.04)	.15 (1.16)	.23 (1.81)
Military expenditures by the federal government	.19 (1.61)	.18 (1.51)	.18 (1.46)	.05 (.36)	.18 (1.56)	.19 (1.60)
Labor force participation		.21 (1.20)				
Change in labor force participation			.08 (.61)			
Educational attainment				.37 (2.36)		
Change in educational attainment					.18 (1.51)	
Social capital						−.04 (.23)
R-squared	.50	.51	.50	.56	.52	.50

Source: Author's analysis; see appendix.
Notes: Standardized coefficients, with absolute t-ratios (based on heteroskedasticity-robust standard errors) in parentheses. Other independent variables were included but were inconsistently signed and had absolute t-ratios smaller than 1.00 in more than half of the regressions: change in nonworking-age population, left government, unionization, change in unionization, union concentration, sunbelt, change in military expenditures. Aside from income inequality, all levels variables are measured as period averages. Change variables are measured as the average annual rate of change. N = 48.

and growth in the U.S. states merely reflects the fact that the best-educated migrate to where the economy is growing most quickly. There very likely is some of that going on. Yet cross-state differences in levels of educational attainment have been relatively stable over time. The correlation between college completion in 1980 and in 2000 is fairly strong (r = .81). And the regression results for the educational attainment variable are only slightly weaker if I use a 1980 measure of college completion rather than a 1980 to 2000 period average. This suggests that reverse causality—growth attracting larger numbers of college graduates, rather than college graduates contributing to growth—was not the main process at work. Furthermore, the association between college completion and growth is consistent with that found in the cross-country analysis, where migration of the college-educated is unlikely to have played a role.

That the distribution of income might affect college-level educational attainment is certainly plausible, for the reasons outlined at the beginning of this chapter. Yet there is reason to question the apparent link between income inequality and differences in college-level educational attainment across the states. As just noted, state differences in the share of those age twenty-five and over with a college degree have been fairly stable over time. If inequality had a dampening effect on college completion during the 1980 to 2000 period, then that effect should be apparent when the initial level of college educational attainment is controlled for. In other words, there should be a negative correlation between 1979 levels of income inequality and 1980 to 2000 *change* in the share of persons age twenty-five and over who have a college degree. But that is not the case. Instead, the correlation is positive (though fairly weak): $r = .21$.

Thus, the ostensible link between inequality and college-level educational attainment, and hence with growth, is probably spurious. In other words, lower inequality is associated with faster growth, but that is because lower inequality is associated with a larger share of college graduates, and it is the latter that has the true causal effect. Since inequality does not seem to have impeded college completion in the 1980s and 1990s (see also Mayer 2001), the most reasonable conclusion is that inequality's apparent negative effect on growth is not genuine.

Even if the link is genuine, it is not particularly strong. The unstandardized coefficient for the inequality variable in the regression reported in column 1 of table 4.2 is –7.07. This suggests that, on average, a difference between two states of one standard deviation (.0165) in income inequality was associated with a difference in the annual (catch-up-adjusted) growth rate of real per capita GSP of about one-tenth of a percentage point. Sustained over a very long period of time, that could amount to a sizable effect. But for a period of twenty years, it is a relatively small one.

The finding for the American states in the 1980s and 1990s is thus similar to that for affluent countries: inequality probably had little or no impact on economic growth.

The U.S. Case

Another way to explore the effect of inequality on growth is to examine longitudinal trends within countries. Because any such effect presumably is a relatively long-term one, it is best to have data stretching over a lengthy period of time. We also need a country in which there has been a nontrivial amount of variation in inequality over time. The United States is a good candidate on both counts, as data are available for many of the relevant variables for the whole of the post–World War II period and the level of inequality changed markedly during a portion of this period.

Here again, I use income inequality data from the U.S. Census Bureau. In addition to the limitations noted earlier, these historical data may be problematic in that they do not encompass single-person households; they are available only for "families," which are defined as households that include at least two related persons. How misleading a picture might we get from these data? Probably not very misleading, since the focus here is on the trend over time rather than the level of inequality at a particular point in time. For the seven years for which LIS data are available for the United States—1974, 1979, 1986, 1991, 1994, 1997, and 2000—the correlation between the Census Bureau Gini for pretax-posttransfer family income and the LIS Gini for posttax-posttransfer household income is .95. An additional measure of inequality is the income share of the top 10 percent. These data have been compiled by Thomas Picketty and Emmanuel Saez (2001) based on tax return records. They include capital gains and corporate income and employer payroll taxes, but not individual income and employee payroll taxes.

Figure 4.3 shows the over-time trends in income inequality in the United States. Both measures reveal a slight decline from the end of World War II through the early 1970s, followed by a fairly sharp rise beginning in the late 1970s and early 1980s. If inequality is good for growth, then savings, investment, work effort, or educational attainment should have declined a bit between the late 1940s and the late 1970s; then it should have risen sharply beginning sometime around the early to mid-1980s. If inequality is bad for growth, the trends for these indicators should have been in the opposite direction. The trend for economic growth, in turn, is expected to be a function of these trends.

Figure 4.4 shows the trends for savings (personal savings as a share of personal disposable income) and investment (net private fixed investment as a share of GDP). Because the values fluctuate so much from year to year, the chart includes trend lines that represent five-year moving averages. For savings, the pattern favors the notion that inequality

Figure 4.3   Income Inequality in the United States, 1947 to 2000

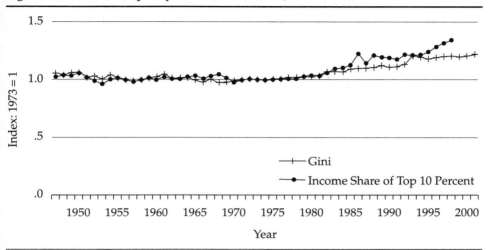

Source: Author's compilation; see appendix.

Figure 4.4   Savings and Investment in the United States, 1947 to 2000

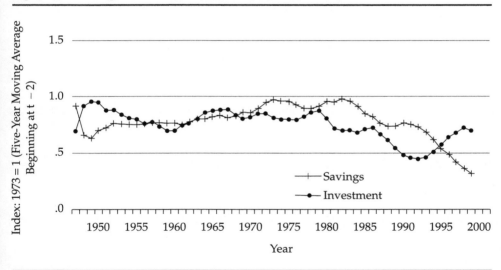

Source: Author's compilation; see appendix.

is bad for growth. Savings increased up to the mid-1970s, then dropped sharply beginning in the mid-1980s. By the end of the 1990s it had fallen to one-quarter of its 1973 level. Yet, to my knowledge, there is no compelling theoretical rationale for why an increase in income inequality would cause a decline in savings. For investment the pattern is very similar, except that, after falling throughout the 1980s, investment began to rise again in the 1990s. I return to this later.

As indicators of work effort, I include the rate of labor force participation and the level of productivity (real GDP per hour worked). The trends are shown in figure 4.5. The labor force participation rate increased steadily beginning in the early 1960s, as did productivity throughout most of this period. Neither indicator of work effort appears to have been responsive to trends in income inequality.

Figure 4.6 shows the trend in the share of persons age twenty-five and over with a four-year college degree. There is no indication that developments in income inequality had any impact; the trend moved steadily upward during the periods of both falling and rising inequality. There was a slight acceleration in the rate of increase in the early 1970s, but this appears to have been due to the massive expansion in the supply of college slots in the mid- to late 1960s coupled with Vietnam War deferments rather than to any effect of income inequality (Kane 2001).

Figure 4.5   Work Effort in the United States, 1947 to 2000

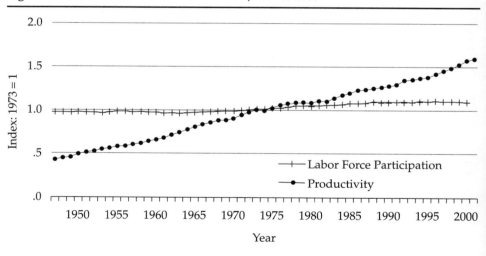

Source: Author's compilation; see appendix.

Figure 4.6   Educational Attainment in the United States, 1947 to 2000

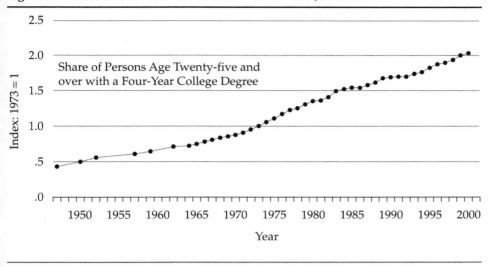

Source: Author's compilation; see appendix.

Lastly, figure 4.7 shows the postwar trends for economic growth. I include a trend curve to summarize the general pattern. There is little indication of an effect of inequality on growth in either direction. Indeed, the year-to-year correlation between income inequality (Gini coefficient, as shown in figure 4.3) and economic growth over the period 1947 to 2000 is just –.01. Lagging the inequality variable up to ten years or using an average for earlier years yields correlations no larger than –.12. The growth rate increased in the period from the mid-1950s to the mid-1960s, which could conceivably have been affected by the declining level of inequality during the preceding two decades. But that decline in inequality was so minimal that it seems extremely unlikely to have had an impact. After the mid- to late 1960s the average rate of growth was a bit lower. Inequality was higher during much of this period (figure 4.3), but the downturn in growth preceded the rise in inequality by nearly a decade. This suggests reason for skepticism that the substantial rise in inequality beginning in the mid-1970s had any appreciable effect on the rate of growth (see also Burtless 2001; Burtless and Jencks 2003).

The reasonably strong U.S. growth performance in the 1980s and 1990s is particularly interesting in light of the significant decline in savings during this period (figure 4.4). Investment also declined in the 1980s, and though it increased for much of the 1990s, it neverthe-

Figure 4.7   Economic Growth in the United States, 1947 to 2000

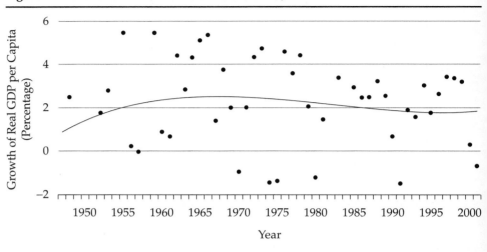

Source: Author's compilation; see appendix.

less was at historically low levels for the bulk of that decade (figure 4.4). By most accounts, U.S. growth during these two decades was driven more by consumption than by investment. This is inconsistent with the Okun-type view, which holds that high investment is critical to strong growth performance. Nor is it consistent with the newer approach to the inequality-growth relationship, which contends that higher inequality might be bad for growth because it reduces consumption. The increase in inequality in the United States did not reduce consumption.

One possible interpretation is that the rise in U.S. inequality was mainly a product of accelerating incomes at the top, and that (contra the Okun logic) these were largely consumed rather than saved. However, as figure 4.8 indicates, that interpretation is at best only partially correct. The chief source of rising income inequality in the United States since the mid-1970s was stagnant incomes in the bottom half of the distribution (Kenworthy, forthcoming). This is what distinguishes the 1980s and 1990s from earlier years. Although incomes at the top did increase, the rate of increase for the 95th percentile in the 1980s and 1990s was no faster than in previous decades. Then again, this figure does not include the incomes of those at the very top, which do indeed appear to have grown more rapidly than they did prior to the 1970s (Picketty and Saez 2001). For instance, the compensation of CEOs relative to that of

Figure 4.8 Family Income Trends in the United States, 1947 to 2001

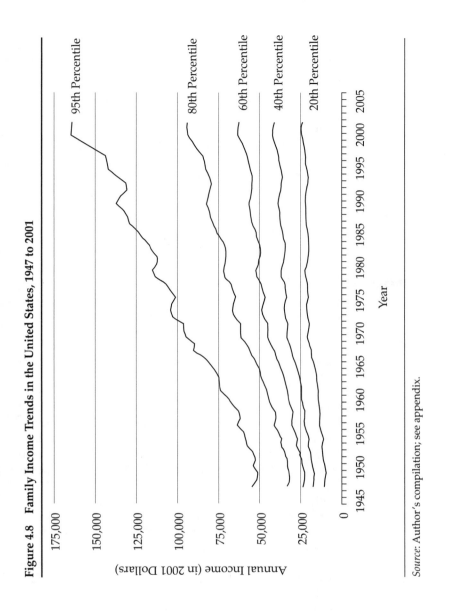

Source: Author's compilation; see appendix.

an average production worker increased moderately leading up to the 1980s, but then skyrocketed (Mishel, Bernstein, and Boushey 2003, 213).

There seem to be three main reasons why consumption was strong in the 1980s and 1990s despite stagnant incomes for the segment that tends to consume a higher portion of its income. First, in the 1980s government spending played a key role as the U.S. government ran record deficits. Second, a cultural change glorifying consumption occurred (Schor 1999). Third, there was a substantial expansion of access to credit, which allowed middle- and low-income households to continue to increase their consumption even when income growth did not support such an increase (Mishel, Bernstein, and Boushey 2003). The consumption boom in the 1990s was fueled to a significant degree by personal debt. Among families in the middle quintile of the income distribution, for example, average personal debt increased by $12,000 between 1989 and 1998 (Appelbaum 2000). None of these three processes is consistent with a story in which rising inequality plays a prominent role in either boosting or reducing economic growth.

On the whole, then, over-time developments in the United States suggest a conclusion similar to that reached in the cross-country and cross-state analyses: income inequality appears to have had little or no effect on economic growth.

Effects of Poverty on Growth

As I noted at the beginning of the chapter, several of the mechanisms through which inequality is hypothesized to adversely affect economic growth would seem to apply with even greater force to poverty. Those at the bottom of the income distribution are the most likely to consume all of their income. The lower their incomes are, the less they have to spend. Lower incomes also reduce the ability to pay for college education. Those in poverty may also be more likely to become discouraged and give up on the prospect of gainful employment. Rather than being spurred to work by their low income, in other words, they may react by withdrawing from the labor market altogether. Some may turn to crime or other socially destructive behavior. The likelihood of this is accentuated to the extent that poverty-level incomes are accompanied by social exclusion. Thus, countries or states with greater poverty may have slower economic growth.

Data are available to explore the impact of poverty on growth. Country-level data are once again taken from the Luxembourg Income Study. I use a relative measure of poverty because the mechanisms just outlined seem most likely to be generated by incomes that are low relative to the norm within a given society. State-level data and over-time data for the United States are again taken from the U.S. Census Bureau.

Figure 4.9   Poverty in the United States, 1959 to 2000

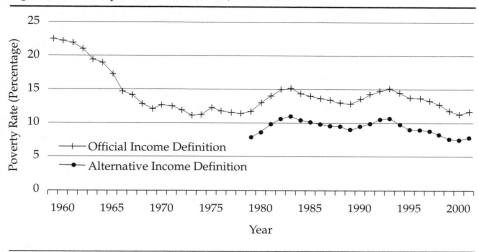

Source: Author's compilation; see appendix.

Across countries, the correlation between inequality (Gini) and poverty is .70. Across the U.S. states, the correlation is .86.

It turns out that poverty performs very similarly to inequality in multivariate regressions (not shown here). There is no indication of either a positive or negative effect of poverty on growth in the cross-country analyses. In the state-level analyses there again is an apparent growth-reducing effect, but it too appears almost certain to be spurious.

Figure 4.9 shows trends in the national U.S. poverty rate over time. According to the official measure, the poverty rate dropped by half between the late 1950s and the mid-1970s. Since then there has been some fluctuation but no sustained upward or downward movement. The same is true using a more comprehensive alternative definition of income for which the Census Bureau has data beginning in 1979. That measure includes capital gains, taxes, noncash government transfers, and noncash benefits provided by employers (such as health insurance). These trends in poverty appear to correspond neither to that for economic growth nor to those for the various mechanisms through which inequality is suspected to affect growth.

Conclusion

The debate about inequality's impact on economic growth has shifted back and forth. For many years the dominant view—based entirely on theoretical reasoning rather than on empirical findings—was that inequality is beneficial for growth. New theorizing coupled with a host of relatively consistent empirical results led to a reversal in the 1990s. The notion that inequality is bad for growth became the dominant perspective among researchers in this field. Since the late 1990s, however, several studies have challenged this view. Strikingly, they find evidence of a growth-enhancing effect of inequality specifically in affluent countries (Barro 2000; Brandolini and Rossi 1998; Forbes 2000).

Given the indeterminacy of theoretical expectations, surprisingly few participants in the debate have taken the position that inequality is unrelated to growth—though that is likely in part an artifact of the bias against "nonfindings" in social science journals. A lack of effect is exactly what the data suggest for the world's richest nations in the 1980s and 1990s. There has been no general tendency for inequality to influence growth in either direction. Across the U.S. states there is an association between low inequality and faster growth, but this association is weak in magnitude, sensitive to the inclusion or non-inclusion of one low-inequality state, and probably spurious in any case. Post–World War II trends in the United States also offer no indication that developments in inequality have mattered for growth. Finally, despite some reason to suspect that it might be poverty more than inequality that affects growth, the cross-country, cross-state, and over-time findings for poverty turn out to be similar to those for inequality.

There surely is some point at which the distribution of income in a country or region would be too egalitarian to be compatible with a desirable rate of economic growth. But the experience of the past two decades suggests that such a point has yet to be reached. Yes, egalitarian Sweden had very poor growth performance in the 1980s and 1990s (figure 4.1). But so did relatively unequal Switzerland. Egalitarian Norway and Finland did much better, and Austria and Belgium did better than most. There are, of course, equality-enhancing institutions and policies in some countries that may have growth-impeding effects. But the analyses here turn up no indication of a general equality-growth trade-off over the past two decades.

═══ Chapter 5 ═══

An Equality-Jobs Trade-off?

I n my examination of trends in inequality among working-age households in chapter 3, employment developments turned out to be a key determinant. What, then, explains employment trends in affluent countries over the past two decades? One of the most prominent explanations focuses on inequality—specifically, the degree of earnings inequality among employed individuals (rather than among households).

Between 1979 and 2000 the share of the working-age population that is employed increased from 68 percent to 75 percent in the United States, but only from 67 percent to 69 percent in Western Europe.[1] The average unemployment rate in the United States dropped from 6 percent in 1979 to 4 percent in 2000, while in Western Europe it jumped from 4.5 percent to 6 percent. On the other hand, earnings for those at the bottom relative to the median are substantially lower in the United States. As of the late 1990s, on average, a Western European at the 10th percentile of the earnings distribution earned two-thirds (68 percent) as much as the median worker, whereas her or his American counterpart earned slightly less than half (48 percent) of the median.

To a number of observers, these differences suggest a trade-off between equality and jobs. In the "U.S. model," wages for those at or near the bottom of the labor market are relatively low. This makes it attractive for companies to hire such workers. The U.S. labor market is thus characterized by low earnings for those at the bottom, but also by extensive job creation and high employment. In the "European model," high relative wages at the low end of the distribution encourage companies to employ fewer workers. Countries in Europe therefore feature relatively high earnings for those at the bottom but little job creation and low employment. This argument has been articulated most prominently in several reports by the Organization for Economic Cooperation and Development (OECD, 1994, 1996b). Although by no means uncontested, the argument has held considerable sway over the past decade among scholars (Becker 1996; Bertola and Ichino 1995; Blanchard and Wolfers 2000; Blau and Kahn 2002a; Esping-Andersen 2000a,

Figure 5.1   Earnings Inequality and Employment in Germany and the United States, 1979 to 2000

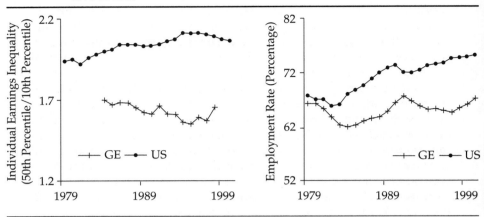

Source: Author's compilation; see appendix.

103; Iversen and Wren 1998; Krugman 1996; Siebert 1997; Wilson 1996, 153) and in the business press (*The Economist* 1997; Samuelson 1996; Wessel and Benjamin 1994).

Germany and the United States illustrate the apparent trade-off. As figure 5.1 shows, inequality in pay between the 50th (median) and 10th percentiles is considerably lower in Germany than in the United States. And the difference between the two countries increased during the 1980s and 1990s as pay inequality widened in the United States while dropping slightly in Germany. But Germany's employment rate was stagnant during these two decades, while in the United States employment increased by seven percentage points. Thus, whereas the two countries began the period with similar employment rates, by the end they had diverged sharply.

Is this trade-off view accurate? Does an egalitarian earnings distribution such as Germany's impede employment growth? The analyses in chapter 4 suggested no adverse effect of low income inequality on economic growth. In this chapter, I examine the effect of earnings (wage) inequality on employment growth across fourteen affluent countries in the 1980s and 1990s.

Existing Theory and Evidence

A number of researchers have highlighted evidence that is inconsistent with the trade-off view. First, cross-country analyses suggest no association between earnings inequality and high employment rates or low unemployment rates (Bazen 2000; Bradley 2002, ch. 3; Galbraith, Conceição, and Ferreira 1999; Howell 2002). However, adverse employment effects of pay compression are likely to have been sufficiently recent that they are not yet apparent in analyses of levels. Instead, they may be evident only in an examination of *changes* in employment performance.

Second, the employment and unemployment rates of low-skilled workers relative to those of high-skilled workers are no better in the United States than in most European nations (Glyn and Salverda 2000, 47; Howell 2002; Mishel, Bernstein, and Schmitt 2001, 402–5; Nickell and Bell 1996; Salverda, Bazen, and Gregory 2001). Yet the relevant comparison might instead be between younger and older workers, as younger workers may be the most likely to suffer if high bottom-end wages reduce the supply of entry-level jobs. The evidence is mixed on whether European countries have poorer employment performance among the young (Blau and Kahn 2002a, 28–38; Goul Andersen and Jensen 2002; OECD 2002a, 53–54).

Third, cross-state differences in minimum-wage levels in the United States have been found to have no adverse effects on minimum-wage employment (Card and Krueger 1995). However, this finding has been challenged (Keil, Robertson, and Symons 2001; Neumark and Wascher 2000), and the debate is not yet resolved.

What evidence is there to support the trade-off view? Proponents frequently point to the contrast between the United States and Western Europe described earlier. But this overlooks a variety of other possible causes of labor market outcomes, such as differing patterns of economic growth, deindustrialization, globalization, and differences in other labor market institutions and policies. It also ignores the considerable diversity in employment and unemployment rates across European countries (Esping-Andersen and Regini 2000; Goul Andersen and Jensen 2002).

In a 1998 article, Torben Iversen and Anne Wren (1998) sharpen the theoretical argument for a trade-off between equality and jobs and provide cross-country multivariate evidence to support it. Iversen and Wren suggest that high relative wages are most likely to reduce the growth of employment in private-sector consumer-oriented services— particularly wholesale and retail trade, restaurants and hotels, and community, social, and personal services. Because productivity in these industries is low and difficult to increase, "the most important source of market-generated expansion of employment in services, apart from the effects of changing consumption patterns, becomes lower wages, which translate into cheaper prices and higher effective demand"

(Iversen and Wren 1998, 512). These industries, according to Iversen and Wren, have been the main locus of job growth in affluent countries in the past several decades. Hence, pay compression is likely to have had an adverse impact on overall employment growth.

Figure 5.2 shows levels of private-sector consumer services employment (as a share of the working-age population) in 1979 and 1995. The equality-jobs trade-off is commonly presumed to have applied to the period since the late 1970s, when demand for less-skilled employees began to decrease owing to globalization, technological change, and other factors. In prior decades pay compression was not an impediment to job creation (Freeman 1995, 64; Howell 2002, 15; Siebert 1997). I thus focus, in these figures and throughout this chapter, on the 1980s and 1990s—though data for private-sector consumer services employment are available only through the mid-1990s. The figure reveals substantial variation across countries in both the level and growth of employment in private-sector consumer services. The Anglo countries and Japan tend to have the highest levels, at approximately 20 to 30 percent of the working-age population. They also feature the fastest growth. The Nordic and continental countries tend to have substantially lower levels of private-sector employment in these industries, ranging for the most part between 10 and 20 percent. Each of the continental countries experienced some growth during this period, whereas there was little or none in the four Nordic countries.

Figure 5.2   Employment in Private-Sector Consumer Services in Fourteen Countries, 1979 and 1995

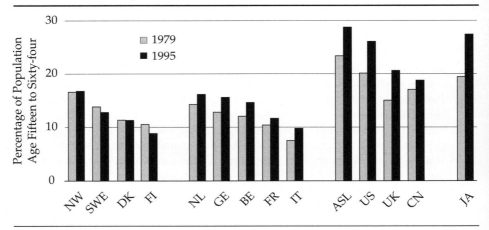

Source: Author's compilation; see appendix.

Figure 5.3   Total Employment in Fourteen Countries, 1979 and 2000

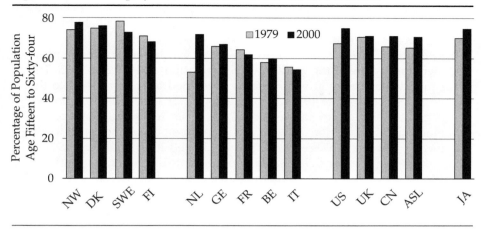

Source: Author's compilation; see appendix.

Figure 5.3 shows parallel data for total employment in 1979 and 2000. The Nordic countries, Anglo countries, and Japan tend to have the highest levels, while the continental nations are lower. Aside from the Netherlands, the most rapid growth was again achieved by the Anglo countries (except for the United Kingdom), while employment rates were largely stagnant in the Nordic and continental nations. Among these latter countries only oil-rich Norway achieved more than a token increase in employment during the two decades.

Figures 5.4, 5.5, and 5.6 illustrate the plausibility of the Iversen-Wren argument. As in figure 5.1, earnings inequality is measured here as the ratio of the annual earnings of a worker at the 50th percentile of the earnings distribution to those of a worker at the 10th percentile, using OECD data.[2] Change in employment, on the vertical axes, is measured as the level at the end of the period—1995 for private-sector consumer services employment, 2000 for total employment—minus the level in 1979. Figure 5.4 suggests a strong positive impact of earnings inequality on employment growth in private-sector consumer-related services. Iversen and Wren do not empirically investigate the second element of their hypothesized causal chain, nor do they examine the overall relationship between earnings inequality and total employment. But the patterns in figures 5.5 and 5.6 are consistent with their argument. Figure 5.5 shows that countries with rapid job growth in private-sector consumer services tended to enjoy faster growth of total employment, and figure 5.6 suggests a positive impact of earnings inequality on total employment growth.

**Figure 5.4   Private-Sector Consumer Services Employment Growth by
Earnings Inequality in Fourteen Countries**

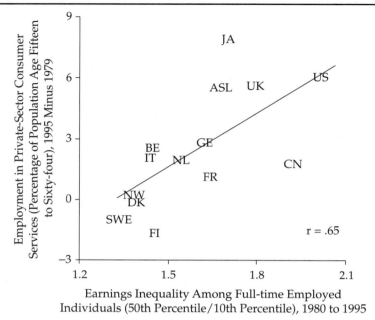

Source: Author's compilation; see appendix.

Slow growth in private-sector service jobs can be offset by the creation of public-sector service jobs. In the 1960s and 1970s the Nordic countries used sizable expansions of public-sector employment to help achieve the highest aggregate employment rates among all affluent nations. Yet, according to Iversen (1999, ch. 6), this strategy may have reached its limit. It depends on relatively high tax rates, which have come under increasing strain due to economic pressures for fiscal austerity coupled with political resistance to heavy tax burdens (see also Esping-Andersen 1999, 153). Recent trends suggest that this may be correct. Among the Nordic countries, only oil-rich Norway continued to expand public employment in the 1990s.

The Iversen-Wren argument seems compelling. And their empirical analysis of employment growth in private-sector consumer services in fourteen OECD countries yields supportive results. Yet there are several reasons to question it. First, the second component of their hypothesized causal chain—the notion that employment growth in private-sector consumer-related services is a key determinant of aggregate

**Figure 5.5   Total Employment Growth by Private-Sector Consumer
Services Employment Growth in Fourteen Countries**

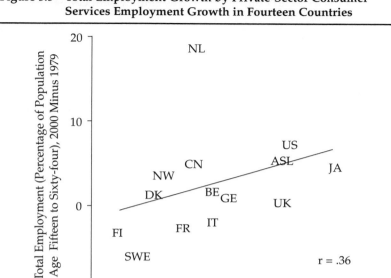

Source: Author's compilation; see appendix.

employment performance—may be suspect. A recent OECD study
(2001a, 107) finds that only half of the employment gap between the
United States and Western Europe lies in low-paying jobs; the other
half is in high-paying positions. Another OECD (2000, 110) study examines employment growth in the 1980s and 1990s and finds that
"countries in which employment grew fastest tended to have above-av-
erage gains across all sectors. This suggests either that economy-wide
factors have been the dominant determinants of international differences in employment growth or that the presence of one or a few especially dynamic sectors generates 'spill-over' effects that raise growth
rates in the rest of the economy." If the first of these alternatives is true,
then earnings compression should be relevant for overall employment
growth only if it has employment-reducing effects across a variety of
sectors. Iversen and Wren do not make this claim; they suggest, for example, that there is likely to be no such adverse impact in manufacturing because higher productivity eases the cost constraint imposed by
high wages. Their findings suggest that is indeed the case (Iversen and

Figure 5.6   Total Employment Growth by Earnings Inequality in Fourteen Countries

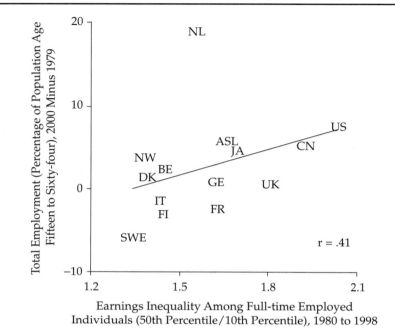

Source: Author's compilation; see appendix.

Wren 1998, 531). If the second alternative is correct, the earnings distribution could have an important impact on overall employment growth even if its direct impact were confined to private-sector consumer-related services, but it would be necessary to show that job growth in private-sector consumer services creates spillover effects that generate job growth in other sectors.

My focus in this chapter, however, is not on this second link in the hypothesized causal chain. Instead, it is on the first link—that between earnings inequality and the growth of private-sector consumer services employment. There are several reasons why high pay levels may not reduce the demand for labor. Efficiency wage theory, for instance, posits that employers willingly pay more in order to increase worker effort and commitment (Akerlof and Yellen 1986). Low-productivity service jobs are among the most likely to be characterized by low employee commitment and high turnover. Employers may therefore find it profitable to pay higher wages to the extent that doing so helps to alleviate these problems. In this context, higher relative pay levels at the bottom of the labor market would not deter employment, and thus countries with less earnings inequality would not be expected to have slower job growth in these low-productivity private-sector services.

More generally, productivity levels in low-wage jobs may differ widely across countries due to differences in skills, work organization, and mechanization, among other factors. For instance, one study found that productivity among hotel cleaning staff in Germany was twice as high as in Britain (Prais, Jarvis, and Wagner 1989). A relatively low 50th percentile/10th percentile ratio therefore might simply be a function of high productivity. If so, wage compression should not be a deterrent to job growth.

Job creation in private-sector consumer services depends not only on wages and productivity but also on the level of consumer demand. Some countries may be blessed by heavy tourism, which heightens demand for hotel, restaurant, and other consumer services. The rate of female labor force participation is also likely to be important. The more women there are in the paid labor force, the greater will be the need to outsource household tasks. Demand for consumer services may also be affected by consumer preferences. Where home cooking and cleaning are more institutionalized, demand for restaurants and house-cleaning services may be lower. Cross-country differences in consumption patterns could substantially weaken or eliminate any impediment to job creation posed by high wages in low-end jobs.

Yet Iversen and Wren do find a positive effect of earnings inequality on employment growth in private-sector consumer services. The chief reason to question this association, which is consistent with that shown in figure 5.4, is that it could be spurious. Iversen and Wren's multivariate analysis does not control for a number of labor market policies and institutions that may affect employment performance, including active labor market policy, public employment, employment regulations, tax rates, the generosity of unemployment benefits, the duration of those benefits, wage-setting coordination, unionization, public child care, and paid maternity leave.

Active labor market policy consists of government expenditures on activities for the unemployed that are aimed at helping them return to work (Martin 2000–2001). Examples include training, assistance with job search, and employment subsidies. During the 1980s and 1990s expenditures on such policies ranged from 0.2 percent of GDP in the United States to 2 percent in Sweden.

The creation of public-sector jobs is a direct employment-boosting policy, and as such it is likely to increase the aggregate employment rate. On the other hand, public employment may have the effect of crowding out private-sector jobs, particularly in the service sector. Public employment as a share of the working-age population ranged from less than 10 percent in Italy, the Netherlands, the United Kingdom, and the United States to more than 20 percent in Denmark, Norway, and Sweden in the 1980s and 1990s.

Employment regulations limit employers' flexibility in labor deployment, most notably by reducing their ability to lay off employees during a downturn. Such regulations may thereby discourage hiring, resulting in slower employment growth. There are various ways to measure employment regulations. I use an index created by Stephen Nickell (1997). It ranges from zero to ten, with each country scored from zero (lax or no legislation) to two (strict legislation) on each of five types of employment regulations: working time, fixed-term contracts, employment protection, minimum wages, and employees' representation rights (on works councils, company boards, and so on). The United Kingdom and the United States have overall scores of zero on this index, while Italy and Sweden have the highest scores at seven.

Payroll, income, and consumption taxes create a "wedge" between gross and net earnings—that is, between the amount paid by an employer and a worker's actual take-home pay. Depending on the institutional setting, this wedge may add to employers' labor costs, since unions are likely to bargain for higher wages to secure the desired levels of net earnings. In addition, payroll tax systems often are structured so that employers pay a portion directly. It is generally expected that higher labor costs reduce employer demand for labor, thereby reducing employment growth. Over the 1980s and 1990s tax rates, measured as the sum of payroll, income, and consumption tax rates, ranged from less than 50 percent in Australia, Canada, Japan, the United Kingdom, and the United States to more than 75 percent in Sweden.

Generous and long-lasting unemployment benefits reduce the incentive for unemployed workers to get a new job. The standard measure of the generosity of such benefits is the replacement rate—the share of former earnings that is replaced by benefits when an individual loses her or his job. Because data on net (after-tax) replacement rates are available only for the late 1990s, I use gross (pretax) rates as the measure. They ranged from less than 10 percent in Italy to more than 85 percent in Denmark and Sweden during the 1980s and 1990s. The duration of unemployment benefits can be measured using a scale that gauges the level of benefits in the second, third, fourth, and fifth year after losing a job relative to those in the first year. Sweden and Italy had the lowest values on this measure, while Australia and Belgium had the highest.

Coordinated wage setting can be expected to reduce the rate of wage increase. If employees bargain aggressively for high wage increases, employers may respond by reducing employment. Where wages are bargained separately for individual firms, those laid off can expect to find work elsewhere because they can presume that high wage increases and consequent layoffs will not be generalized throughout the economy. Thus, where bargaining is uncoordinated, there is an incentive for unions to pursue a strategy of wage militancy. But if most unions adopt this reasoning, layoffs may indeed be generalized, resulting in lower employment. By contrast, if wage negotiations are coordinated across a large share of the workforce, union bargainers can be reasonably sure that a large wage increase will have an adverse employment impact on union members. Coordinated wage setting thus generates an incentive for wage moderation and may therefore contribute to higher employment. Scored on a scale of one to five, the degree of wage-setting coordination during the 1980s and 1990s ranged from one (uncoordinated) in Canada, the United Kingdom, and the United States to four or more (highly coordinated) in Belgium, Germany, Japan, the Netherlands, Norway, and Sweden.

Holding constant the degree of wage coordination, higher levels of unionization may lead to higher rates of wage increase, resulting in lower employment. Unionization levels in the 1980s and 1990s ranged from less than 20 percent in France and the United States to more than 70 percent in Denmark, Finland, and Sweden.

As I pointed out in chapter 3, the bulk of change in employment rates in many affluent countries in the 1980s and 1990s consisted of women moving into or out of the paid workforce. Supportive policies, such as public provision of child care and paid maternity leave, may therefore have played a key role in accounting for cross-country differences in employment trends.

Most of these labor market policies or institutions are moderately or strongly correlated with earnings inequality. The correlations across fourteen OECD countries over the 1980s and 1990s are:

Active labor market policy: −.73

Public employment: −.45

Employment regulations: −.70

Tax rates: −.64

Generosity of unemployment benefits: −.42

Duration of unemployment benefits: −.12

Wage-setting coordination: −.71

Unionization: −.69

Public child care: −.59

Paid maternity leave: −.69

Thus, the earnings inequality variable in Iversen and Wren's analysis may have in fact been capturing effects of some or all of these other labor market policies and institutions rather than the effect of earnings inequality itself. Consider figure 5.7, which replicates figure 5.4 but with earnings inequality replaced on the horizontal axis by the tax rate on a typical worker. The pattern looks strikingly similar (in the opposite direction). Indeed, the relationship is even stronger than that in figure 5.4. Figure 5.8 suggests a similar association, though not quite as strong, for employment regulations. This suggests that including the tax rate, employment regulations, and other institutional features of labor markets in the analysis may yield a different conclusion than that reached by Iversen and Wren and others about the effect of relative pay levels on employment growth.

Figure 5.7   Private-Sector Consumer Services Employment Growth by the Tax Rate in Fourteen Countries

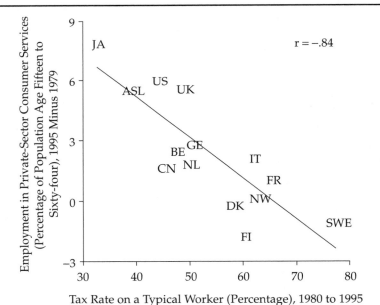

Source: Author's compilation; see appendix.

Figure 5.8   Private-Sector Consumer Services Employment Growth by Employment Regulations in Fourteen Countries

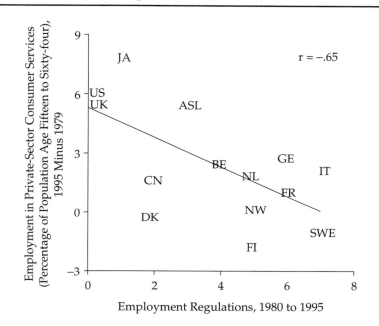

Source: Author's compilation; see appendix.

Data and Measures

The analyses in this chapter include fourteen countries: Australia, Belgium, Canada, Denmark, Finland, France, Germany, Italy, Japan, the Netherlands, Norway, Sweden, the United Kingdom, and the United States. Data on employment in private-sector consumer services are not available for Austria and Switzerland. All of the variables are described and their data sources listed in the appendix. The dependent variables are change (level for the most recent year for which data are available minus the level in 1979) in private-sector consumer services employment and in total employment, both measured as a share of the working-age population. The key independent variable is earnings inequality among full-time year-round employed individuals. As noted earlier, this is measured as the ratio of earnings at the 50th percentile of the earnings distribution to earnings at the 10th percentile.[3]

Why examine effects on *employment* rather than on unemployment?

One reason is that unemployment rates can be misleading to the extent that unemployment is "hidden" by low levels of labor force participation or by various types of active labor market, early retirement, and other social-welfare policies (Scharpf 1997; Smith 1999). Thus, employment is arguably a better barometer of the macroeconomic performance of affluent countries. In addition, as I discussed in chapter 1, high employment is increasingly critical to the long-run financial viability of welfare states.

Why focus on cross-country differences in *inequality* of earnings rather than in the level of earnings at the low end of the distribution? After all, the key assumption underlying the conventional wisdom is that high wages at the bottom create a disincentive for employers to hire, thus impeding employment growth in low-productivity private-sector services. The reason for focusing on inequality is that consumer services in most countries remain heavily domestic. In manufacturing there is extensive cross-country trade, so employers in that sector may use wage levels in other countries as the principal benchmark in making decisions about hiring. But in consumer services, where there is little or no trade, the frame of reference for employers is more likely to be the median (50th percentile) wage in the domestic economy rather than the 10th percentile wage level in other nations.

As in previous chapters, my analyses of the impact of earnings inequality on employment performance consist of single-period regressions that focus on cross-country differences in change over time. I regress employment growth in the 1980s and 1990s on the level of earnings inequality and other potentially relevant causal factors. The impact of earnings inequality on employment growth is best assessed over a reasonably long period of time (as with the effect of household income inequality on output growth in chapter 4).[4] I focus on the *level* of earnings inequality, rather than change in earnings inequality, for substantive reasons. It is the degree of earnings inequality, rather than how it changes over time, that is suspected to be an impediment to job creation in private-sector consumer services. In addition, the variation in inequality across countries is much greater than the variation over time within countries. The coefficient of variation for 50th percentile/10th percentile earnings ratios across the fourteen countries is .13, while the average coefficient of variation for 50th percentile/10th percentile ratios within each country during the 1980s and 1990s is .02.

Poor employment performance may increase earnings inequality, and reverse causality of this form would bias the regressions against finding an adverse effect of pay compression on employment. Such bias can be avoided by using a measure of earnings inequality at the beginning of the period, since change in employment during the 1980s and

1990s cannot have caused a country's level of earnings inequality in 1979. As a practical matter, this makes no difference, because there is so little within-country variation over time. In fact, earnings inequality measured in 1979 (or the earliest available year) correlates at .99 with earnings inequality measured as a 1979 to 1998 period average. Thus, there is little likelihood of a reverse causality problem in these analyses.

A number of variables tapping the general economic environment and labor market policies and institutions are included in the regressions (the expected direction of effect follows in parentheses): growth of real GDP (+); agricultural and manufacturing employment as a share of total employment in 1979 (– for total employment); trade as a share of GDP (±); outward direct foreign investment as a share of GDP (–); real long-term interest rates (–); public employment (– for private-sector consumer services employment, + for total employment); tax rate on a typical worker (–); unemployment benefit replacement rate (–); duration of unemployment benefit eligibility (–).[5] Each has been found in previous studies to affect employment performance and is correlated with earnings inequality (Blau and Kahn 2002a; Bradley 2002; Franzese 2001; Kenworthy 2002a; Korpi 1991; Nickell and Layard 1999; Palley 2001; Scarpetta 1996; Scharpf 2000). Most of these variables are measured in two ways: as levels, using a period average for 1980 to 1995–2000, and as changes, using the end-of-the-period value minus the beginning value. Because they are too highly correlated with earnings inequality (r > ±.65), I do not include active labor market policy, employment regulations, wage coordination, unionization, paid maternity leave, or left government in these analyses. I also leave out public child care, because data are available for only ten countries. In regressions not reported here, it does not turn out to be of importance in predicting variation in employment trends across those ten countries.

In chapter 4, I adjusted rates of economic growth for catch-up effects to control for the tendency of countries with lower per capita GDP to grow more quickly. It seems reasonable to assume that the same pattern would hold for employment: countries beginning the period with high employment levels would find it difficult to increase employment further, while countries beginning at low levels would find it easiest to increase them. However, empirically this turns out not to have been the case. For employment growth in private-sector consumer services, countries with higher levels as of 1979 actually tended to experience faster, rather than slower, job growth. For total employment, countries beginning with higher levels experienced slower job growth, but the relationship is of no substantive significance. Hence, I do not adjust employment growth for catch-up effects in these analyses.

As in previous chapters, the number of cases here is small relative to the number of explanatory factors. I therefore begin by estimating a series of regressions that include all possible combinations of three or fewer of the independent variables. I use this procedure to weed out empirically irrelevant variables—ones that have inconsistent signs and t-statistics less than 1.00 (in absolute value) in more than half of the regressions in which they appear. I then estimate models that include all possible combinations of the surviving variables in order to find the model that accounts for the largest portion of variation in employment growth (the "best" model). Because it is the explanatory variable of interest in these analyses, I include earnings inequality in all of these latter models.

Changes in Private-Sector Consumer Services Employment

I begin with growth of employment in private-sector consumer-related services. The minimum, median, and maximum standardized coefficients for the variables are shown in table 5.1. The earnings inequality variable always has the expected positive sign, and it has a t-statistic greater than 1.00 in more than three-quarters of the regressions. Apparently, countries with lower 50th percentile/10th percentile earnings ratios tended to experience slower growth of employment in private-sector consumer services. This suggests possible support for the notion of a trade-off between equality and jobs.

What is the magnitude of the effect? One interpretation is that the most reasonable estimate of earnings inequality's true effect is the median coefficient in the regressions that include all possible combinations of the explanatory variables. The median unstandardized (metric) coefficient is 6.10. This estimate suggests that if we compare two countries that differ by one standard deviation (.22) in the 50th percentile/10th percentile earnings ratio, the country with less earnings inequality will have had approximately 1.3 percentage points less growth in private-sector consumer services employment between 1979 and 1995 (6.10 multiplied by .22). Note that this represents the total amount of employment growth over the period, not the annual rate of growth.

Another way to get a sense of the magnitude of the estimated effect is to consider two extreme cases: the United States and Sweden. Between 1979 and 1995 private-sector consumer services employment in the United States increased from 20 percent of the working-age population to 26 percent, while in Sweden it fell from 14 percent to 13 percent. The difference between these two countries was thus 7 percentage points (plus six for the United States, minus one for Sweden). The United States had the highest 50th percentile/10th percentile earnings

Table 5.1   Regression Results: Effect of Earnings Inequality and Other Variables on Employment Growth in Private-Sector Consumer Services, 1979 to 1995

	All Possible Models of Three or Fewer Variables			Best Models	
	Minimum	Median	Maximum	1	2
Earnings inequality	.03	.45	.66	.07	.16
among full-time	.44	6.10	8.91	.96	2.15
year-round employed individuals	(.72)	(1.79)	(1.85)	(.34)	(.84)
Other variables					
Growth of real GDP	.00	.45	.75	.21	
	(.00)	(2.00)	(3.31)	(1.34)	
Change in outward	−.89	−.44	−.08		
direct foreign investment	(3.32)	(2.14)	(.39)		
Public employment	−.64	−.41	.09		
	(3.05)	(1.76)	(.33)		
Change in public	−.86	−.53	−.27	−.33	
employment	(4.99)	(2.11)	(1.19)	(2.28)	
Tax rate on workers	−.90	−.74	−.57	−.42	−.57
	(5.43)	(3.32)	(2.77)	(2.76)	(3.12)
Unemployment	−.81	−.47	.03	−.20	−.31
benefit replacement rate	(3.79)	(1.55)	(.08)	(2.21)	(2.97)
Change in	−.86	−.51	−.16		
unionization	(3.57)	(2.20)	(.54)		

Source: Author's analysis; see appendix.
Notes: Standardized coefficients, with absolute t-ratios (based on heteroskedasticity-robust standard errors) in parentheses. The numbers in the second row for the earnings inequality variable are unstandardized coefficients. OLS regressions. Results in columns 1, 2, and 3 are from regressions using all possible combinations of three or fewer of the independent variables (16 variables, 696 regressions). Variables included in these regressions but not reported here owing to inconsistent signs and lack of absolute t-ratios greater than 1.00 in at least half of the regressions are: trade, change in trade, outward direct foreign investment, real long-term interest rates, change in tax rate on workers, change in unemployment benefit replacement rate, unemployment benefit duration, and change in unemployment benefit duration. "Best models" regressions are those with the largest adjusted R-squared. Active labor market policy, employment regulations, wage coordination, unionization, and left government are not included in these regressions because they are too highly correlated with earnings inequality. Levels variables are measured as period averages. Change variables are measured as 1995 value minus 1979 value. Minimum and maximum R-squared: .01, .91. N = 14.

ratio during this period, averaging 2.02, while Sweden had the lowest at 1.33. If we multiply the median earnings inequality regression coefficient, 6.10, by the difference between these values for the earnings inequality variable, .69 (2.02 minus 1.33), we get an estimate of earnings inequality's contribution to the difference between these two countries in employment growth in private-sector consumer services: 4.2 percentage points. That is more than half of the actual difference of 7 percentage points.

Using the variables that survive the "all possible models" regressions, I estimate a variety of additional regressions, allowing more variables to be included in the models. In terms of explanatory power (adjusted R-squared), the best regression in which the earnings inequality variable appears includes earnings inequality, growth of real GDP, change in public employment, the tax rate, and the unemployment benefit replacement rate. These five variables account for 87 percent of the cross-country variation in employment growth in private-sector consumer services during the 1980s and 1990s. But earnings inequality has an unstandardized coefficient of only .96 in this equation. Based on this coefficient, the difference in employment growth between two countries that differed by one standard deviation in earnings inequality would have been only one-fifth of a percentage point (0.96 multiplied by .22). And earnings inequality would have accounted for only .67 percentage points of the 7-percentage-point difference between the United States and Sweden (.96 multiplied by .69).

Including five variables in a regression with just fourteen cases may be asking too much of the data, however. Several of these variables are moderately correlated with earnings inequality, so its coefficient may be reduced by multicollinearity. The best three-variable regression in which earnings inequality is included is shown in the last column of table 5.1. The other two variables are the tax rate and the unemployment benefit replacement rate. The coefficient for earnings inequality doubles in size compared to the five-variable best model, but it is still quite small.

Five variables that prior studies have found to be relevant in explaining cross-country differences in employment performance—active labor market policy, employment regulations, wage coordination, level of unionization, and left government—are not included in these regressions because they are too highly correlated with earnings inequality. In separate regressions not reported here, I have tried entering each of these five variables in combinations with all of the others aside from earnings inequality. Only two of the five perform well: employment regulations and the level of unionization. Their results are very similar to those for the earnings inequality variable shown in table

5.1: the median standardized coefficient is around −.45, and the t-values are generally reasonably large. It therefore seems likely that the earnings inequality variable is picking up some of the effect of employment regulations and/or unionization.

Thus, while the results reported in table 5.1 do indicate some support for the notion that earnings inequality helped to boost the growth of private-sector consumer services employment, this effect appears to be fairly small in magnitude. In addition, the results indicate that cross-country differences in a variety of other factors—particularly the tax rate but also GDP growth, public employment, the unemployment benefit replacement rate, outward direct foreign investment, and very likely employment regulations and unionization as well—contributed to the variation in job growth in low-productivity private-sector consumer services.

Changes in Total Employment

What effect did earnings inequality have on aggregate employment growth? In analyzing changes in total employment, I omit the Netherlands from the regressions. As figure 5.6 makes clear, employment growth was far more rapid in the Netherlands than in any other country in the 1980s and 1990s. This was not a fluke, and in chapter 7 I discuss the sources of employment growth in the Netherlands in some detail. But in statistical terms, the Dutch case is a clear outlier, and as such it is likely to have disproportionate influence on the regression estimates. Regressions not reported here indicate that that is indeed the case.

Table 5.2 shows the results. In the "all possible models" regressions, the earnings inequality variable performs about the same as in the regressions for private-sector consumer services employment growth. It has the expected positive sign in all of the regressions in which it appears, and in most instances it has a t-statistic greater than 1.00. Its median standardized coefficient is .58, which is fairly large.

The median unstandardized coefficient is 10.10. This is one estimate of earnings inequality's true effect on total employment growth. If we compare two countries that differ by one standard deviation (.22) in the 50th percentile/10th percentile earnings ratio, this coefficient suggests that the country with less earnings inequality will have had approximately 2.2 percentage points less growth in total employment between 1979 and 2000. Once again, the United States and Sweden represent extreme cases (if we disregard the Netherlands), with the former experiencing an increase of 7 percentage points in total employment between 1979 and 2000 and the latter a decline of 6 percentage points. The me-

Table 5.2   Regression Results: Effect of Earnings Inequality and Other Variables on Total Employment Growth, 1979 to 2000

	All Possible Models of Three or Fewer Variables			Best Models	
	Minimum	Median	Maximum	1	2
Earnings inequality	.17	.58	.87	.09	.08
among full-time	2.72	10.10	15.19	1.59	1.38
year-round employed	(.69)	(2.08)	(2.88)	(.78)	(.40)
individuals					
Other variables					
Growth of real GDP	.31	.63	.85	.23	
	(1.54)	(2.55)	(3.57)	(.99)	
Agricultural and	−.82	−.40	−.23	−.35	−.33
manufacturing	(5.53)	(2.29)	(1.11)	(3.71)	(2.68)
employment in					
1979					
Outward direct	−.71	−.36	−.12	−.28	
foreign investment	(3.62)	(1.39)	(.52)	(3.36)	
Tax rate on workers	−.96	−.76	−.48	−.44	−.69
	(4.03)	(3.18)	(2.01)	(2.48)	(5.28)
Change in tax rate	−.76	−.40	−.09		
on workers	(3.70)	(1.45)	(.34)		

Source: Author's analysis; see appendix.
Notes: Standardized coefficients, with absolute t-ratios (based on heteroskedasticity-robust standard errors) in parentheses. The numbers in the second row for the earnings inequality variable are unstandardized coefficients. OLS regressions. Results in columns 1, 2, and 3 are from regressions using all possible combinations of three or fewer of the independent variables (17 variables, 833 regressions). Variables included in the regressions but not reported here owing to inconsistent signs and lack of absolute t-ratios greater than 1.00 in at least half of the regressions are: trade, change in trade, change in outward direct foreign investment, real long-term interest rates, public employment, change in public employment, unemployment benefit replacement rate, change in unemployment benefit replacement rate, unemployment benefit duration, change in unemployment benefit duration, and change in unionization. Active labor market policy, employment regulations, wage coordination, unionization, and left government are not included in these regressions because they are too highly correlated with earnings inequality. Levels variables are measured as period averages. "Best models" regressions are those with the largest adjusted R-squared. Change variables are measured as 2000 (or most recent year) value minus 1979 value. Minimum and maximum R-squared: .01, .86. N = 13 (Netherlands is omitted).

dian regression coefficient suggests that earnings inequality accounted for approximately 6.6 percentage points out of the total difference of 13.

Again, however, it is important to be cautious about these estimates of the impact of earnings inequality. The earnings inequality variable performs rather poorly in some of these regressions. For instance, in the "best" overall model, its unstandardized coefficient drops to only

1.59. Even if we permit only three variables in the regression (best model 2), the unstandardized earnings inequality coefficient is no larger. If this represents the true effect of earnings inequality, a one-standard-deviation difference in inequality is associated with a difference in total employment growth of about one-third of a percentage point over the 1980s and 1990s. And earnings inequality accounts for just 1.2 percentage points of the 13-percentage-point difference between the United States and Sweden during this period.

Like those for employment growth in private-sector consumer services, these regressions do not include variables representing active labor market policy, employment regulations, wage coordination, unionization, or left government. Separate analyses indicate that among these five only the employment regulations variable is robustly related to total employment growth. But the coefficients for earnings inequality in table 5.2 may be overestimated to the extent that the inequality variable is picking up some of the effect of employment regulations.

For total employment only a few explanatory factors are consistently signed and have reasonably large t-values. Economic growth and outward direct foreign investment appear to matter. The share of total employment accounted for by agriculture and manufacturing in 1979 was an important factor, with countries having larger employment shares in these declining sectors suffering worse aggregate employment performance. The tax rate again appears to be the most influential determinant of the cross-country variation. Its standardized coefficients are quite large, as are its t-statistics. Changes in the tax rate also appear to have been relevant. A regression with outward direct foreign investment, tax rates, and employment regulations accounts for 85 percent of the cross-country variation in aggregate employment growth.

Conclusion

Sluggish job growth and large-scale unemployment have been arguably the prime economic, social, and political issues in Western Europe over the past two decades. Europe's jobs problem is frequently said to be a product of labor market "rigidities." Although the institutional features of European labor markets are sometimes lumped together, it is helpful to distinguish among them. They are of five main types: employment regulations regarding job protection, working time, and related matters; the unemployment compensation system; the tax wedge; wage-setting arrangements; and high relative earnings for workers at the low end of the labor market.

The findings in this chapter suggest that portions of the conventional wisdom regarding the deleterious effects of labor market rigidities on employment growth are accurate. Specifically, more extensive employment regulations, a larger tax wedge, higher unemployment benefits, and higher unionization rates appear to have had adverse effects on employment growth in private-sector consumer services, and for the tax wedge and employment regulations these effects carried over to growth of total employment (see also Garibaldi and Mauro 2002).

The fifth rigidity—high relative earnings at the bottom of the labor market—has received perhaps the most attention of the five in policy discussions. Yet there has been only one prior multivariate cross-country empirical study on this issue (Iversen and Wren 1998), and it does not include controls for a variety of factors that influence employment performance and are correlated with earnings inequality. My analysis in this chapter of employment patterns in fourteen OECD countries during the 1980s and 1990s suggests that higher relative pay levels in low-wage jobs may indeed have reduced the growth of low-productivity private-sector services employment and of overall employment. However, this effect appears to have been a relatively mild one.

What implications do these findings have for future labor market performance in affluent nations? Iversen (1999, ch. 6) and Esping-Andersen (1999) have suggested recently that such nations have two principal options if they wish to generate an ample supply of jobs. One is to reduce wages at the bottom of the earnings distribution in order to stimulate job creation in low-productivity private-sector services. The other is to rely on the expansion of public employment. Countries such as the United States and the United Kingdom have pursued the former strategy, while the Nordic nations have traditionally relied on the latter. However, both Iversen and Esping-Andersen contend that the public employment route is likely to encounter increasing economic pressure and political resistance, limiting countries' ability to sustain the high tax rates necessary to finance extensive public-sector job creation. Thus, in their view, a solution to the jobs problem in Western Europe is likely to require increased pay inequality (Esping-Andersen 1999, 173; Iversen 1999, 174).

The findings in this chapter suggest some alternatives to these two options. The distribution of earnings is only one among a number of factors that influence employment growth. In particular, some countries may be able to stimulate job growth just as (or more) effectively by reducing tax rates or employment regulations. That is to say, even if the public-sector route to high employment is now effectively blocked, nations with a jobs problem could potentially go a long way toward alleviating it without having to increase pay differentials.

To illustrate, let me return to the comparison between Germany and the United States with which I began this chapter. Germany's employment rate is about eight percentage points lower than that of the United States. In a recent study, Richard Freeman and Ronald Schettkat (2000) find that low-wage services—eating, drinking, and care facilities, retail trade, and so on—account for a large portion of this difference in aggregate employment rates. Yet they also find that, although Germany's overall pay structure is more egalitarian than that of the United States, the ratio of wages in the lowest-paying service sectors to average wages is approximately the same in the two countries. In other words, German employers in low-wage private-sector services do not have to pay higher relative wages than their American counterparts. That is because Germany does not have a statutory minimum wage, and many of these jobs lie outside the collective bargaining system and so are not affected by the minimum wage established there.

So why are there fewer jobs in these industries in Germany than in the United States? One view is that the problem lies on the supply side of the labor market. According to this perspective, there is sufficient employer demand for workers in such jobs, but people are unwilling to accept the jobs—either because the jobs are considered demeaning or because they pay less than the "social wage" (unemployment benefits and/or social assistance). Another potential problem on the supply side is that, as I discuss in chapter 8, a variety of German policies and institutions discourage women from entering or remaining in the labor force.

Others suggest that the problem lies primarily on the demand side of the labor market: too few jobs are created. Why might that be the case? Aside from high wage levels, there are several possibilities. One is a sluggish macro economy, which limits consumer demand. German monetary policy and fiscal policy were more restrictive than in the United States in the 1980s and 1990s. Yet there are other European countries (Denmark and the Netherlands, for example) that have had higher employment or faster employment growth despite similar macroeconomic policy.

Employment protection regulations may be too strict. This creates a disincentive for employers to hire, because they are unable to get rid of workers during a downturn. Yet since the mid-1990s employers have been able to hire workers on fixed-term contracts (up to two years), which in principle should allow considerable flexibility if the need to downsize arises.

The most important factor, in my view, is Germany's high payroll tax rates (Manow and Seils 2000a; Scharpf 1997, 2000; Streeck 2001). Payroll taxes average 42 percent of gross wages, compared to 15 percent in the United States. This creates a substantial wedge between a worker's actual take-home pay and the cost a firm bears in hiring the worker, resulting in a significant disincentive for employers to hire. Reducing these contributions, rather than reducing wages, seems likely to prove most effective in generating low-end service jobs in Germany. One way to do this would be to shift to a social insurance system funded primarily out of general revenues rather than payroll taxes. An alternative, which is being tried in Belgium, France, and the Netherlands, is to subsidize employers who hire workers in low-productivity jobs—either by paying them or by exempting them from social security contributions for part or all of their workforce (Ferrera and Hemerijck 2003; OECD 2003a, ch. 3).

In the past several years the German government has opted for a different strategy: it has aimed to increase employment in private-sector services by subsidizing employees. Because productivity in such jobs tends to be low and steep payroll taxes substantially increase the cost of labor, employers can afford to pay only a relatively low wage. It is thought that too few Germans are willing to take such jobs at the low offered wages because unemployment insurance and related benefits—the "social wage"—provide a better net income. In early 2002 the government introduced an employee subsidy in the form of a reduction in payroll contributions for workers in low-wage jobs. As for employers, the standard payroll contribution for an employee is 21 percent of earnings. In 2003 this policy was amended to fully exempt from payroll contributions workers in jobs paying less than 400 euros per month and to partially exempt those in jobs paying between 400 and 800 euros. In addition, the generosity of unemployment benefits and the duration of eligibility are scheduled to be reduced in 2004. There have been two noteworthy government initiatives on the demand side: One is an employer subsidy for companies that hire an unemployed person on a permanent basis. The other is a reduction in the payroll taxes a household must pay when hiring repair, cleaning, or other in-home services. It is plainly far too early to tell what impact these initiatives will have on employment.

I do not mean to suggest that altering the structure of the tax system or reducing employment regulations will always and everywhere stimulate private-sector consumer services job growth just as effectively as reducing wage levels. The experiences of the Nordic countries in the 1980s and 1990s suggest that this is probably not the case. As figure 5.4 shows, these four countries had similar (low) levels of earnings inequality through the two decades. But they differed in their tax systems and employment regulations. Sweden had higher tax rates than Denmark, Finland, and Norway (figure 5.7), and its tax system relied more heavily on payroll taxes than did those of the other three countries. Denmark had significantly weaker employment protection regulations than the other three (figure 5.8). Based on the regression results in this chapter, we would therefore expect Denmark to have had the best performance of the four countries in employment growth in private-sector consumer services. In fact, however, private-sector consumer services job growth differed only marginally across the four countries during the 1979 to 1995 period. Denmark's performance was only slightly better than those of Sweden and Finland. In the Nordic countries, then, it may be high wage levels at the low end of the distribution that constitute the chief obstacle to growth of private-sector jobs in consumer services.

What should we conclude about the need for lower wages in European economies? The comparative evidence is inconclusive. The regression analyses suggest that in the 1980s and 1990s pay compression tended to contribute to slower employment growth in private-sector consumer services. But they also suggest that the effect was not terribly strong and that other labor market policies and institutions may have played an equal or more important role. In the end, whether or not lower wages are a prerequisite for employment growth depends on the particular national context. As Esping-Andersen (1999, 138) has observed: "Welfare state programs and labor market institutions are, in each nation, inserted within a particular societal framework; visible rigidities may be offset by informal flexibilities and vice versa; an individual may react very differently to an identical welfare or regulatory program, depending on who he or she is, in what kind of labor market he or she operates, or in which society he or she resides."

It is worth emphasizing that even if a country can achieve job growth by lowering tax rates rather than lowering wages, that might not be the best choice from an egalitarian point of view. Since earnings typically are pooled within households, the distribution of earnings among households should be of greater concern to egalitarians than the distribution of earnings among employed individuals. The latter contributes to the former, of course, but if greater earnings inequality among employed individuals leads to rising earnings inequality among households, this can be offset by government redistribution (see chapter 8). Doing so requires sizable tax revenues, which in turn depend to some degree on high tax rates. Since other factors contribute to household earnings inequality—household size and structure, marital homogamy, as well as employment patterns (see chapter 3)—it might be wise to choose government tax and transfer programs rather than pay compression as the chief instrument for ensuring a reasonably low level of household income inequality (see also chapter 8; Ferrera, Hemerijck, and Rhodes 2000).

═ Chapter 6 ═

An Equality-Incomes Trade-off?

The analyses in chapter 4 indicated no adverse effect of low levels of income inequality on economic growth, but the findings in chapter 5 suggested that low levels of pay inequality may have impeded employment growth in the 1980s and 1990s. The asserted trade-off that is potentially most damning to egalitarians, in my view, has to do with the real income levels of those at the low end of the distribution. The focus here is on the effects of redistribution. Many welfare state critics (Friedman and Friedman 1979; Lindbeck 1995; Murray 1984; Tullock 1997) and even some supporters (Arrow 1979; Okun 1975) contend that, over time, generous social-welfare programs reduce the growth of economic output and/or employment. As a result, redistribution may produce stagnant or even declining real incomes for the very segment of society it is most directly aimed at helping—those at the bottom.

The incomes of those at the bottom of the distribution are typically studied by analyzing poverty. Most analysts of cross-country differences in poverty prefer a *relative* poverty measure, which sets the poverty line for each country at a certain percentage (usually 50 percent) of the median income within that country. The poverty line thus differs across countries. However, to assess the possibility that redistribution is bad for real income growth, it is necessary to use an *absolute* measure of poverty. An absolute measure uses the same poverty line (in converted currency units) across all nations. Consider two hypothetical countries. Suppose that both the median level and the distribution of pretax-pretransfer income are identical in the two nations. Country A's social-welfare programs redistribute more money from rich to poor, so after taxes and transfers only 10 percent of its citizens have incomes below half the median whereas 20 percent of country B's do. This would suggest that the welfare state helps to reduce poverty. But suppose that over the next several decades country A's generous welfare state has the additional effect of reducing the growth of its GDP and/or employment compared to country B. Given its more extensive redistribution, country A might continue, at this later point in time, to have a lower rate of *relative* poverty than country B—that is, a smaller share of its citizens with posttax-posttransfer incomes below half of *its* median. Yet because of the differences in GDP growth and/or employment growth, the rate of *absolute* poverty—calculated using the same poverty line for both countries rather than country-specific poverty lines—might be higher in country A.

A variety of recent studies have found that, across the most affluent OECD nations, welfare state generosity is associated with low relative poverty (Brady 2001; DeFina and Thanawala 2002; Goodin et al. 1999; Kenworthy 1999a; Kim 2000; Moller et al. 2003; OECD 2001e; Smeeding 1998; Smeeding, Rainwater, and Burtless 2001). Figure 6.1 illustrates this relationship for fourteen countries as of the mid-1990s.[1]

Given the finding in chapter 3 that redistribution helps to reduce income inequality, it is no surprise that welfare state generosity tends to reduce relative poverty. Since relative poverty is measured as the share with incomes below a certain percentage of the median within each country, it is essentially a measure of inequality. It differs from standard

Figure 6.1   Relative Poverty by Welfare State Generosity, Fourteen Countries, Mid-1990s

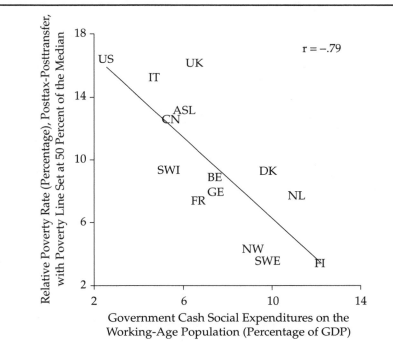

inequality measures, such as the Gini coefficient or the 90th percentile/10th percentile ratio, in that it takes into account only the bottom portion of the income distribution. But it shares with other inequality measures the fact that it is based strictly on the distribution of income rather than on income levels. Indeed, for the fourteen countries shown in figure 6.1, the correlation between the relative poverty rate and the Gini coefficient as of the mid-1990s is .93.

There are sound reasons for using a relative measure of poverty in comparative analyses of affluent countries. As Robert Goodin and his colleagues (1999, 28) note: "People feel themselves to be poor, and think others to be poor, in ways that matter both sociologically and ultimately morally, if they have substantially less than what is commonplace among others in their society" (see also Brady 2003; Iceland 2003). Yet the assertion that the poor may be harmed in an absolute sense if the welfare state worsens macroeconomic performance should not be lightly dismissed.[2] If it is correct, egalitarians face a troubling dilemma: redistribution may help to reduce inequality and relative poverty but also contribute to lower real incomes for those at the bottom. Hence, there is a compelling rationale for examining the welfare state's impact on absolute poverty.

To date there has been very little cross-national research on the relationship between welfare state generosity and absolute poverty. In an earlier study (Kenworthy 1999a), I found welfare state generosity from 1960 to 1990 to be associated with lower absolute poverty as of the early 1990s across fifteen countries, but the cross-sectional framework of that analysis may have missed informative longitudinal developments. A number of studies have examined over-time patterns in the United States, yielding mixed conclusions (for example, Bane and Ellwood 1994; Blank 1997, 2000; Danziger and Weinberg 1994; Freeman 2001; Murray 1984; Sawhill 1988). Maria Hanratty and Rebecca Blank (1992) find that absolute poverty decreased in Canada in the 1980s while it remained constant in the United States, and they attribute this to Canada's more generous social-welfare programs. Unfortunately, temporal variation in a variety of potentially important factors—particularly demographics and the state of the economy—makes it difficult for a one- or two-country analysis to isolate the effect of the welfare state on poverty. Also, the generalizability of the U.S. and Canadian cases is questionable. My aim in this chapter is to shed some light on the welfare state's over-time effects on absolute poverty using data from the Luxembourg Income Study.

What should we expect to find? The critics' argument is centered on a presumption that generous welfare states impede the growth of economic output (and therefore incomes) and/or employment. An adverse effect on economic growth is expected to work primarily through the channels I discussed in chapter 4: reduction of investment and/or work incentives. Since those with high incomes account for a disproportionate share of savings and investment, redistributing money to those with lower incomes may reduce investment. It may also reduce work incentives: those with high earnings lose a larger share to taxes and may therefore choose to work less, while those with low earnings may find it more attractive to live off government benefits instead of working. In addition, the high tax rates necessary to finance a generous welfare state may interfere with the market allocation of resources, thereby causing some loss of efficiency.

On the other hand, by transferring money to those who tend to spend a larger portion of their incomes, redistribution may bolster consumer demand. It also may increase the ability of those with low earnings to invest in skill development—particularly a college education. In these ways redistribution may have a positive impact on growth that partially or fully offsets any negative impact due to reduced investment, diminished work effort, or resource misallocation.

There is an extensive empirical literature on the effects of social-welfare programs on economic growth in affluent countries, but it has yielded nothing close to a consensus. In his survey of this research, Anthony Atkinson (1995, 196) concludes that "while popular argument often refers in a casual way to the experience of Sweden or other countries with sizeable levels of spending, the results of econometric studies are mixed, and provide no overwhelming evidence that high spending on social transfers leads to lower growth rates." Gøsta Esping-Andersen (1994), Ian Gough (1996), and Peter Lindert (2003) come to a similar conclusion in their reviews of this research.

What about employment? Generous benefits and high income tax rates may reduce the supply of labor by lowering its payoff relative to nonwork, and high payroll tax rates may reduce the demand for labor. Recent research on employment developments has tended to yield findings that do suggest adverse effects of certain elements of the welfare state. A variety of cross-country studies have found detrimental effects of tax rates and the level and/or duration of unemployment benefits on unemployment or employment (Adsera and Boix 2000; Blanchard and Wolfers 2000; Kenworthy 2003; Nickell and Layard 1999; Nickell et al. 2001; OECD 1994, ch. 8). The analyses in chapter 5 suggested an adverse effect of high tax rates on employment growth in the 1980s and 1990s. On the other hand, as I noted in chapter 5, across countries these welfare state–related policies tend to be fairly closely correlated with various labor market policies and institutions, such as employment regulations, union strength, and the degree of pay inequality. This makes it somewhat difficult to isolate the causal effects of particular elements of these configurations. In addition, there are some elements of welfare state generosity that may have pro-employment effects. In particular, government provision or subsidization of child care may boost employment by facilitating women's labor market participation.

Suppose generous welfare states do tend to have an adverse effect on economic growth or employment growth. This may result in increasing pretax-pretransfer absolute poverty in such countries. But whether absolute poverty increases *after taxes and transfers are taken into account* depends on the structure and size of the tax-transfer system. For instance, social-welfare programs may be structured in such a way as to create significant work disincentives but without being generous enough to lift many people out of poverty. Conversely, such programs may create only minimal work disincentives (for example, because they are available for only a short period of time) while also transferring enough money to the pretax-pretransfer poor to pull a substantial portion above the poverty line. It is impossible to be sure on theoretical grounds whether posttax-posttransfer absolute poverty in countries with generous welfare states will increase, decrease, or remain constant relative to countries with less generous social-welfare programs. The issue can only be settled empirically.

Data and Measures

As I noted in chapter 3, in the LIS database the first available year for many affluent nations is in the early or mid-1980s, and the most recent is in the mid-1990s. This is problematic for an assessment of long-run trends in incomes and poverty. There are five countries, however, for which LIS data are available from the mid-1970s through the year 2000: Sweden, Germany, the United Kingdom, Canada, and the United States (the most recent year being 1998 for Canada and 1999 for the United Kingdom). I examine developments in these nations during this twenty-five-year period. Although the LIS country surveys are not from exactly the same year within each wave, the years are close enough to make comparison reasonable. An obvious potential complication is German unification, which occurred in the middle of the period being analyzed. It turns out, however, that the level of absolute poverty in unified Germany as a whole has tended to be very similar to that for the former West German regions (see table 6A.1).

For my purposes, these five countries happen to be useful ones. They include a representative of each of the three types of welfare regime highlighted by Esping-Andersen (1990, 1999): Sweden the social-democratic, Germany the conservative, Canada and the United States the liberal. The United Kingdom is classified by Esping-Andersen as a hybrid social-democratic and liberal welfare state. As table 6.1 shows, the five countries differ on a variety of measures of welfare state size and generosity. The variation on these measures between the high-end and low-end nations, Sweden and the United States, is fairly pronounced. For instance, Sweden is about three times as high as the United States on Esping-Andersen's (1990) index of decommodification and nearly twice as high in its level of government transfers and its tax rate on a typical worker.

The first three measures in the table tap the size and generosity of the welfare state as a whole. On each of these measures the five countries can be rank-ordered from high to low as follows: Sweden, Germany, United Kingdom, Canada, United States. However, since work disincentives are a key reason why critics believe the welfare state is ultimately ineffective at reducing poverty, I focus throughout this chapter (as in chapter 3) on the working-age population. I include only households with heads age twenty-five to fifty-nine, thus excluding those most likely to be students or retirees. The three measures in the bottom portion of the table attempt to tap the size and generosity of welfare state programs that primarily or exclusively benefit working-age households. For these, Sweden remains at the high end (despite the very limited duration of unemployment benefits) and the United States at the low end, but the rank-ordering for the other three countries is less straightforward. The level of unemployment benefits is highest in Canada, the duration of benefits is longest in the United Kingdom, and the share of GDP going to benefits for the working-age population is the same in all three. Overall, in my estimation, the five countries can be grouped into three categories with regard to welfare state size and generosity:

High: Sweden

Intermediate: Germany, United Kingdom, Canada (not necessarily in that order)

Low: United States

It is important to keep in mind that these measures emphasize only one aspect of welfare states: cash benefits. Governments also typically provide a variety of services, such as health care, education, and child care. These services are a central component of the supports that welfare states offer to citizens, though their role varies across countries (Huber and Stephens 2001). I focus exclusively on cash benefits because poverty measurement is based on income rather than on actual consumption of goods and services. This is a reasonable approach to

Table 6.1   Indicators of Welfare State Size and Generosity in Five Countries, Mid-1970s to 2000

	Sweden	Germany	United Kingdom	Canada	United States
Overall					
Esping-Andersen decommodification[a]					
1980	39	28	23	22	14
Government transfers as percentage of GDP[b]					
1965 to 1975	11	13	9	8	7
1990 to 2000	21	18	14	13	13
Tax rate on a typical worker[c]					
1965 to 1975	57	45	43	40	38
1990 to 1995	78	52	47	50	45
Working-age population					
Government cash expenditures on the working-age population as percentage of GDP[d]					
1980	7	4	5	5	3
1990 to 1999	9	6	6	6	3
Unemployment benefit replacement rate[e]					
1965 to 1975	42	42	39	49	27
1990 to 1998	90	38	27	57	28
Unemployment benefit eligibility duration[f]					
1965 to 1975	.00	.57	.59	.31	.17
1990 to 1995	.04	.61	.70	.22	.18

Source: Author's compilation; see appendix.

[a]1980 is the only year for which these data are available. *Source*: Esping-Andersen (1990, 52).

[b]*Source*: My calculations from data in OECD (various years [b], table 6.3).

[c]Sum of the average income, payroll, and consumption tax rates for a typical worker. 1995 is the most recent year for which data are available. *Source*: Nickell et al. (2001, 32).

[d]Sum of cash family benefits and benefits for unemployment, disability, occupational injury and disease, sickness, and "other contingencies" (mainly low income) as a share of GDP. 1980 is the earliest year for which these data are available. *Source*: My calculations from data in OECD (2001c).

[e]Gross replacement rate (share of previous earnings) for a worker with earnings at the thirty-third percentile, in the first year after losing the job. *Source*: OECD (n.d., a).

[f]Duration of eligibility for unemployment compensation (index). 1995 is the most recent year for which data are available. *Source*: Nickell et al. (2001, 27).

poverty measurement, since income is an important resource for acquiring goods and services and there are no reliable comparative data on household consumption levels. But it is clearly an incomplete approach. In countries where governments provide services that are universal (available to all), low-cost, and reasonably high-quality, income-based poverty measures understate the well-being of those with low incomes to a nontrivial degree. I return to this issue later in the chapter.

Since my principal interest here is in the effects of redistribution on incomes at the low end of the distribution, I examine trends in real income levels directly rather than focusing solely on poverty. Incomes for households at various percentiles of the distribution can be calculated for each country using the LIS database. For purposes of cross-country comparison, these incomes must then be converted into a common currency. I do so using purchasing power parities (PPPs) from the OECD. Unlike exchange rates, PPPs are based on the cost of living for a typical household in each country. They therefore provide a better (albeit imperfect, as I discuss later) gauge of real living standards across countries. After using the PPPs to convert incomes into U.S. dollars, I adjust for inflation using the U.S. consumer price index (CPI-U-RS). As noted in chapter 2, I adjust these income figures for household size using a conventional equivalence scale: household income is divided by the square root of the number of persons in the household. All income levels are thus expressed in year-2000 U.S. dollars per equivalent person.

Given that real incomes can be examined directly, the chief advantage of calculating a poverty rate is data reduction. A measure of absolute poverty allows us to express information about real income levels at the bottom of the distribution with a single number. Following convention, I calculate the poverty rate for each nation as the percentage of persons living in households with incomes below the poverty line. I compute two poverty rates for each country in each year: one for pretax-pretransfer household income and the other for posttax-posttransfer household income (see chapter 2 for a list of the types of income and taxes included in these two income measures). I set the poverty line at $12,763, which is 50 percent of the 2000 median posttax-posttransfer household income per equivalent person in the United States.[3] For a single-person household, the poverty line is thus $12,763. For a household of two, it is $18,050 ($12,763 multiplied by the square root of 2). For a household of four it is $25,526 ($12,763 multiplied by the square root of 4).

The choice of $12,763 per equivalent person is an arbitrary one, of course. But any other number would be equally arbitrary. The question is whether it is a substantively sensible choice. There is no easy answer to this question; analysts differ greatly in their assessment of how much income is sufficient these days to ensure a minimally adequate standard of living in an affluent country (see, for example, Bernstein, Brocht, and Spade-Aguilar 2000; Citro and Michael 1995, 6; Schwarz and Volgy 1992, 44). Most researchers who use a relative measure of poverty set the poverty line at 50 percent of the median within each country. A poverty line set at 50 percent of the median in the United States, which is the richest country, might therefore seem too high. On the other hand, a recent study of the cost of living in metropolitan and rural areas throughout the United States finds that the amount of money required to meet a "basic family budget" is two to three times the official U.S. poverty line (Boushey et al. 2001, 11). This comes to more than $35,000 for a family of four. And the median response of Americans to a 1996 Gallup poll asking "How much income do you feel your family would need just to get by?" was $30,000 (cited in Schiller 2001, 18). These levels are substantially higher than the poverty line I use here, which amounts to just over $25,000 (in 2000 dollars) for a family of four.[4]

The poverty rate, or "headcount," is by far the most commonly used measure of poverty. But it is incomplete and thus potentially misleading. Also relevant is the depth of poverty, commonly measured using the poverty gap (Blank 1997; Sen 1976).[5] The poverty gap is calculated by subtracting the average income among the poor from the poverty line and then dividing this difference by the poverty line.

The measure of poverty I use here, which I refer to as the "poverty level," is calculated as *the poverty rate multiplied by the poverty gap*. If 15 percent of the working-age population live in households with incomes below the poverty line, the poverty rate is 15.0. If the average income among the poor is two-thirds of the poverty line, the poverty gap is .333. The rate-times-gap measure of poverty would therefore be 15.0 multiplied by .333, which equals 5.0. The figures for the poverty rates and poverty gaps themselves are shown, for selected years, in table 6A.1.

Changes in Pretax-Pretransfer Incomes and Poverty

Figure 6.2 shows trends from the mid-1970s through 2000 for real pretax-pretransfer incomes at the 5th, 10th, 15th, 20th, and 25th percentiles of the distribution. The United States had the best performance among the five countries, in that incomes at each of the percentiles were higher at the end of the twenty-five-year period than at the beginning. That improvement was due entirely to the late 1990s. Between the mid-1970s and the mid-1990s real income levels declined at the 5th, 10th, 15th, and 20th percentiles and were stagnant at the 25th percentile.

Figure 6.2   Real Pretax-Pretransfer Incomes at the 5th, 10th, 15th, 20th, and 25th Percentiles in Five Countries, Mid-1970s to 2000

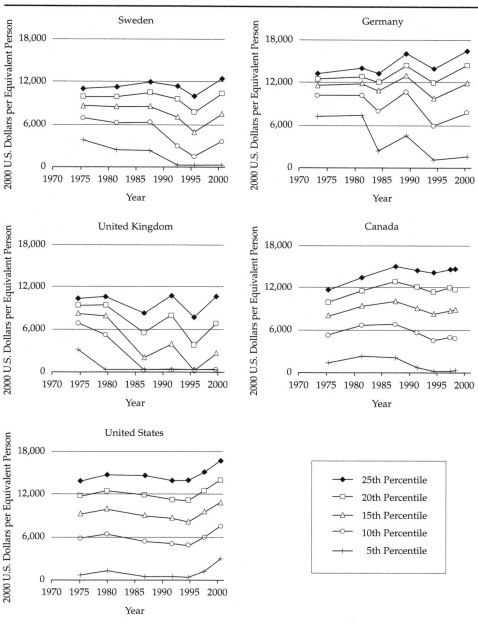

Source: Author's compilation; see appendix.

Canada and Germany were the next-best performers. In both countries incomes increased somewhat at the 20th and 25th percentiles, were stagnant at the 15th, and declined at the 5th and 10th. The drop at the bottom was somewhat more severe in Germany than in Canada.

In Sweden incomes at each of the five percentiles held roughly constant from the mid-1970s through the end of the 1980s, but then fell sharply during the economic crisis of the first half of the 1990s. By 2000 income levels at the 15th, 20th, and 25th percentiles had nearly or fully returned to their pre-crisis levels, but at the 5th and 10th percentiles they remained significantly lower.

Finally, in the United Kingdom incomes in 1999 were lower than in the mid-1970s for all except the 25th percentile. During the recessions of the early 1980s and early 1990s real incomes dropped dramatically at the 5th, 10th, and 15th percentiles.

Figure 6.3 shows trends in pretax-pretransfer absolute poverty, measured as described earlier. The figures for market poverty correlate strongly with those for real incomes at the 10th, 15th, and 20th percentiles of the distribution: $r = -.95, -.98,$ and $-.94,$ respectively. In other words, examining real income levels at these spots in the income distribution provides essentially the same information as a measure of absolute poverty. For the 5th and 25th percentiles the correlations are not quite as strong: $r = -.65$ and $-.82.$

The United Kingdom, Sweden, and to a lesser extent Germany experienced rising market poverty, whereas the level in Canada and the United

Figure 6.3   Pretax-Pretransfer Absolute Poverty in Five Countries, Mid-1970s to 2000

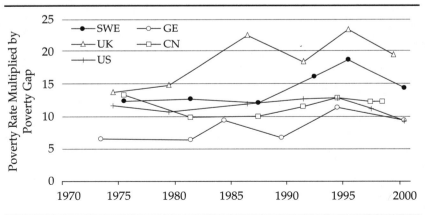

Source: Author's compilation; see appendix.

States decreased slightly over the twenty-five-year period. According to the measures in table 6.1, the Swedish, German, and British welfare states were as generous as Canada's and clearly more generous than that of the United States during these years. So did welfare state generosity contribute to increases in pretax-pretransfer absolute poverty?

We can begin by investigating the purported causal paths. The mechanism through which welfare state generosity is most commonly asserted to increase absolute poverty is reduced economic growth. Trends in GDP per capita are shown in the left side of figure 6.4 ("GDP per Capita"). The trend was fairly similar for each of the five countries, though growth was a bit more rapid in the United States than elsewhere. There is little indication that the countries with more generous welfare states had notably slower economic growth. The scatter plot in the lower-left corner of figure 6.4 suggests no association between patterns of growth and trends in market poverty.

A second possibility is that generous welfare states raised absolute poverty by reducing employment. Figure 6.4 shows trends in employment rates as well (right side). Here the United States performed particularly well, starting at the second-lowest level among the five countries and finishing at the highest. Canada also had fairly strong employment performance. Sweden, Germany, and the United Kingdom each experienced stagnation or slight declines in employment. Sweden's trend was the most volatile. It had by far the highest employment rate from the mid-1970s until 1990, but then suffered a severe economic crisis. Between 1990 and 1995 the Swedish employment rate dropped from 81 percent to 72 percent. In the late 1990s it began to increase again, and by 2000 it had returned to its 1970 level—the second-highest among the five countries and only slightly lower than the U.S. rate.

The scatter plot on the "Employment" side of figure 6.4 shows that the three countries in which employment did not increase, the United Kingdom, Sweden, and Germany, suffered increases in pretax-pretransfer absolute poverty, whereas the two countries with employment increases, the United States and Canada, experienced decreases in pretax-pretransfer absolute poverty. This parallels the finding in chapter 3 that employment declines between the mid-1980s and the mid-1990s were associated with increases in household earnings inequality. Was poor employment performance the main reason for the disappointing trends in pretax-pretransfer incomes in Sweden, Germany, and the United Kingdom? After all, other factors could have contributed to declining real market incomes among those at the bottom of the distribution. For example, wages may have fallen among low-skilled workers. Or the share of households with just one adult, and therefore probably only one earner, may have increased.

Figure 6.4   Potential Macroeconomic Determinants of Change in Pretax-Pretransfer Absolute Poverty in Five Countries, Mid-1970s to 2000

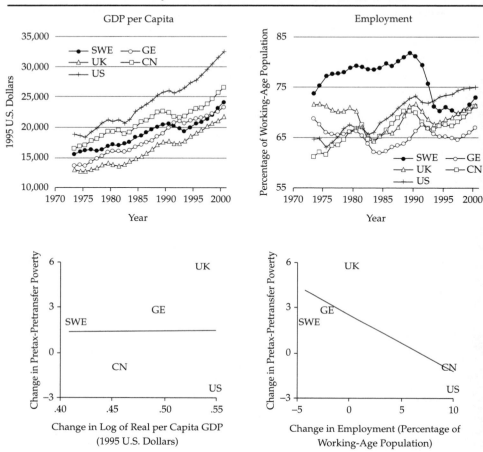

Source: Author's compilation; see appendix.

The small number of LIS observations for each country restricts the kind of analysis one can conduct in assessing the relative contributions of these various potential causes. But the limited data that are available can be used to at least get a sense of the likely causal story. Figure 6.5 shows trends from 1975 to 2000 for one of these countries, Sweden, in employment, real annual earning levels at the 10th percentile among individuals employed full-time year-round, the share of households that have only one adult, and the level of pretax-pretransfer absolute poverty. The trend for employment corresponds closely to that for mar-

Figure 6.5   Employment and Other Potential Determinants of Change in Pretax-Pretransfer Absolute Poverty in Sweden, Mid-1970s to 2000

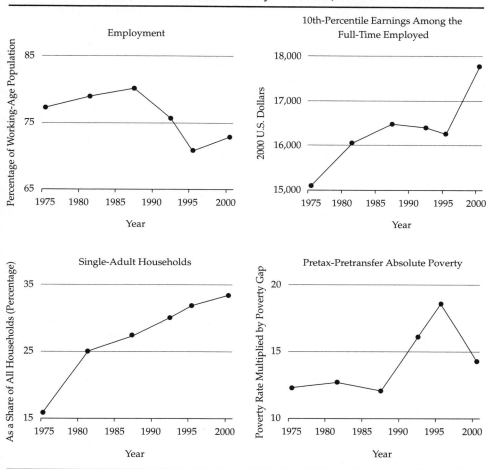

Source: Author's compilation; see appendix.

ket poverty. The correlation between these two variables is –.85. For earnings levels the correlation with market poverty is .22, which is weak and in the opposite direction to what we would expect. For single-adult households the correlation with market poverty is .63. This is not much weaker than the correlation for employment, but the trend in single-adult households does not account for the sharp increase in poverty in Sweden in the early 1990s, nor for the decline beginning in the mid-1990s. As I noted in chapter 3, the share of Swedish households with *no* employed person increased substantially during the early 1990s, and employment losses during that period were most severe among workers with low skills and earnings. On the whole, employment appears to have been the chief culprit in Sweden. The same turns out to be true for the United Kingdom and Germany, though I do not show the data for those two countries here.

Needless to say, employment is not always a cure for poverty. Much research in the past two decades has emphasized the large number of working poor in the United States—people who have paying jobs but whose earnings are below the poverty line (see, for example, Edin and Lein 1997; Schwarz and Volgy 1992). Still, in comparative terms employment seems to have been important in influencing trends in pretax-pretransfer absolute poverty.

As noted earlier, recent cross-country studies have found apparent adverse effects of high tax rates, unemployment benefit replacement rates, and unemployment benefit duration on employment performance. Figure 6.6 shows, for the five countries examined here, the relationship between average levels over the mid-1970s-to-2000 period for these three welfare state components and change in the employment rate during this period. It also includes a summary welfare state indicator: Esping-Andersen's decommodification score, which is a composite measure of the rules governing access to various government benefits, the degree of income replacement provided by those benefits, and the range of entitlements they encompass. All four charts reveal an inverse association, suggesting that welfare state generosity may indeed have hindered job growth. There is reason, then, to suspect that generous welfare states may have increased pretax-pretransfer absolute poverty by contributing to employment declines.

But this conclusion is based on the aggregate cross-country pattern. Does it hold if we examine the individual cases?

Let's begin with Sweden. As the data in table 6.1 indicate, Sweden's welfare state was already the most generous of the five toward working-age households by the mid-1970s. Perhaps most indicative, government cash transfers to the working-age population totaled 7 percent of GDP in Sweden as of the 1980s, compared to 5 percent or less in each of the other four countries. Yet in seeming contradiction to the critics' view, Sweden's economy fared reasonably well through the 1970s and 1980s. Its rate of economic growth was not as rapid as in the other four countries, but the difference was relatively small. And Sweden's employment rate was by far the highest. Pretax-pretransfer absolute poverty remained flat through the late 1980s, and at the end of this period it was at a level equal to that of the United States, well below that of the United Kingdom, and not much higher than that of Canada.

Figure 6.6 **Potential Welfare State Determinants of Change in Employment, Five Countries, Mid-1970s to 2000**

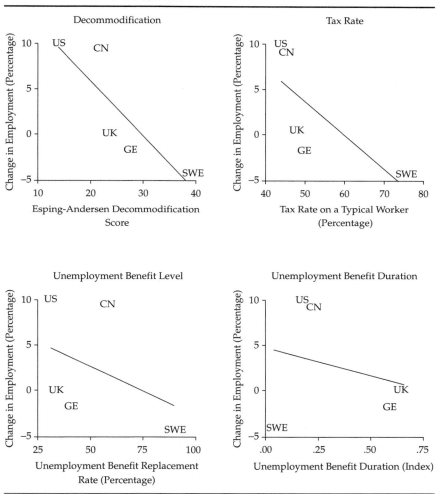

Source: Author's compilation; see appendix.
Notes: Employment change (vertical axes) is change in employment as a share of the working-age population: 2000 value minus mid-1970s value. Welfare state measures (horizontal axes) are averages of levels from the mid-1970s to 2000 (or the most recent year for which data are available).

In the first half of the 1990s, however, Sweden's level of pretax-pretransfer absolute poverty shot up. This was a product of the economic crisis of the early 1990s, particularly the sharp drop in employment that occurred. Was the economic crisis due to Sweden's generous welfare state, as the welfare state critics' view would suggest? That is certainly the contention of some observers (Lindbeck 1997, 1312). In this view, the excessive generosity of the Swedish welfare state was causing economic strain through the 1970s and 1980s. Its adverse impact on macroeconomic performance was masked by heavy public expenditures, and particularly by increases in government employment. The welfare state's adverse effects were therefore manifested not in a gradual deterioration but rather in a dramatic crisis.

There is little doubt that by the end of the 1980s some components of the Swedish welfare state were creating adverse work incentives. The prime example is sickness leave, which had been made progressively more generous since the early 1960s. As Jonas Agell (1996, 1767) notes:

> According to the rules in place by the end of the 1980s, employees were entitled to a 90% compensation level from the first day of reporting sick. Due to supplementary insurance agreements in the labour market, however, many employees had a compensation level of 100%. For the first seven days of sickness leave, a physician's certificate was not required. If individuals ever respond to economic incentives, work absenteeism ought to have been widespread in Sweden. The increase in the average number of sickness days per insured employee from 13 days in 1963 to 25 days in 1988 can hardly be attributed to a deteriorating health status of the population.

Yet other components of Sweden's welfare state seem likely to have increased employment. Most notably, the gradual extension of public provision and subsidization of child care for preschool-age children almost certainly increased labor force participation by mothers.

Many observers attribute the economic crisis of the early 1990s mainly to policy choices (Benner and Vad 2000, 426–28; Furåker 2002; Palme et al. 2002, 162–64; Scharpf 2000, 90; Wilensky 2002, 111). Of particular importance was the decision to tie Sweden's currency, the kronor, to the European currency unit (ECU) in May 1991, which put the Swedish economy at the mercy of the German Bundesbank's hard-core monetarism. By the time the policy was abandoned in November 1992, Sweden's unemployment rate had shot up from 2.5 percent to 7 percent, and it climbed to more than 9 percent in 1993. Then, in the midst of the recession, the Swedish government raised taxes and reduced government expenditures (along with public employment), electing to focus on price stability and a balanced budget rather than on stimulation of the economy.

The health of the Swedish economy has improved considerably since the mid-1990s. As of 2002 unemployment was down to 5 percent, the employment rate was up to 75 percent, and real per capita GDP had grown by as much since 1995 as it did during the two decades between 1975 and 1995. Welfare state critics might attribute the recent economic improvement to cutbacks in social-welfare programs. In the early and mid-1990s the replacement rates for sickness, occupational injury, and unemployment benefits were reduced, eligibility criteria were tightened, and waiting periods were increased (Huber and Stephens 2001, 241–57; Palme et al. 2002; Ploug 1999, 100–2). However, these reforms were relatively minor. For instance, the unemployment benefit replacement rate was reduced only from 90 percent to 80 percent, which was still higher than in any other affluent nation. It seems unlikely that such fairly minor cutbacks have been the chief impetus for the Swedish economy's buoyancy since the mid-1990s.

It is difficult to reach a firm judgment about the causes of the early 1990s Swedish economic crisis or of the ensuing turnaround. Yet despite the fact that as of 2000 Sweden's welfare state remained by far the most generous among the five countries examined here, its per capita GDP was third highest, its employment rate was second highest, and its level of market poverty, although second highest, was not markedly above that of most of the other countries (figures 6.3 and 6.4).

The United Kingdom had the highest level of pretax-pretransfer absolute poverty as of the mid-1970s, but up to 1979 it was only marginally higher than the levels in several other nations. Then, in the four years from 1979 to 1983, the employment rate in the United Kingdom dropped from second highest among the five countries to nearly the lowest. Market poverty increased dramatically. Since then the level of market poverty has moved up and down in concert with the employment rate. Welfare state critics might suggest that the steep decline in employment in the early 1980s was the product of an excessively generous welfare state, but it seems clearly to have been the result instead of the Thatcher government's monetarist orientation and privatization efforts (Rhodes 2000).

Germany is the third country in which pretax-pretransfer absolute poverty increased. This is probably in part because of its starting point. As of the mid-1970s, the level of market poverty was substantially lower in Germany than in any of the other four countries. As in Sweden and the United Kingdom, however, the rise in market poverty appears to be a direct product of employment declines. In Germany there were two key periods of decline: the early 1980s and the early 1990s. The latter may be attributable partly to reunification with the East in 1990, which put considerable strain on the economy. Yet Germany's employment decline in the early 1990s was not notably more severe than the declines in other countries. Perhaps the most important employment barrier in Germany has been its tax system. As noted in chapter 5, German social-welfare programs are funded largely through heavy employer payroll taxes, which increase the cost of hiring. These taxes are certainly related to the level of welfare state generosity, but analysts who have studied this most carefully suggest that it is the *structure* of the German tax system rather than its level that constitutes the chief obstacle to a higher employment rate (Manow and Seils 2000a; Scharpf 1997, 2000).

Examining the individual country experiences suggests, then, that there is reason to question the importance of welfare state generosity in causing employment declines and hence rising pretax-pretransfer absolute poverty in Sweden, the United Kingdom, and Germany. It may have played some role, but other factors appear to have had greater causal significance. Furthermore, Canada's welfare state was comparable to those of Germany and the United Kingdom in generosity toward the working-age population (table 6.1), and Canada's record of employment growth and hence market poverty was fairly strong during this period (figure 6.4).

Changes in Posttax-Posttransfer Incomes and Poverty

What ultimately matters to people is not their market income but rather their posttax-posttransfer income. Figure 6.7 shows trends in absolute poverty levels with taxes and transfers included. As with pretax-pretransfer poverty, the poverty line is set at $12,763 per equivalent

Figure 6.7   Posttax-Posttransfer Absolute Poverty in Five Countries, Mid-1970s to 2000

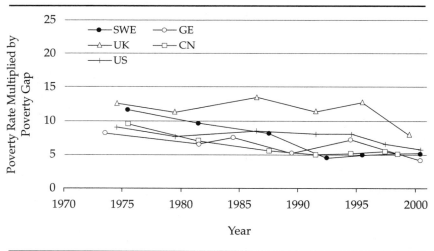

Source: Author's compilation; see appendix.

Figure 6.8   Real Posttax-Posttransfer Incomes at the 5th, 10th, 15th, 20th, and 25th Percentiles in Five Countries, Mid-1970s to 2000

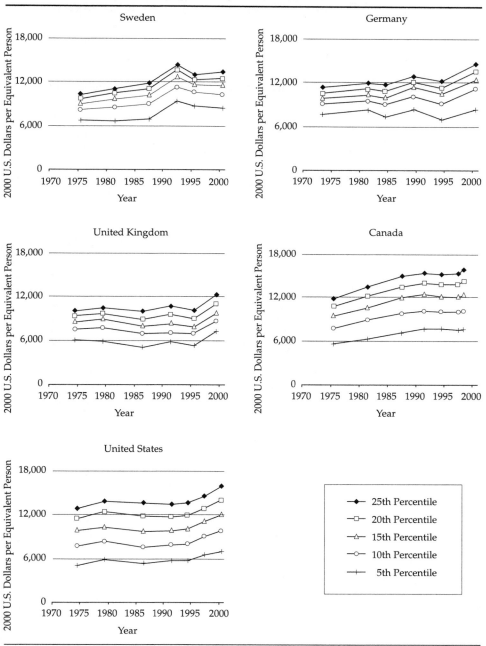

Source: Author's compilation; see appendix.

person in 2000 U.S. dollars, poverty is measured as the poverty rate multiplied by the poverty gap, and the figures are for working-age households only.[6] Figure 6.8 shows trends in real posttax-posttransfer income levels at the low end of the distribution. Once again, the correlations between poverty levels and real incomes at the 5th, 10th, 15th, 20th, and 25th percentiles are strong: r = −.77, −.92, −.96, −.92, and −.85, respectively.

Figure 6.9 shows actual government transfers to working-age households with market incomes below the poverty line. The figures represent net transfers: cash and near-cash transfers received minus taxes paid. They are averages for each country, in 2000 U.S. dollars per equivalent person. Like the figures for actual redistribution in chapter 3, they are a product of both the level of intended generosity, as expressed, for example, in the replacement rates for unemployment and sickness, and the level of need, as determined, for example, by the unemployment rate or by low wages for those in low-end jobs.

As of the mid-1970s, the country rank-ordering for levels of posttax-posttransfer absolute poverty, from low to high, was: Germany, the United States, Canada, Sweden, and the United Kingdom. During the ensuing twenty-five years all five countries experienced reductions. In most of the countries posttax-posttransfer poverty levels and low-end

Figure 6.9   Net Government Transfers to the Poor in Five Countries, Mid-1970s to 2000

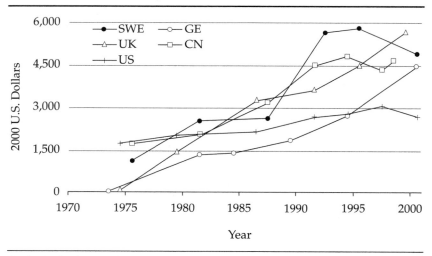

Source: Author's compilation; see appendix.
Note: Average transfers (cash and near-cash) minus taxes to working-age households with pretax-pretransfer incomes below the poverty line.

real incomes tracked relatively closely with pretax-pretransfer poverty and incomes. That was especially true in the United States, where net government transfers to the poor increased only minimally. In Germany and the United Kingdom the average amount of net transfers increased significantly. As a result, in the early 1980s and early 1990s posttax-posttransfer poverty did not rise nearly as much as market poverty. Similarly, a sizable increase in net transfers allowed Canada to maintain a relatively low level of posttax-posttransfer poverty in the early 1990s despite a jump in market poverty.

The most striking change occurred in Sweden. As noted earlier, Sweden suffered a deep employment crisis in the early 1990s. Largely as a result of this employment decline, pretax-pretransfer incomes at the low end of the distribution fell steeply, and market poverty increased by approximately half (the poverty rate multiplied by the poverty gap jumped from 12 in 1987 to 18 in 1995). Indeed, by the early 1990s Sweden had the second highest level of pretax-pretransfer absolute poverty among these five countries. Yet the average net transfer to poor households more than doubled in inflation-adjusted terms between the late 1980s and the early 1990s, and as a result, the posttax-posttransfer poverty level actually decreased and real incomes rose. Sweden's posttax-posttransfer poverty level was the second highest as of the mid-1970s, but by 2000 it had dropped to the second lowest, despite the fact that pretax-pretransfer poverty continued to be the second highest among the group. Sweden's welfare state appears to have been particularly effective at raising the incomes of households with market incomes below the poverty line.

The LIS database makes it possible to explore the impact of social-welfare benefits in greater detail. Table 6.2 splits those with market incomes below the poverty line into four subgroups, based on level of market income as a percentage of the poverty line. The data are for the year 2000 (1998 for Canada, 1999 for the United Kingdom). As before, the poverty line is $12,763 per equivalent person. Thus, the first column, for people in households with market incomes from 0 to 25 percent of the poverty line, represents those in households with incomes from $0 to $3,191 per equivalent person; the second column represents those in households with market incomes from $3,192 to $6,382 per equivalent person; and so on.

Among all four subgroups, government transfers provided the least income support in the United States. Germany, the United Kingdom, and Canada were fairly similar to one another in transfer levels. Sweden stands out as the most generous. For instance, among the very poorest, those with market incomes below 25 percent of the poverty line, the average amount of government transfer income was more than

Table 6.2   Sources of Income for Four Segments of the Pretax-Pretransfer Poor in Five Countries, 2000

	Market Income as a Percentage of the Poverty Line			
	0 to 25 Percent	26 to 50 Percent	51 to 75 Percent	76 to 100 Percent
Sweden 2000				
Share of all persons	10%	4%	5%	8%
Income				
Market income	$853	$4,824	$8,184	$11,273
Government transfer income	10,312	8,535	6,355	6,085
Other income	148	393	520	422
Taxes	−2,000	−3,176	−3,620	−4,615
Posttax-posttransfer income	9,313	10,576	11,439	13,165
Germany 2000				
Share of all persons	7%	2%	3%	5%
Income				
Market income	$838	$4,807	$8,017	$11,157
Government transfer income	7,349	5,338	4,432	4,011
Other income	973	744	295	549
Taxes	−277	−830	−1,650	−2,355
Posttax-posttransfer income	8,883	10,059	11,094	13,362
United Kingdom 1999				
Share of all persons	16%	4%	4%	5%
Income				
Market income	$582	$4,769	$7,933	$11,217
Government transfer income	8,641	5,207	3,988	2,779
Other income	135	630	255	333
Taxes	−208	−838	−1,569	−2,601
Posttax-posttransfer income	9,150	9,768	10,607	11,728
Canada 1998				
Share of all persons	8%	4%	4%	5%
Income				
Market income	$786	$4,484	$8,019	$11,154
Government transfer income	6,789	4,960	4,301	3,976
Other income	144	625	614	468

(*Table continues on p. 117.*)

Table 6.2   *Continued*

	Market Income as a Percentage of the Poverty Line			
	0 to 25 Percent	26 to 50 Percent	51 to 75 Percent	76 to 100 Percent
Taxes	−126	−344	−782	−1,372
Posttax-posttransfer income	7,593	9,725	12,152	14,226
United States 2000				
Share of all persons	5%	3%	4%	5%
Income				
Market income	$938	$4,956	$8,042	$11,182
Government transfer income	4,898	3,675	2,747	1,914
Other income	485	503	452	372
Taxes	−60	−417	−744	−1,171
Posttax-posttransfer income	6,261	8,717	10,497	12,297

Source: Author's calculations from LIS data; see appendix.
Note: All income figures are averages, in 2000 U.S. dollars per equivalent person. "Other income" includes child support and alimony, interpersonal transfers, and income from unidentified sources.

$10,000 in Sweden, compared to $8,500 or less in each of the other four countries and less than $5,000 in the United States. The very poor paid more in taxes in Sweden than in any of the other four countries, but even when this is taken into account, the welfare state's net contribution was still most substantial in Sweden. As a result, average posttax-posttransfer incomes for the very poor—those with incomes from 0 to 25 percent and from 26 to 50 percent of the poverty line—were higher in Sweden than in the other countries.

As I noted at the outset of this chapter, it can be misleading to infer trends in posttax-posttransfer absolute poverty from trends in pretax-pretransfer poverty. The aggregate pattern of developments in pretax-pretransfer absolute poverty for these five countries corresponds roughly to what welfare state critics predict: the nations with the most generous welfare states tended to experience rising market poverty and falling real incomes for those at the low end of the distribution. Yet no such pattern is evident for posttax-posttransfer absolute poverty. It declined a bit more in the countries with more generous welfare states than in those with less generous ones. And it fell most of all in Sweden, the country with by far the most generous welfare state.

Comparing Levels of Real Income

Although my focus is on cross-country differences in change over time, a comparison of *levels* of income across the five countries is certainly of interest too. Figure 6.10 shows real posttax-posttransfer income levels as of 2000 throughout the income distribution. The top chart shows the entire distribution, from the 5th percentile to the 95th. The lower chart focuses on the 5th through the 25th percentiles, allowing a clearer view of cross-country differences at the low end of the distribution. The figures include only the working-age population.

Poverty reduction is not the chief aim of the liberal welfare state. Instead, the aim is to maximize average well-being (Goodin et al. 1999). The top chart in figure 6.10 suggests some support for the notion that a liberal welfare state is most conducive to achievement of that aim. Median incomes are highest in the United States and Canada, and in the top third of the distribution the United Kingdom has the next-highest levels. Germany and especially Sweden trail behind.

Lowering poverty levels is also not the chief goal of a social-democratic welfare state such as Sweden's or a conservative welfare state such as Germany's. Instead, the goal is achieving social equality and community (Goodin et al. 1999). Low absolute poverty certainly contributes to this aim, but low *relative* poverty, which refers to the degree of inequality in the bottom half of the distribution, is arguably more important. Figure 6.1 indicates that relative poverty is lower in Sweden and Germany than in the United States, Canada, and the United Kingdom (see also Smeeding and Rainwater 2002; Smeeding, Rainwater, and Burtless 2001). And the top chart in figure 6.10 reveals that there is less dispersion in incomes throughout the entire distribution in Sweden and Germany than in the other three countries. The size and characteristics of the Swedish welfare state also contribute to the goal of social equality directly, not merely indirectly through poverty reduction: extensive public services and universal-type transfer programs, from which everyone receives a benefit and on which everyone is taxed, foster a climate of solidarity (table 6.2; Rothstein 1998, 163).

Yet as the top chart in figure 6.10 makes clear, low income inequality in Sweden and Germany is in large part a function of the fact that incomes from the 20th percentile up are lower than in the United States and Canada. Is that a good thing? In other words, is low inequality better than high inequality if it entails lower incomes for most of the population?

There are two responses. One is that low inequality can be considered desirable not merely on grounds of fairness but also because it contributes to other social goods. A society with less dispersion be-

Figure 6.10   Real Income Levels in Five Countries, 2000

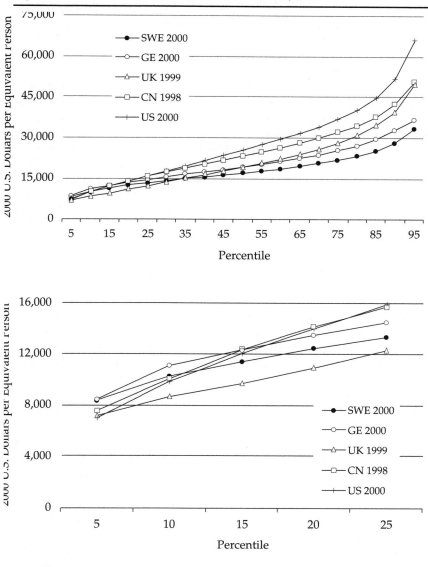

Source: Author's compilation; see appendix.

tween those at the bottom and those at the top may be characterized by greater social harmony and solidarity. Less inequality may also help to keep the political influence of the rich in check, thereby contributing to a more democratic polity.

A second response is that lower incomes at the middle and top may be a price worth paying if incomes at the bottom are higher (Rawls 1971). Yet the bottom chart in figure 6.10 indicates that, as of 2000, real incomes were highest in Sweden and Germany only at the 5th percentile. At the 10th percentile income levels in Sweden were no higher than in the United States and Canada, and the same is true for Germany at the 15th percentile. From the 20th percentile on up, Swedish and German incomes were lower. This seems to suggest that, relative to their counterparts in countries with liberal welfare states, many of those at the low end of Sweden's and Germany's income distributions have not benefited in terms of real income levels from their country's generous social-welfare programs.

Recall, however, that the LIS income data do not include the value of government-provided services such as health care, education, and child care. An obvious difference between Sweden, Germany, and the United States is in health care. Fifteen to 20 percent of Americans do not have health insurance. Most with very low incomes are covered by Medicaid, so those without coverage tend to have incomes between the 5th and 25th percentiles of the distribution. A conservative estimate of the average yearly cost of purchasing health insurance through the private insurance market in the United States is $2,000 per equivalent person—$2,000 for an individual adult, $4,000 for a family (Jencks and Edin 1995; Musco and Wildsmith 2002). Thus, the income figures for the United States at the 10th, 15th, 20th, and perhaps the 25th percentiles would need to be lowered by at least this amount to make them truly comparable to those in the other four countries, where health insurance is provided for all citizens at little or no direct cost to households.[7]

The quality of the public educational system is also likely to differ across countries. Every child in the United States has access to free public schooling from kindergarten through twelfth grade, but because school funding is based heavily on local property taxes, schools in low-income areas tend to be considerably less well funded than those in moderate- and high-income areas. This has obvious consequences for the quality of teachers, educational materials, and infrastructure (Biddle and Berliner 2002; Kozol 1991). Given that average spending per student is similar across countries (once administrative costs are taken into account), many American children whose parents are at the low end of the income distribution are likely to attend lower-quality schools than their counterparts in countries where funding is more equally distributed. The results of a cross-country OECD study on levels of functional literacy among adults in the mid-1990s illustrate the effects. Individuals were scored on a scale of 1 to 5, with 1 indicating functional illiteracy and 5 indicating a very high level of functional literacy. Figure 6.11 shows the share of the population in each country that scored at level 1 and at levels of 4 or 5. The United States had the largest percentage scoring at level 1, followed by the United Kingdom and Canada. Sweden and Germany had by far the smallest share scoring at the lowest level, and Sweden had the largest share scoring at the top levels.

In many Western European countries there is no tuition charge for college, and students from low-income families often receive a subsidy to help with housing and other living expenses. As noted in chapter 4, in the United States many students from lower-income families pay a relatively large amount to attend college. Among students from families with incomes below $25,000, the average yearly cost of attending college as of 1996 was $6,000. Of this, an average of $3,000 was covered by financial aid, leaving the remaining $3,000 to be paid by the student or her or his parents (Boggess and Ryan 2002, table 6a).

Sweden's array of public services also includes extensive provision of high-quality public child care for preschool-age children. According to figures compiled by Janet Gornick and Marcia Meyers (2003, ch. 7), approximately 50 percent of one- and two-year-olds and 80 percent of three-, four-, and five-year-olds in Sweden are enrolled in public child

Figure 6.11   Functional Literacy Among Adults in Five Countries, Mid-1990s

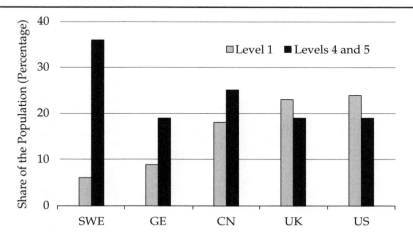

Source: Based on the OECD's 1994–1995 International Adult Literacy Survey (OECD 1998a, 54).
Note: Level 1 is the lowest possible score (indicating functional illiteracy); level 5 is the highest.

care and preschool programs, compared to just 5 percent and 50 percent, respectively, in the United States. Although the average child care cost paid by parents for preschool children appears to be similar in the two countries—around $400 per month (Gornick and Meyers 2003; Smith 2002)—the quality of care purchased for this price tends to be superior in Sweden. The Swedish government spends around $5,000 per child on public child care programs for young children, and both centers and staff are carefully regulated. In the United States, by contrast, most child care for preschool-age children tends to be of low quality, in unregulated home settings rather than in child care centers (Blau 2001; Gornick and Meyers 2003; Kamerman and Kahn 1995). This too may contribute to the difference between the two countries in functional literacy.

In addition to excluding the value of services, the LIS data do not incorporate cross-country differences in the quality of housing and neighborhoods. The quality of apartment one can rent for, say, $500 per month is generally better in Swedish and German cities than in U.S. cities. This difference pertains also to the attractiveness and safety of the neighborhood in which such an apartment is likely to be located, and particularly to public spaces such as parks, libraries, and roads.

Finally, it is worth noting that Americans work longer hours for their incomes than do their counterparts in Sweden and Germany—or in any other rich country, for that matter. Figure 6.12 shows average annual hours worked in the five countries. The typical German works 350 fewer hours per year than her or his American counterpart. That amounts to about 45 fewer eight-hour days over the course of a year.

Figure 6.12   Annual Hours Worked in Five Countries, 2000

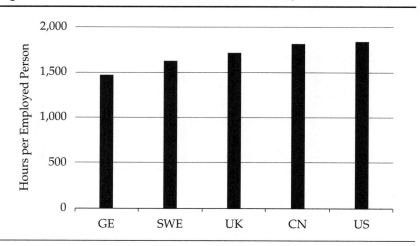

Source: Author's compilation; see appendix.

In short, despite the fact that real incomes are lower in Sweden and Germany than in the United States from the 20th percentile up, incorporating the value of public services, the quality of housing and neighborhoods, and the quantity of working time suggests higher real living standards for low-income Swedish and German households than for their U.S. counterparts. Clearly at some point in the distribution American living standards are higher, but it is difficult to tell exactly where that point is. Nor is it clear how the real living standards of low-income Canadians compare with those of their Swedish and German counterparts. Better data on non-income sources of material well-being are needed to make such comparisons possible (see Mayer 1995).

Conclusion

In this chapter I have explored the over-time effects of welfare state generosity on real incomes at the low end of the distribution in Sweden, Germany, the United Kingdom, Canada, and the United States. The countries with more generous welfare states tended to experience declines in pretax-pretransfer low-end incomes (increases in pretax-pretransfer absolute poverty) between the mid-1970s and 2000. Welfare state generosity may have contributed to employment losses and hence to lower real incomes for the poor. However, examination of the individual country histories suggests that the case for a significant causal role in the three nations that experienced employment declines (Sweden, Germany, and the United Kingdom) is tenuous.

Several aspects of the findings are clearly inconsistent with the notion of an equality-incomes trade-off. For example, despite having a relatively generous welfare state, Germany has maintained the lowest levels of both pretax-pretransfer and posttax-posttransfer absolute poverty among the five countries. This record is even more impressive when we take into account the cost and strain of reunification with the East, where incomes generally were much lower.

Proponents of a generous welfare state can also point to the Swedish case. Of the five countries, Sweden experienced the largest drop in posttax-posttransfer absolute poverty between the mid-1970s and 2000. Critics may counter that Sweden "purchased" low posttax-posttransfer absolute poverty through a sizable expansion of its welfare state in the 1970s and 1980s (which was only partially offset by cutbacks in the 1990s). Eventually, in this view, Sweden's bloated welfare state will severely inhibit the growth of its GDP and/or employment, leading to very high rates of market poverty that even its generous social-welfare programs will not be able to overcome. Sweden's economic turnaround since the mid-1990s appears to contradict this assertion, but we will have to wait another decade or two to make a full assessment.

Appendix

Table 6A.1   Absolute Poverty Rate and Poverty Gap Data in Five Countries, Selected Years

	Poverty Rate	Poverty Gap	Rate Multiplied by Gap
Sweden 1975			
Pretax-pretransfer	34.6%	.355	12.3
Posttax-posttransfer	49.7	.234	11.6
Sweden 2000			
Pretax-pretransfer	26.2	.545	14.3
Posttax-posttransfer	21.6	.237	5.1
Germany 1973			
Pretax-pretransfer	22.4	.288	6.5
Posttax-posttransfer	35.6	.227	8.1
Germany 2000			
Pretax-pretransfer	16.4	.566	9.3
Posttax-posttransfer	16.9	.251	4.2
West German regions 2000			
Pretax-pretransfer	13.5	.568	7.7
Posttax-posttransfer	15.1	.260	3.9
United Kingdom 1974			
Pretax-pretransfer	39.6	.345	13.7
Posttax-posttransfer	47.3	.265	12.5
United Kingdom 1999			
Pretax-pretransfer	28.3	.687	19.4
Posttax-posttransfer	26.7	.298	8.0
Canada 1975			
Pretax-pretransfer	28.8	.458	13.2
Posttax-posttransfer	29.2	.335	9.5
Canada 1998			
Pretax-pretransfer	21.6	.567	12.2
Posttax-posttransfer	16.3	.313	5.1
United States 1974			
Pretax-pretransfer	22.7	.512	11.6
Posttax-posttransfer	24.6	.364	9.0
United States 2000			
Pretax-pretransfer	18.1	.506	9.2
Posttax-posttransfer	16.8	.344	5.8

Source: Author's compilation; see appendix.
Notes: Poverty line is $12,763 per equivalent person, in 2000 U.S. dollars. Working-age households only. Poverty rate is the percentage of persons in households with incomes below the poverty line. Poverty gap is the poverty line minus the average income among households with poverty-level incomes, divided by the poverty line.

═ Chapter 7 ═

Lessons from Country Experiences

M ust we give up on the vision of a dynamic and productive yet relatively egalitarian form of capitalism? This is the question I set out to address in this book. The comparative analyses in chapters 3 through 6 suggest that the answer is no.

In chapter 3, I examined developments in income inequality among the working-age population in the 1980s and 1990s. Some of the more egalitarian countries—most notably Sweden and Finland, but also Norway and Denmark—experienced employment declines, which led to increased earnings inequality among households. But this triggered an increase in government redistribution, as more people were eligible for unemployment benefits and social assistance. As a result, there was little change in posttax-posttransfer income inequality in these countries. By contrast, redistributive programs are less well designed to compensate for rising household earnings inequality that results from increases in wage inequality, increases in single-earner households, or increases in marital homogamy. Moreover, in the countries where rising household earnings inequality was driven mainly by these factors—such as the United States, the United Kingdom, and Italy—welfare states are less generous. Hence, even though household earnings inequality increased less in these countries than in the Nordic nations, posttax-posttransfer income inequality increased more. Cross-country variation in posttax-posttransfer income inequality therefore widened in the 1980s and 1990s, since inequality tended to increase more in the countries that began the period with higher levels. Sustained employment declines could potentially lead to an erosion of the generous social welfare programs in some of the more egalitarian countries and thereby push them up to a higher "equilibrium" level of posttax-posttransfer inequality, but so far that has not happened.

In chapter 4, I explored the impact of inequality on economic growth. Egalitarian countries may have succeeded in maintaining lower levels of income inequality through the 1980s and 1990s, but did they do so at the expense of healthy growth performance? The cross-country evidence suggests not. There is no apparent relationship be-

125

tween income inequality and growth in either direction during those two decades. The same is true across the U.S. states. An examination of longitudinal developments in the United States during the post–World War II period yields the same conclusion. There is no indication, in other words, of a trade-off between equality and growth.

In chapter 5, I examined the effect of pay inequality in the bottom half of the distribution on employment growth. Here there *is* some indication of a trade-off. Countries with greater pay compression among employed individuals tended to experience slower employment growth (or outright employment decline) in private-sector consumer-related services and in the aggregate during the 1980s and 1990s. But this effect was relatively weak, and other labor market institutions and policies, such as tax rates and employment regulations, appear to have been of equal or greater importance in determining cross-country differences in employment growth.

In chapter 6, I assessed the impact of welfare state generosity on real income growth for those at the bottom of the distribution in Sweden, Germany, the United Kingdom, Canada, and the United States between the mid-1970s and 2000. A trade-off here would be particularly alarming for egalitarians, as it would suggest that equality is achieved at the cost of stagnant or falling real living standards for the poor. In the countries with more generous welfare states—Sweden, Germany, and the United Kingdom—pretax-pretransfer income levels at the low end of the distribution declined (and hence absolute poverty increased) during this twenty-five-year period, largely because of falling employment rates. However, social-welfare programs do not appear to have been the chief culprit in any of these three cases. Posttax-posttransfer incomes increased slightly more rapidly in the nations with generous welfare states than in those with less generous programs. And they increased most rapidly in Sweden, the country with the most generous programs. Thus, across these five countries redistribution appears to have been beneficial for the absolute well-being of those at the low end of the income distribution.

Because they focus on the average effects of institutions and policies across countries rather than on how such institutions and policies fit together in a particular nation, comparative statistical analyses can take us only so far in exploring the viability of a model that combines low inequality with high living standards and high employment. In this chapter, I therefore examine the individual experiences of some of these countries during the 1980s and 1990s.

An Overview

Figures 7.1, 7.2, and 7.3 show country trends in inequality, employment, welfare state generosity, and real living standards at the low end of the distribution in the 1980s and 1990s. The upper-left chart in each figure shows earnings inequality among full-time employed individuals. The upper-middle chart shows household earnings inequality. (Recall from chapter 3 that household earnings inequality is virtually identical to household pretax-pretransfer income inequality.) The upper-right chart shows posttax-posttransfer household income inequality. The lower-left chart shows the employment rate. The lower-middle chart shows government cash social expenditures aimed primarily at the working-age population, measured as a share of GDP. These include family benefits and payments for unemployment, sickness, occupational injury or disease, disability, and other contingencies such as low income. Finally, the lower-right chart shows household income at the 10th percentile, in inflation-adjusted U.S. dollars. The upper three charts of each figure are measures of inequality; the lower charts represent employment, welfare state generosity, and real income levels for the poor. Thus, the most successful performance, from an egalitarian perspective, would consist of low values across the top row and high values across the bottom row.

The countries are separated into three groups—Nordic, continental, and Anglo—to highlight the differences across the groups as well as within each group. The Nordic countries shown in figure 7.1 are Denmark, Finland, Norway, and Sweden; the continental European nations in figure 7.2 are France, Germany, Italy, and the Netherlands; and the Anglo countries in figure 7.3 are Australia, Canada, the United Kingdom, and the United States.

Only twelve of the sixteen nations featured in this book are included in these figures. There are no LIS data for Japan and only two LIS observations for Austria and Switzerland. There also are very few observations for each of the latter two countries in the OECD's individual-level earnings inequality database. Belgium is not included because the Belgian LIS datasets switch from net income to gross income in the middle of this period, rendering an assessment of over-time trends problematic (see chapter 3).

The Nordic countries featured the lowest levels of individual earnings inequality and posttax-posttransfer household income inequality. They also featured the highest real income levels for households at the 10th percentile. In the 1980s these countries had the highest employment rates and the lowest levels of household earnings inequality as well. Then, in the first half of the 1990s, Finland and Sweden suffered deep economic recessions—the deepest since the 1930s—with employment in both countries dropping by more than ten percentage points. Denmark and Norway also experienced downturns, though not nearly as severe. As a result of the employment declines, household earnings inequality jumped in all four countries. However, despite some social-

Figure 7.1 Developments in the Nordic Countries, 1979 to 2000

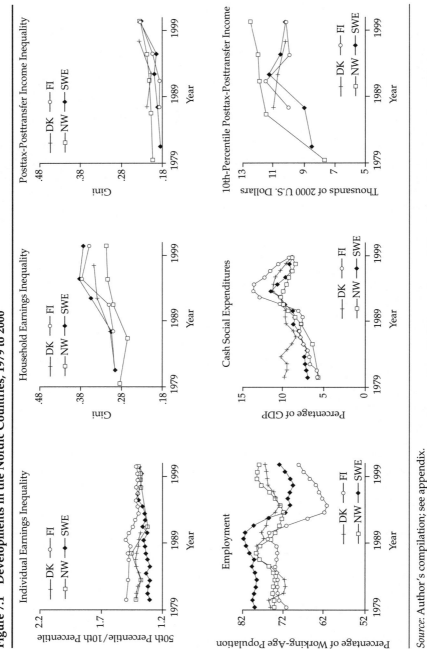

Source: Author's compilation; see appendix.

Notes: Individual earnings inequality data refer to those employed full-time year-round. Data for household earnings inequality, posttax-post-transfer household income inequality, and 10th-percentile household income levels refer to working-age households. Employment refers to the share of the working-age population that is employed. Cash social expenditure data refer to government benefits aimed mainly at the work-ing-aged. 10th-percentile income levels are converted to U.S. dollars using purchasing power parities and adjusted for inflation using the CPI-U-RS. For variable descriptions and data sources, see the appendix.

Figure 7.2 Developments in the Continental Countries, 1979 to 2000

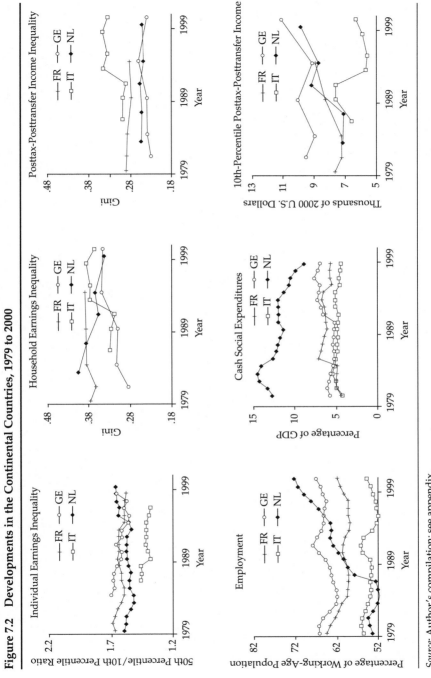

Source: Author's compilation; see appendix.
Note: See note to figure 7.1.

Figure 7.3 Developments in the Anglo Countries, 1979 to 2000

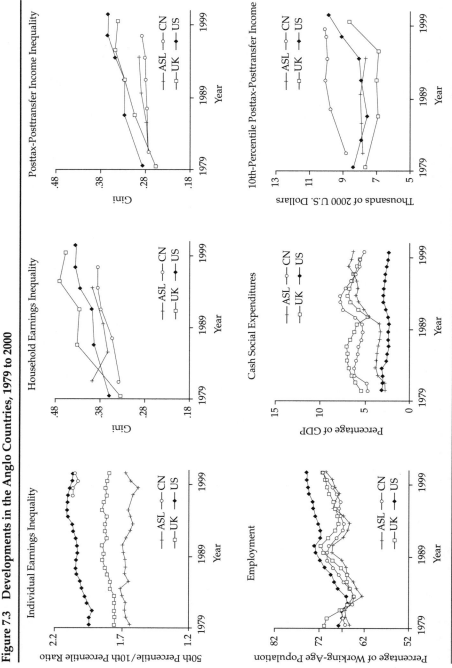

Source: Author's compilation; see appendix.
Note: See note to figure 7.1.

welfare program retrenchment in eligibility requirements and benefit levels, automatic compensatory increases in redistribution prevented any significant rise in levels of posttax-posttransfer income inequality. In addition, through the early 1990s slump, and in spite of some decentralization of wage bargaining during these two decades, there was virtually no change in levels of pay inequality among the employed. Indeed, pay inequality decreased in three of the four Nordic countries between the start of the period and the late 1990s, rising only in Sweden (and there only slightly).

The continental countries were characterized by moderate levels on all three measures of inequality—individual earnings, household earnings, and disposable household income—and by moderate real 10th-percentile income levels. Their chief weakness was low employment rates. There were a few exceptions to these general characterizations. Italy had less pay inequality, far lower employment rates and 10th-percentile income levels, and, since the mid-1990s, higher posttax-posttransfer income inequality than the other three continental countries. And the Netherlands stood apart on employment, jumping from the lowest level in the mid-1980s to by far the highest at the end of the 1990s.

The Anglo countries had relatively high employment rates, with the United States particularly strong in this area. However, they were characterized by comparatively high levels of inequality. Individual earnings inequality tended to be high, though Australia stood out with only a moderate level. These countries also had the highest levels of household earnings inequality. Except for the United States, they featured moderate levels of social expenditures on the working-age population. Along with Italy and France, they had the highest levels of posttax-posttransfer income inequality. Finally, real income levels at the 10th percentile tended to be moderate. Employment increased in all four Anglo countries during the 1980s and 1990s, but at the same time inequality increased substantially in two of them—the United Kingdom and the United States. In Australia and Canada, by contrast, there was no rise in either pay inequality or posttax-posttransfer household income inequality.

Success Stories

What do the country experiences tell us about the potential for a successful model of egalitarian capitalism? Let me highlight what I take to be some of the most useful lessons we can draw from developments in six of these nations: Denmark and Sweden from the Nordic group, the Netherlands and Germany from the continental group, and Australia and Canada from the Anglo group.

Denmark

At the end of the 1990s Denmark was considered by some analysts to be the most successful of the Nordic countries at maintaining healthy macroeconomic performance without sacrificing equality (Auer 2000; Hemerijck and Schludi 2000; Iversen 1999; Scharpf 2000). (Norway's overall performance was better. But as noted in chapter 4, Norway owes its economic success in part to its oil resources. Hence, it may be misleading to characterize the country as an exemplar in terms of combining equality and jobs.) Although the employment rate in Denmark increased only slightly during the 1980s and 1990s, the rate was very high to begin with. As of 2002 Denmark's employment rate of 76 percent was the third highest among OECD countries, behind only Switzerland and Norway. As figure 7.4 indicates, it succeeded in maintaining a high level of employment despite no expansion of public-sector jobs since the early 1980s. It also appears to have done so without a rise in its relatively low degree of pay inequality. Although there are no Danish data for the 1990s in the OECD earnings dispersion dataset, other data suggest no increase in earnings inequality through the decade (Goul Andersen 2002, 144; Goul Andersen and Jensen 2002, 53).

The sudden unwillingness to further expand public employment beginning in the early 1980s contributed to a jump in Denmark's unemployment rate toward the end of that decade. Then, in the early 1990s, the country was hit hard by the international economic recession, and

Figure 7.4   Public Employment in Twelve Countries, 1979, 1989, and 1997

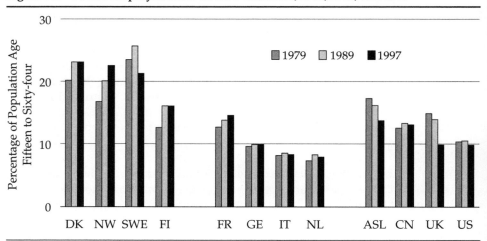

Source: Author's compilation; see appendix.

employment dropped while unemployment increased even further. However, in 1994 and 1996 the Danish government introduced two major labor market reforms: it initiated several new active labor market measures to facilitate the transition from unemployment to a job, and it reduced the duration of unemployment benefit eligibility.[1] Between 1994 and 2002 the Danish unemployment rate fell from 8.2 percent to 4.3 percent, and the employment rate climbed from 73 percent to 76 percent. While the two policy reforms by no means deserve full credit for this improvement, they do appear to have helped (Auer 2000; Benner and Vad 2000; Björklund 2000; Goul Andersen 2002; Kvist and Ploug 2003; Madsen 1999).

Denmark's high employment level may also be aided by the country's comparatively easy job dismissal rules, which should encourage hiring. It ranks with the Anglo countries in having minimal employment regulations (figure 5.8). Dismissals and employee turnover are more common in Denmark than elsewhere in Europe, and there is less long-term unemployment (Esping-Andersen 2000b, 94–95; OECD, various years[a]). Weak employment protection is politically sustainable in Denmark in part because generous unemployment benefit levels cushion the financial pain of job loss (Benner and Vad 2000, 459; Madsen 1999, 76). In the 1980s and 1990s the unemployment benefit replacement rate averaged 62 percent for a worker with median earnings and 88 percent for a worker with earnings at two-thirds of the median.

On the other hand, it is not clear to what extent weak employment regulations have really contributed to Denmark's successful employment performance. As I noted at the end of chapter 5, the country was only marginally more successful at generating private-sector consumer services jobs than Sweden and Finland, each of which had much stricter regulations. Furthermore, Denmark's superior employment record compared to Sweden and Finland is entirely a function of the fact that its employment decline in the early 1990s was less severe (figure 7.1). Given that the severe drops in Sweden and Finland during those years were arguably a product of policy choices (see chapter 6) and an exogenous shock (the collapse of the Soviet market for Finnish exports), respectively, there is reason to question the role of employment regulations in accounting for Denmark's relative success.

Inequality among households increased in Denmark in the middle of the 1990s, though only slightly. Whether this represents a temporary blip or the beginning of a longer-term trend toward rising inequality remains to be seen. Given Denmark's high employment rate, low pay inequality, and still very generous welfare state, the former seems more likely.

Sweden

Sweden has a number of institutions and policies that are commonly thought to impede high employment rates and/or rapid employment growth. Its level of pay inequality is one of the lowest among affluent countries (figure 5.6). It has the highest replacement rates for unemployment, sickness, and disability compensation. Its tax rates are the highest (figure 5.7). Social security contributions and payroll taxes, which are the types of taxes most likely to impede employment growth, are nearly the highest (Scharpf and Schmidt 2000, table A.26). Its employment regulations are the strictest, though rules discouraging the use of temporary employees have been loosened (figure 5.8; Furåker 2002). It has the one of the highest rates of public employment, which may not hinder total employment but is widely presumed to crowd out the growth of private-sector consumer services jobs (figure 7.4). To some observers, it thus came as no surprise that Sweden suffered a deep economic recession in the early 1990s. In this perspective, the bill for decades of unrivaled pursuit of equality had finally come due (Lindbeck 1997).

The picture now looks considerably less dire. As of 2002 Sweden's employment rate was 75 percent, one of the highest among affluent nations, and its unemployment rate of 5.0 percent was one of the lowest. Real per capita GDP increased by 17 percent between 1995 and 2001, and real median household income rose by 14 percent. Earnings inequality among employed workers has remained very low by comparative standards. Household income inequality increased between 1995 and 2000, owing largely to a sharp jump in capital gains income at the top of the distribution. But thus far the increase has been relatively small—similar to the increase in Denmark and Finland.

Key components of the Swedish model are public employment and active labor market policy. Because private-sector consumer services jobs are squeezed by high wages and steep payroll taxes, maintenance of a high employment rate depends on public employment. As figure 7.4 indicates, public employment dropped during the early 1990s crisis and had not regained its 1980s level by the end of the 1990s. Even so, the government still employs approximately one in five working-age Swedes. Active labor market measures help to keep employment reasonably flexible in the private sector. Retraining and job placement through the active labor market boards, coupled with fairly strict limits on the duration of eligibility for unemployment compensation, enable displaced workers to move back into the workforce relatively quickly and with limited loss of earnings.

There are two chief threats to Sweden's ability to combine a high employment rate with these and other institutions and policies that foster equality. Both are related to the tax revenues needed to finance the system. One is capital flight. There is no indication, however, that Sweden has been a victim of investor withdrawal to a greater extent than other rich nations (Steinmo 2002).

The second threat is popular resistance. Survey data indicate that Swedish attitudes toward redistribution and taxes shifted back and forth in the 1970s and 1980s, with the long-run pattern showing considerable stability (Goul Andersen et al. 1999). For the 1990s, data are available from the International Social Survey Program (ISSP). The ISSP has a "social inequality" module that was conducted in 1987, 1992, and 1999, though Sweden was included only in the 1992 and 1999 surveys. Table 7.1 shows the percentages of Swedes in each response category for two questions that tap attitudes toward redistribution and taxes. The data suggest an increase, rather than a reduction, in support for redistribution, and no decrease in support for progressive taxation. At the moment, then, there is no evidence of a turn in public opinion against the high taxes necessary to finance Sweden's approach to combining equality with employment. It also is worth emphasizing that Swedes' responses to these questions indicate a greater degree of egalitarianism than in most other affluent nations. For instance, in the 1999 survey, 24 percent of Swedes strongly agreed that it is government's responsibility to reduce income differences. This compares to 9 percent in Australia, 16 percent in Canada, 37 percent in France, 19 percent in Germany, 19

Table 7.1   Attitudes Toward Redistribution and Taxes in Sweden, 1992 and 1999

		1992	1999
"It is the responsibility of the government to reduce the differences in income between people with high incomes and those with low incomes."	Strongly agree	17%	24%
	Agree	36	36
	Neither	18	22
	Disagree	19	13
	Strongly disagree	10	6
"People with high incomes should pay a [. . .] share of their income in taxes than those with lower incomes."	Much larger	14	16
	Larger	62	60
	The same	23	22
	Smaller	1	1
	Much smaller	0	0
Number of respondents		749	1,100

Source: ISSP (1992, 1999).
Notes: Because of rounding, numbers do not always sum to 100. "Neither" = neither agree nor disagree.

percent in Norway, 19 percent in the United Kingdom, and 11 percent in the United States.

Despite the resilience of popular support for redistribution and high taxes, Swedish governments instituted a variety of cutbacks in the generosity of social-welfare programs in the 1990s. Eligibility rules were tightened and replacement rates were reduced. But from a comparative perspective, these changes were minor (Palme et al. 2002; Steinmo 2002). For instance, the replacement rates for unemployment, sickness, and parental leave stood at 90 percent in 1990. At the end of the decade each had been lowered, but only to 80 percent. The commitment to a high-equality, high-employment society remains largely intact in Sweden, and as of this writing the effort can be judged rather successful.[2]

The Netherlands

Dutch employment performance in the 1980s and 1990s was unique in several respects. First, the country had by far the fastest employment growth among affluent countries. This extraordinary growth needs to be placed in context: the employment rate in the Netherlands was the lowest among these countries at the end of the 1970s, so the improvement started from a very low base. Even so, it has been impressive. By 2000 the Dutch employment rate, at 72 percent, was seventh highest (after Switzerland, Norway, Denmark, Japan, the United States, and Sweden). Unemployment also declined substantially, though this change is a bit less impressive given the large number of people who are classified as "disabled" and therefore do not count as unemployed (Becker 2001; Gorter 2000).

Second, the Netherlands achieved rapid employment growth despite a relatively high tax rate (see figure 5.7), relatively stringent employment regulations (figure 5.8), and a moderately egalitarian distribution of earnings among the employed (figure 7.2). Given these institutional and policy conditions, it is perhaps not surprising that employment growth in the Netherlands was not based on an increase of jobs in private-sector consumer services. Indeed, in its level and rate of growth of private-sector consumer services employment, the country is in the middle of the pack (figure 5.2). Job growth was fastest in business services (OECD 2000, 87).

As figure 7.5 makes clear, underlying the rise in employment in the Netherlands was a substantial increase in part-time employment. Part-time jobs have been an important source of employment expansion in a number of countries (OECD 2003a, 49), but they grew more rapidly in the Netherlands than anywhere else, climbing from 18 to 31 percent of total employment between 1983 and 2000. (Unfortunately, reliable part-

Figure 7.5   Part-Time Employment in Twelve Countries, 1983 and 2000

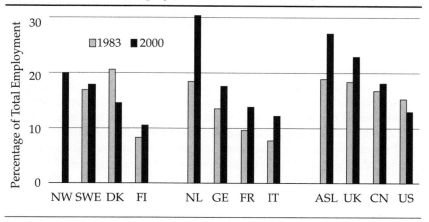

Source: Author's compilation; see appendix.

time employment data are not available for many countries prior to 1983, and for Norway not even then.) Indeed, in the 1980s and 1990s part-time jobs accounted for two-thirds to three-quarters of total job growth in the Netherlands, depending on the estimate (Hartog 1999; Salverda 1998). A large majority of Dutch part-time workers say they prefer not to have a full-time job, so there does not appear to be great cause for concern about underemployment (Auer 2000, 19; Salverda 1998).

But what about earnings? The upper-left chart in figure 7.2 shows that earnings inequality in the Netherlands held more or less constant through the 1980s, before increasing a bit starting in 1994. However, these OECD earnings data include only full-time workers. Since part-time employees tend to be paid less per hour than their full-time counterparts, there is reason to suspect that if part-timers were included in the figures, we would find a more substantial rise in earnings inequality. Then again, for Dutch women, who account for most part-time employment, the median hourly earnings of part-time employees were 93 percent of those for full-time employees as of 1995 (OECD 1999b, 24; Visser 2002, 33).

Wiemer Salverda (1998) has calculated hourly wages at the 10th and 50th percentiles in the Netherlands with both full-time and part-time workers included. As it turns out, the over-time trend for these figures is no different from that for the full-time annual pay data shown in figure 7.2, though Salverda's data extend only through the late 1980s. In addition, Joop Hartog (1999, n.p.) has examined the industries in which there was an increase in employment, including part-time employment, between 1987 and 1995. He finds that "employment growth is really across the board of the entire wage distribution, with neither support for a marked dualization nor for a concentration of employment growth in low-wage pockets." The overall degree of pay inequality in the Netherlands thus does not appear to have been adversely affected by the acceleration of part-time employment. And while pay inequality has increased somewhat since the mid-1990s, it remains a good bit below the level of the United States. The Dutch-style "one-and-a-half jobs" economy therefore may offer another reasonably egalitarian option for affluent countries (see also Visser and Hemerijck 1997).

Over the past several decades the Dutch welfare state has been one of the world's most generous.[3] Although the level of social expenditures on the working-age population in the Netherlands has declined steadily since the early 1980s, it remains on par with the Nordic countries (figure 7.2). The chief reason for the drop in spending is higher employment. Employment has increasingly replaced the welfare state as the principal source of income for many individuals and households at the low end of the distribution. By most accounts, that is a desirable development (for critical perspectives, see Goodin 2001; Keman 2003).

Germany

At the end of the 1980s the German economy was regarded by some as perhaps the most successful among affluent nations (Albert 1993; Carlin and Soskice 1990; Porter 1990; U.S. Congress 1990). German manufacturers were thriving exporters, economic growth was healthy, pay levels were the highest in the world, pay inequality was fairly low, and the degree of posttax-posttransfer income inequality was the lowest outside of the Nordic countries.

Recent assessments of the German economy tend to be less enthusiastic (Manow and Seils 2000a; Scharpf 1997, 2000; Streeck 1997, 2001, forthcoming). Rising inequality is not the source of this pessimism. As the charts in figure 7.2 indicate, both pay inequality among the employed and posttax-posttransfer income inequality among working-age households have remained relatively low. Instead, at the heart of the gloom is Germany's mediocre employment performance during the 1980s and 1990s. The problem is not lack of competitiveness in sectors exposed to international competition. Despite very high wages, high productivity levels have kept German firms competitive in international markets. Instead, as I noted at the end of chapter 5, Germany's employment deficit is in consumer services jobs. Private-sector consumer services employ about five percentage points less of the working-age population in Germany than in the typical Anglo country, and ten percentage points less than in the United States (figure 5.2). The level of private-sector consumer services employment is higher in Germany than in three of the four Nordic countries, but those countries use extensive public employment (in a variety of sectors) to compensate for their low levels in private-sector consumer services. Public employment in Germany, by contrast, is much lower (figure 7.4).

Although there are a variety of potential culprits, the chief barrier to the creation of private-sector consumer services jobs in Germany seems to be high payroll taxes. A good account is provided by Fritz Scharpf (1997, n.p.):

> The negative impact on service employment is particularly acute in those countries which, like Germany and France, rely to a large extent on payroll taxes for the financing of the welfare state. In Germany, for instance, 74% of total social expenditures were financed through workers' and employers' contributions to social insurance systems in 1991, and in France that was true of 82%. In Germany, these contributions presently amount to about 42% of the total wage paid by the employer. . . . If the net wage of the worker cannot fall below a guaranteed minimum [the level of unemployment benefits and social assistance], the consequence is that any social insurance contributions, payroll taxes, and wage taxes that are levied on jobs at the lower end of the pay scale cannot be absorbed by the employee but must be added to the total labor cost borne by the employer. Assuming that additional overhead costs are proportional to total labor cost, the implication is that the minimum productivity that a job must reach in order to be viable in the market is raised by more than 50% above the level of productivity required to pay the worker's net wage. As a consequence, a wide range of perfectly decent jobs, which in the absence of payroll taxes would be commercially viable, are eliminated from the private labor market.

For a brief period in the late 1990s there was hope that an "Alliance for Employment" composed of union, employer, and government representatives would reach agreement on reform of the tax structure. But no agreement was reached, and the German government has been unwilling to impose such reform unilaterally (Streeck, forthcoming).

Failure to address the payroll tax problem has meant that, in a de facto sense, Germany has begun to encourage private-sector consumer services jobs through widening pay differentials. A range of "off-the-books" jobs in such services has developed in recent years, usually at low pay levels and without unemployment insurance or pension entitlement. One recent estimate suggests that the underground economy accounts for 15 percent of GDP (Streeck 2001, 704). Because these jobs are outside the formal labor market, they generate no tax revenue (from either payroll or income taxes) and hence do not contribute to the funding of the welfare state. As I noted in chapter 5, the German government has recently introduced subsidies to employees in low-wage jobs in the form of partial or full exemption from social security contributions. The aim is to encourage less-skilled workers to take jobs in the formal sector despite the low wages. But this does nothing to address the impediment on the demand side—that is, from the employer's point of view.

Steep payroll taxes are not the only obstacle to employment growth in Germany. As I discuss in chapter 8, there also are a range of policies that explicitly or implicitly support the traditional male breadwinner model, thereby discouraging women from entering or remaining in the paid workforce.

As with the Dutch employment experience, it is important to place the German record in context. Considering the enormous burden imposed by unification with the East, the maintenance of relatively low inequality, high real incomes for those at the bottom of the distribution, and a moderate employment rate can be considered a substantial success. Moreover, the employment rate poses a problem mainly in terms of *future* welfare state generosity. Germany has been able to maintain a generous welfare state through two decades of stagnant employment. It is whether and how long this can continue that is the pressing question.

Australia

Within the Anglo group of countries, Australia stands out as successful in several respects. Foremost among these is that it has achieved solid employment performance without a high level of pay inequality. The degree of pay inequality in Australia is well below that of the other countries in this group. Indeed, it is similar to most of the continental nations. Yet its record of job growth in the 1980s and 1990s was on par with that of Canada, slightly better than that of the United Kingdom, and only slightly weaker than that of the United States.

Several factors appear to have contributed to Australia's success at achieving employment growth without high earnings inequality (Lansbury and Niland 1995; Schwartz 2000). Its tax rate is a bit lower than those of the other Anglo nations (figure 5.7), but it has more stringent employment regulations (figure 5.8); hence, these two factors would appear to offset one another. Over the 1980s and 1990s a series of tripartite "accords" were reached by unions, employers, and the government.

These were explicitly modeled on the centralized wage bargaining arrangements common in the Nordic and other northern European nations. These accords, coupled with the central arbitration system of pay awards, produced relatively moderate real wage increases throughout this period. In the early 1990s the government created a "family payment" program that encourages employment by supplementing the incomes of working families with low earnings. The government also instituted a new active labor market policy, which included a commitment to subsidize a private-sector job or provide a public-sector job to anyone unemployed for more than eighteen months.

The arbitration system has helped to keep a lid on pay inequality. In the 1990s wages for about one-third of workers were determined directly by arbitration, and the tribunal set a "basic" or minimum wage each year. Wage setting in Australia has become increasingly decentralized, but it remains less so than in the other Anglo countries. As in the Netherlands, part-time jobs have played an important role in Australia's employment growth (figure 7.5). As of 1995 median hourly earnings for part-time workers in Australia were 89 percent of the median for full-time employees, a higher ratio than in virtually any other country (OECD 1999b, 24). This suggests that the surge in part-time employment probably has not increased the degree of overall earnings inequality markedly. The level and trend in earnings inequality for full-time employees shown in the upper-left chart in figure 7.3 are thus likely to reflect those for the workforce as a whole.

Earnings inequality among households in Australia did increase over this period, but not much. As a result, Australia's position within the Anglo group shifted from worst to nearly best between the early 1980s and the mid-1990s (figure 7.3). The fact that employment increased without a rise in earnings inequality among the employed meant that there was little increase in earnings inequality among households. What limited increase did occur seems to have been due in large part to heightened inequality of employment among households—more two-earner households and more zero-earner households (Saunders 2002, ch. 7).

Posttax-posttransfer income inequality also barely changed. The most recent LIS dataset for Australia is for 1994. However, Peter Saunders (2002, 192) has used more recent versions of the same source from which the LIS data for Australia come, the Survey of Income and Housing Costs by the Australian Bureau of Statistics, to calculate Gini coefficients for disposable income through 1999–2000 (see also Australian Bureau of Statistics 2003). These data indicate only a very slight increase in inequality since the mid-1990s, similar to that which occurred between 1989 and 1994 (see figure 7.3, upper-right chart). This success in holding household inequality at bay seems to have been a product of a limited increase in earnings inequality among households together with heightened welfare state generosity. Cash social expenditures aimed primarily at the working-aged jumped significantly in the early and mid-1990s, moving Australia to the top of the Anglo group (figure 7.3). This increase in expenditures was coupled with a shift toward greater means-testing, thereby probably yielding a more effective targeting of benefits to the most needy.

In sum, Australia's record in the 1980s and 1990s differs from that of the United States and the United Kingdom in several respects. It too has achieved healthy employment growth, but without a high or increasing degree of pay inequality among the employed. It also has raised social expenditures on the working-age population. As a result, it has been comparatively successful at combining employment growth with a reasonably attractive level of equality.

Canada

The Canadian experience over the past two decades suggests that, even within the confines of the liberal welfare state model, it is possible to do better than the United States at reducing inequality without severely impairing employment growth. Figure 7.3 shows that Canada's record of job growth has been nearly as strong as that of the United States. It has accomplished this in combination with a more generous welfare state and consequently less household income inequality.

The key to Canada's success relative to the United States is both higher spending levels and more effective targeting of expenditures (Hanratty and Blank 1992; Myles 1996; Zuberi 2001). Canada's social-welfare programs are more generous than those of the United States in several areas where such generosity is particularly helpful in boosting low incomes. For instance, Canada's principal means-tested transfer program, social assistance, has for some time been available to individuals and couples without children, which was not true of Aid to Families with Dependent Children (AFDC) in the United States, and the benefit levels are substantially higher than those of AFDC-TANF (Temporary Assistance for Needy Families). Canada provides a guaranteed income supplement to the elderly that ensures that elderly individuals and couples have an income no less than 55 to 60 percent of the nation's median; in the United States supplemental security income (SSI) and food stamps ensure the elderly an income only 35 to 40 percent of the median. Canada also provides a special widow's benefit to assist elderly women living alone, who make up the largest single poverty group.

Perhaps the most significant difference between Canada and the United States is in health care. Approximately 15 percent of the U.S. population has no health insurance (U.S. National Center for Health Statistics, n.d.), whereas in Canada (and every other affluent country) all citizens are covered. This difference is not reflected in data on income levels or income inequality, but it obviously matters for real living standards.

The United States

The United States has the world's largest, most affluent, and most influential economy, and it has attracted a great deal of attention in the past decade as a potential model for other rich nations to emulate. Is the United States a success story?

Employment growth in the American economy has been strong for several decades, and the employment rate is high. In 1979, 68 percent of the working-age population was employed; by 2000 the share had risen to 75 percent. Much concern has been expressed about the quality of the new jobs, but the best study on this issue finds that a disproportionate share of the jobs created in the 1980s and 1990s were in high-paying occupations and sectors (Wright and Dwyer 2003). This study found that in the 1990s the distribution of new employment was U-shaped, with a relative shortage of job growth in mid-paying occupations. This represented a sharp contrast with prior decades. Still, concern that the *bulk* of the net new employment in the American economy consists of poorly paid positions with little opportunity for advancement appears to be misplaced.

America's deficit is in equality. As the charts in figure 7.3 show, inequality of earnings and income is quite high in comparative terms, and it has been rising. The limited available comparative data suggest that this holds for wealth as well (Wolff 1995/2002).

Some dismiss high and rising inequality as irrelevant in the American context, because the United States is said to have a high and increasing amount of mobility. That is, the overall distribution of pay or household income may be widening, but individuals and households shift around within the distribution to a greater degree than in other countries, and to an increasing degree over time. Although many Americans probably believe this, the available evidence suggests that it is false. It is a claim about relative intragenerational mobility—the degree to which individuals or households move up or down during their lifetimes relative to others in their cohort. Longitudinal data—from the Panel Study of Income Dynamics (PSID) and the National Longitudinal Survey (NLS)—suggest that, if anything, such mobility has declined slightly in the United States over the past three decades (Bernhardt et al. 2001; Bradbury and Katz 2002; Gottschalk and Danziger 1998; McMurrer and Sawhill 1998). The findings of an OECD (1996a) study suggest that the degree of earnings mobility among employed individuals was very similar across affluent countries as of the late 1980s and early 1990s; it was no greater in the United States than in Denmark, Finland, France, Germany, Italy, Sweden, or the United Kingdom. Aaberge and his colleagues (2002) find that earnings mobility in the United States was similar to that in Denmark, Norway, and Sweden during the 1980s. And data from panel income surveys indicate that the degree of income mobility among households is about the same in the United States as in Denmark, Germany, the Netherlands, Norway, and Sweden (Aaberge et al. 2002; Goodin et al. 1999, 191–93). In fact, the comparative data suggest that, if anything, there may be slightly *less* relative intragenerational mobility in the United States than elsewhere.

Others emphasize that the income of middle-class households is higher in the United States than in other nations. That is true. Figure 7.6 shows median posttax-posttransfer income per equivalent person for working-age households as of the mid-1990s, calculated from the LIS database. As with the 10th-percentile income levels shown earlier in this chapter, I have converted these incomes to 2000 U.S. dollars using purchasing power parities and an adjustment for inflation. The United States does indeed have the highest median household income among affluent countries (see also Smeeding and Rainwater 2002). In fact, it is

Figure 7.6   Median Household Income in Twelve Countries, Mid-1990s

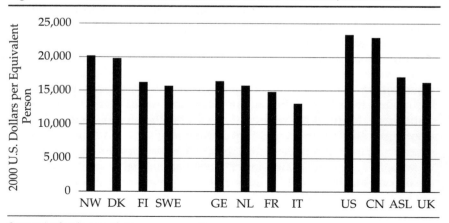

Source: Author's compilation; see appendix.

significantly higher than the median in many other nations. This is certainly a positive aspect of the American economy.

Still, a few qualifications should be noted. First, the median in countries such as Canada, Norway, and Denmark is not terribly far behind that of the United States. Second, the average American works longer to achieve her or his high income than is true in other countries (Jencks 2002; OECD, various years[a]; Pontusson, forthcoming). Employed Americans work more hours than their counterparts in any other affluent nation.

The challenge for the United States is to find a way to reduce income inequality without impeding the strong employment growth that has characterized the past several decades. U.S. social-welfare programs have moved steadily in the direction of encouraging (paid) work in recent years. In my view, this is a positive development. Indeed, it has been central to the approach pursued by the Nordic countries. The question is whether the United States will become a society that merely *requires* work by those at the low end of the labor market or one that also *enables* and *rewards* work. Pursuing the latter course would move the United States much closer to being a high-employment, moderate-equality society.

Conclusion

Plainly, developments in some affluent countries during the 1980s and 1990s cannot be considered successful from an egalitarian perspective. Sharp increases in inequality occurred in the United States and the United Kingdom. Italy suffered rising income inequality, stagnant employment (starting from a very low level), and falling real incomes at the bottom of the distribution. In Finland employment dropped dramatically and remains well below the level in the other Nordic countries, although this decrease was due in significant measure to an exogenous shock (the collapse of the Soviet market beginning in 1990).

In the face of growing economic pressures and challenges, however, some nations succeeded in maintaining relatively low levels of inequality, moderate or high employment rates, and reasonably high real income levels for the least well-off. They did so to differing degrees, and they achieved their successes through varying sets of institutions and policies. The success stories were not the rule, but neither were they the exception. They offer reason for optimism about the future viability of egalitarian capitalism.

═ Chapter 8 ═

Which Way Forward?

The findings in this book suggest that low income inequality can be sustained and that it need not severely impede the growth of economic output, employment, or living standards for those at the bottom of the distribution. I suggested in the introductory chapter that a sensible contemporary vision of an egalitarian capitalist society would prioritize low income inequality, high living standards (especially at the low end), and high employment. In this final chapter, I outline an approach to egalitarianism that I believe would be particularly promising for pursuing these aims in the early years of the twenty-first century. It centers on employment-friendly egalitarianism and equality of opportunity. I describe the contours of such an approach and explore a variety of policy options for the Nordic, continental, and Anglo countries.

As I argued in chapter 1, a high employment rate is likely to be increasingly necessary to achieve and maintain a relatively low level of household income inequality. Welfare states face rising costs owing to population aging at the same time that capital mobility increasingly constrains their capacity to raise tax revenues. The most reasonable way to increase revenues without raising tax rates, and thereby ensure the viability of a generously redistributive welfare state, is to increase the share of the working-age population that is employed. Access to employment is critical for reducing gender inequality as well. More and more women want paid work; impediments to their finding employment thus constitute a severe barrier to equality. Employment also has intrinsic benefits: it provides social interaction in an age of weakening family and neighborhood ties, and it imposes regularity and discipline on people's lives.

Countries need to not only maximize labor force participation but also ensure that the labor force is mobile. Relying on firms to provide lifetime employment is no longer practical, as heightened competition increasingly necessitates a substantial degree of flexibility in labor deployment.

If everyone is in the paid labor force, what happens to housework and child care? Housework is the less problematic of the two. Much of it can be done at a time of a household's own choosing, and if wages are high enough, many dual-earner couples, and even some single adults, are able to outsource at least part of their cooking and cleaning tasks. The key question is: who will care for preschool-age children? How can societies balance the need to have a high proportion of working-age adults in paying jobs with the need to provide attention and cognitive stimulation to infants and young children?

In some national contexts, a commitment to employment-friendly egalitarianism is by no means novel. In Sweden, and to an extent the other Nordic countries as well, high and mobile employment has been a key aim for half a century, and the provision of paid parental leave and high-quality public child care has been a policy concern since the 1970s. Indeed, most of the policies I recommend for pursuing high employment and high equality have existed in one or another country for quite some time. Nevertheless, even in the Nordic countries a somewhat different policy approach may now be required, at least with respect to employment promotion.

I noted in chapter 1 that a considerable portion of the existing inequality of earnings and incomes is a product of genetics, parents' assets and traits, and the quality of one's childhood neighborhood and schools. The fact that these factors are beyond the control of most individuals is the chief rationale for institutions and policies that reduce unequal outcomes. A more direct way to confront the influence of luck is to attempt to equalize opportunity. Indeed, citizens in affluent countries tend to attach greater importance to equality of opportunity than to equality of outcomes. Efforts to reduce the extent or impact of family and schooling disparities should appeal to egalitarians both in and of themselves and because they are likely to reduce inequality of outcomes. Although all rich countries take steps to reduce barriers stemming from low parental income, lack of cognitive stimulation early in life, poor schools, inadequate health care, and lack of assets, in most nations much more could be done.

Employment-Friendly Egalitarianism

Achieving and sustaining a high rate of employment requires that jobs be created in the private and public sectors and that working-age adults be motivated to seek a paying job. From an egalitarian standpoint, it also is important to "make work pay," which can be achieved through a reasonably high wage floor and/or an earnings subsidy. Employment mobility requires retraining and job placement to assist individuals who lose a job involuntarily in getting a new one. Also needed are programs to provide income maintenance during work interruption: unemployment, sickness, and disability benefits along with a catchall social assistance type of benefit. Finally, policy supports for ensuring care and cognitive stimulation for young children are critical to the long-term success of a high-employment, high-equality society.

Job Creation

Agriculture and manufacturing almost certainly will no longer be significant sources of new jobs in affluent countries. Service jobs are the key to future employment growth. In the past two decades the chief locus of employment growth has tended to be consumer-related services—retail and wholesale trade, restaurants and hotels, and community, social, and personal services. That seems likely to continue. What fosters job creation in consumer services? In chapter 5, I examined cross-country differences in employment growth in private-sector consumer services industries in the 1980s and 1990s. According to the findings, three types of institutions and policies appear to have played an important role (together with economic growth and limited outward direct foreign investment) in promoting such growth: pay inequality (low wages at the bottom of the distribution), low tax rates, and weak employment regulations.

The Anglo countries were quite successful at generating private-sector consumer services job growth in the 1980s and 1990s (figure 5.2). Hence, they tended to have very strong aggregate employment growth. These countries feature low wages (with the exception of Australia), low tax rates, and limited employment regulations (figures 5.4, 5.7, and 5.8).

The Nordic countries, by contrast, tend to have low levels of private-sector consumer services employment, and they also had little or no increase in such jobs during the 1980s and 1990s (figure 5.2). Pay levels at the low end of the distribution are high, tax rates are high, and, except in Denmark, employment regulations are stiff. In these countries consumer services jobs are likely to be government jobs rather than in the private sector. Because the public sector is not profit-sensitive, wages can be relatively high even for low-productivity positions. As long as capital does not flee and public support for high taxes holds up, this approach can probably be continued. But massive public employment imposes a cost burden on the state that may eventually prove unsustainable, particularly when a number of such jobs provide pay that exceeds productivity levels (Esping-Andersen 1999; Ferrera and Hemerijck 2003; Iversen and Wren 1998). Hence, the Nordic countries may find themselves forced to stimulate more aggressively the creation of private-sector consumer services jobs.

Loosening employment restrictions is one option. But as I noted in chapter 5, the experience of the past two decades suggests that this might not prove sufficient. Employment regulations are much less stringent in Denmark than in the other three Nordic countries, yet Denmark was no more successful at generating new private-sector consumer services jobs in the 1980s and 1990s. The Nordic countries may find it necessary to permit individual earnings inequality to rise a bit— by allowing wages to fall at the low end of the distribution—in order to keep the welfare state on sound financial footing and thereby maintain low inequality of incomes across households.

But there is a practical impediment. Even if policymakers in the Nordic countries were to agree that wages need to fall somewhat for private-sector jobs in low-productivity consumer services, there may be little they can do about this. Wage levels in these countries are determined largely by collective bargaining between unions and employers, and union leaders tend to face strong pressures from their membership to promote pay compression (Swenson 1989). Policymakers may be able to convince unions to allow wages in low-productivity jobs to drop in exchange for the introduction of an earnings subsidy, which would supplement the incomes of low-earning households (discussed later in this chapter). An alternative would be to allow wages in low-productivity service jobs to remain relatively high but to encourage hiring by subsidizing employers (Ferrera and Hemerijck 2003; Miller 2003, ch. 8; OECD 2003a, ch. 3; Phelps 1996). This could be done through a direct payment to employers or a reduction of their payroll tax contributions.

As various commentators have suggested (Esping-Andersen 1999; Ferrera and Hemerijck 2003; Scharpf 1997, 2000; Streeck 2001), increasing employment is the principal challenge facing the continental countries (aside from the Netherlands). Meeting this challenge is mainly, though not exclusively, a matter of increasing the labor force participation of women. As more women move into the paid labor force, the demand for consumer services rises, which creates more jobs, which lures more women into the workforce, and so on.

Several reforms could help. One would be to loosen employment protection regulations. Since employers could more easily dismiss workers during hard times, presumably they would become less reluctant to hire new ones. But would there be substantial adverse effects on the existing workforce? That depends on the broader context of labor market institutions and policies. In a country such as Sweden the negative impact would probably be minor, because Sweden has generous unemployment benefits to cushion the loss of earnings and an active labor market policy to help the displaced find new jobs (and get retrained if necessary). In a country such as Italy, on the other hand, the consequences would be much more severe. Unemployment benefits in Italy are minimal, and there is no active labor market policy to speak of. For a weakening of employment protection to not only promote jobs but also enhance well-being in a context such as Italy's, it would have to be accompanied by other policy changes.

A second possible reform strategy would be to reduce payroll taxes. The best option here would be to radically overhaul the tax system so that the welfare state is funded mainly out of general revenues. However, this poses a substantial political challenge. Such efforts in Germany have had no success, and in the past several decades payroll contributions have accounted for a steadily increasing proportion of Germany's welfare state financing (Manow and Seils 2000b, 143). In 1990 France introduced a new tax on personal income (the CSG) to partially shift funding away from payroll contributions, but the latter still account for about 80 percent of social expenditures (Palier 2000). A perhaps more politically feasible alternative is to offer employers a partial or full exemption from payroll taxes on workers in low-productivity jobs.

A third helpful reform would be to allow wage levels at the bottom of the distribution to drop a bit, though this may be more important in Belgium and Italy, which have levels of pay inequality similar to those in the Nordic countries, than in Germany and France (see figure 5.4). Lowering wages would increase the degree of earnings inequality among those in the workforce. But it need not contribute to a rise in household income inequality, which is more relevant to people's living standards than their individual earnings. As I suggest later, governments can use an employment-conditional earnings subsidy to supplement low household incomes.

An employer subsidy might serve as an effective substitute in helping to offset high wage costs. Employer subsidies have been used over the past decade in Belgium, Denmark, France, and the Netherlands to try to increase private-sector job creation in low-productivity services. Sweden has long used employer subsidies on a case-by-case basis for new or unemployed workers who have trouble finding a job, and the United Kingdom has done so in recent years. Studies suggest that such subsidies do tend to boost employment (Bartik 2001; Katz 1998; OECD 2003a, ch. 3). The chief worry has to do with their cost-efficiency. Employers may qualify for the subsidy by hiring workers they would have hired anyway, or they may hold wage levels at an artificially low level in order to qualify.

Another helpful change in the continental countries would be the provision of affordable care for children under age three, full-day year-round schooling for children age three and over, and a restructuring of parental leave policies (discussed later in the chapter). These types of measures would be likely to stimulate greater labor force participation by women.

Also beneficial would be an easing of restrictions on part-time employment. The dramatic expansion of part-time jobs in the Netherlands largely preceded the loosening of such restrictions there, but that loosening has probably helped it to continue.

Although low-productivity jobs in consumer-oriented services are a key to overall employment growth, they need not and should not be the whole story. Countries can take steps to promote job expansion in high-productivity, high-paying positions as well. Indeed, a recent report by the OECD (2001a, 111) concludes that "the continued growth of service sector employment in all countries over the 1990s has not been driven by an expansion of low-paid jobs. In most countries, including the United States, employment grew more rapidly in high-paying jobs than in low-paying or medium-paying ones." Low-end service jobs should be a key policy concern, both because they are an important source of aggregate employment growth and because they are the jobs in which the least fortunate in society—individuals with less cognitive ability, education, training, or work experience—are most likely to be employable. Yet the larger the share of the working-age population in high-skill, high-paying positions, the better off the society is likely to be in terms of individual and households earnings as well as tax revenues to fund the welfare state.

How can countries stimulate high-end job growth? Buoyant consumer demand is critical. This can be influenced by monetary and fiscal policy, along with an orientation toward external markets. Consumer demand also depends in part on income levels among the lower and middle classes, which can be affected by social-welfare policies (see chapter 6). Another important factor is the skill level of the workforce, which can be influenced by formal schooling (including, as I discuss later, child care beginning very early in life) and by opportunities for training and retraining. A final policy lever relates to programs that affect competition and entrepreneurship. Regulations on business play a vital role in achieving key social objectives in affluent countries, such as environmental quality, worker safety, and consumer access. Yet regulations ought to be subject to regular scrutiny. It is of little help for egalitarians to blindly oppose deregulation just because anti-egalitarians tend to blindly favor it. One issue that has been discussed in some European countries recently is the option of opening the heretofore strictly public university system to private-sector competitors. Germany, for one, has allowed the opening of a few private universities on an experimental basis. This holds the potential for increasing one type of high-

Bad for the environt

end occupation: teachers and researchers. In addition, the basic and applied research performed at universities, along with the human capital enhancement created by teaching, tend to have multiplier effects on local and national economies.

Active Labor Market Policies

All affluent countries have active labor market policies (ALMPs), such as retraining and job placement assistance, to aid those who lose a job in getting a new one. In an economic environment in which lifetime employment with the same firm is increasingly rare, such programs take on heightened importance. There is a vast difference across countries in the level of resources committed to such programs. At the end of the 1990s the United States spent only 0.2 percent of its GDP on ALMPs, and the United Kingdom spent just 0.3 percent, whereas Denmark and Finland each spent 1.5 percent and Sweden spent 2.0 percent (OECD 2001c). An alternative measure of ALMP effort is expenditures per unemployed person, expressed as a percentage of the average production worker's wage. As of the late 1990s this ranged from just 8 percent in the United States and 9 percent in the United Kingdom to 47 percent in the Netherlands and Norway and 51 percent in Sweden (Martin 2000–2001, 86).

Sweden has long been at the forefront in the use of active labor market policy (Ginsburg 1983; Rehn 1985). Swedish ALMP is administered by the National Labor Market Board, but its functions are largely decentralized and carried out by local boards. Its main thrust is training and job placement. Firms must notify their local board in advance when employees are to be laid off and when they have job openings that have lasted more than ten days. Workers who are displaced or who leave their job by choice can receive subsidized training through the employment service. Officials keep in close communication with firms and with officials in other areas regarding trends in skill needs. The training programs are full-time and range in duration from two weeks to more than a year. The service then helps place workers in new positions. If necessary, an employer subsidy may be used to encourage a private-sector employer to hire, or a public-sector job may be created. There is an element of compulsion in the system: after a short time displaced workers can receive unemployment compensation only if they participate in a training and placement program. Recent research suggests that such limits, when coupled with skill enhancement and job placement assistance, contribute to better outcomes for program participants (Martin 2000–2001, 103–4; OECD 2003a, 202–14).

Labor market policy in the United States contrasts starkly with that of Sweden (Osterman 1988, 1999). Funding for public training assistance programs has been insufficient to reach more than a minuscule portion of the workforce. Job placement efforts have tended to be similarly underfunded, as well as inadequately integrated with local labor markets.

Active labor market policies are by no means a panacea. Where programs provide insufficient assistance to participants, lack adequate incentives for participants to move back into the workforce, or are poorly coordinated with firms in the local labor market, the results are likely to be less than optimal. And regardless of the scale and structure of the programs, their success is contingent on the availability of jobs. Nevertheless, the most comprehensive recent survey of research on the effectiveness of such policies concludes that "they remain a potentially important weapon in the fight against unemployment" (Martin 2000–2001, 107). The successful experiences of Sweden over the past several decades and Denmark since the mid-1990s (see chapter 7) support that assessment.

Employer of Last Resort

In every country, even those with an effective active labor market policy, some of the unemployed are unable to find a new job for long periods of time. Long-term unemployment—defined formally as joblessness that lasts more than a year—ranges from less than 10 percent of the unemployed in Norway and the United States to more than 50 percent in Italy and Belgium (OECD 2003a, 325). Involuntary long-term unemployment can be substantially reduced by having government serve as the employer of last resort (Gottschalk 1998; Kaus 1992). Anyone jobless for more than a year could be offered a temporary "public works" position performing socially useful tasks such as assisting with neighborhood beautification or caring for the elderly. The wage level could be set at or just below the (statutory or collectively bargained) minimum wage in order to encourage recipients to seek private-sector or regular public-sector employment. By guaranteeing a job to anyone who wants but cannot find one, such a policy would affirm the value of work.

Minimum Wage

A high employment rate may be increasingly needed to fund a generous welfare state, and employment may have intrinsic benefits, but simply encouraging or forcing people into the labor market has limited appeal if many end up in jobs that do not pay very well. One way to ensure that work pays decently is through a wage floor. Some countries, such as the United States, the United Kingdom, and France, establish a minimum wage through legislation. In many others a de facto minimum is determined through collective bargaining.

There are well-known arguments against a high minimum wage. One is that not all of the benefits go to low-income households. Some minimum-wage recipients are students in middle-income households or have spouses with moderately high earnings. Nevertheless, a nontrivial share of workers whose wages are at or slightly above the minimum are in low-income households. For the United States, the Economic Policy Institute (2003) estimates that if the minimum wage were increased from its present $5.15 per hour to $6.65 per hour, 6 percent of the workforce would receive an increase in their hourly wage, and an additional 9 percent whose wages are less than one dollar above the minimum would also be likely to benefit. Approximately half of the benefits of such an increase would go to workers in households with an annual income below $25,000.

The chief concern about a high minimum wage is the possibility of adverse employment effects. If employers are forced to pay a higher wage to workers in low-productivity positions, they may hire fewer workers. In chapter 5 I examined this possibility, though with a focus on the degree of inequality between the bottom and the middle rather than on the absolute level at the bottom. The findings suggested an employment-dampening effect of low pay inequality, but one that may be fairly small in magnitude. In the U.S. context, state governments are permitted to set the minimum wage at a higher level than the federal minimum, and one widely cited study that compared hiring in fast-food restaurants in similar, neighboring states found no adverse employment impact of a higher minimum (Card and Krueger 1995). That study has been the subject of extensive reassessment, and the verdict is not yet in (Houseman 1998). However, evidence about the effects of increases in the federal minimum on employment in the country as a whole seems less ambiguous: there appears to have been no adverse impact (Bernstein and Schmitt 1998). Other research has examined the effects of "living wage" ordinances enacted in a number of American cities since the mid-1990s. These typically require businesses that contract with the city government to pay their employees a minimum wage of around $7.00 per hour. The most thorough study finds a small employment-reducing impact of these ordinances but an overall positive impact on the incomes of low-income households (Neumark 2002).

Given the need for job creation, in some countries the minimum wage may at present be too high rather than too low. This is most likely to be the case in Sweden, Denmark, and Norway, and perhaps also in Belgium, Italy, and Finland (see figure 5.4). The high wages that employers must pay in these countries may impede job creation in consumer-related services. If so, and if these countries wish to stimulate private-sector employment, they may decide it is advantageous to allow wages at the bottom to drop somewhat. As noted earlier, an obstacle to doing so lies in the fact that the minimum wage in such countries tends to be set through collective bargaining rather than by government policy. Unions may be ideologically opposed to letting the wage floor drop and powerful enough to impose that preference. An alternative in such a scenario is for government to subsidize employers who hire workers into low-productivity positions. This stimulates hiring by offsetting the high (relative to productivity) cost of labor.

Earnings Subsidy

When wages in low-productivity jobs are low enough to encourage job creation, the chief problem tends to be large numbers of individuals and households with very low earnings. Earnings subsidies can help to redress this problem. They can be targeted either to individual workers or to households.

An earnings subsidy for individual workers increases their take-home pay relative to what they receive from their employer. One way to implement this is with a cash supplement paid directly to low-wage workers (Haveman 1997). Another is with a combination of tax breaks and benefits for workers. As noted in chapter 5, Germany has recently instituted a policy along these lines: low-income workers receive a full or partial exemption from social security contributions (OECD 2003a, 118, 153).

The drawback to subsidizing individuals is similar to that of a minimum wage: any given individual may or may not be part of a low-earning household. Since earnings tend to be pooled within households, households arguably are the unit to which subsidies should be provided. An effective way to boost the incomes of those in low-productivity jobs is through an employment-conditional negative income tax, such as the Earned Income Tax Credit (EITC) in the United States or the Working Tax Credit in the United Kingdom.

The EITC was created in 1975. Its aim is to supplement the incomes of low-earning households without creating work disincentives. As of 2002 it provided a tax credit to households with at least one working adult and a pretax household income of up to $34,000. The amount of the credit depends on household size and income. Figure 8.1 shows the benefit levels in 2002 for a married couple with two or more children, for a single adult with one child, and for a single adult with no children. For a household with two or more children, the EITC gave a 40 percent

Figure 8.1   U.S. Earned Income Tax Credit, 2002

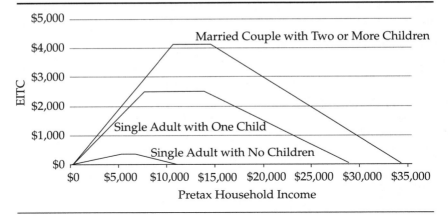

Source: CBPP (2002).

earnings subsidy for those with earnings up to $10,500, a flat subsidy of $4,140 to those with earnings between $10,500 and $14,500, and a $4,140 subsidy minus 21 percent of earnings above $14,500 for those with earnings between $14,500 and $34,000. The EITC is refundable, which means that if it amounts to more than the household owes in federal income taxes (as is often the case), the household receives the difference as a cash refund.

The EITC is effective in several respects. First, it directly boosts the incomes of low-earning households and, in doing so, reduces the poverty rate. In 1999 the EITC moved nearly 5 million Americans above the official U.S. poverty line (CBPP 2002). Notably, two-thirds of EITC dollars go to single-parent (mainly single-mother) households, one of the sociodemographic groups most vulnerable to poverty (Meyer and Holtz-Eakin 2002). The EITC has been found to be more effective at increasing the incomes of low-earning households than employer hiring subsidies and the minimum wage (Dickert-Conlin and Holtz-Eakin 2000; Hotz and Scholz 2000). Second, studies consistently find that the EITC tends to encourage labor market participation (Blank, Card, and Robins 2000; Hoffman and Seidman 2003; Hotz and Scholz 2000; Meyer and Rosenbaum 2002). Third, because the EITC is implemented through the tax system, recipients avoid the discomfort and stigma associated with going to a public office to apply for assistance. Fourth, the EITC is relatively inexpensive to administer. It has far lower administrative costs than more bureaucratic American social-welfare programs such as AFDC-TANF and food stamps (Hotz and Scholz 2000).

Figure 8.2   U.S. Social-Welfare Program Recipients, 1975 to 2002

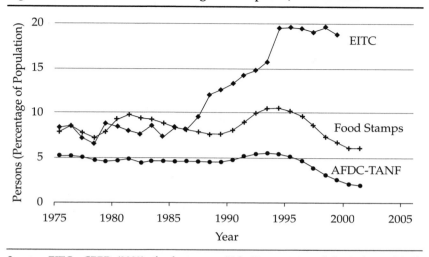

Sources: EITC—CBPP (2002); food stamps—U.S. Department of Agriculture (2003); AFDC-TANF—U.S. Department of Health and Human Services (n.d.).
Note: EITC figures are estimates (tax units multiplied by average household size).

As figure 8.2 indicates, the Earned Income Tax Credit has become by far the most widely used cash or near-cash transfer program for Americans with low incomes. Although the share of AFDC-TANF and food stamp recipients has dropped steadily since the mid-1990s, EITC use has remained high. This is a function of increased labor market participation among those with low skills and an expansion of eligibility criteria in 1993. In 2000, $26 billion was spent on the EITC, compared to $14 billion on TANF (Moffitt 2003, 134).

The EITC could and should be made more generous. Since the mid-1990s the EITC has been set at a level (adjusted annually for inflation) designed to ensure that a family of four with one full-time minimum-wage worker has an income at or above the poverty line through a combination of earnings, the EITC, and food stamps (Ellwood 1996). Yet this is a rather low income—$18,244 as of 2002. About one-third of the U.S. states offer an additional state Earned Income Tax Credit, but the benefit level in most instances is quite modest (Johnson, Llobrera, and Zahradnik 2003). The EITC's most glaring weakness is that, as indicated in figure 8.1, it provides very limited benefits to households with no children. (Prior to 1993 it offered no benefit at all to childless households.) The United Kingdom's Working Tax Credit is more generous to households without children.

One limitation of the EITC is underutilization, which results from the fact that a household cannot receive the credit without filing a federal income tax return. An estimated 15 to 20 percent of those eligible fail to claim the credit (CBPP 2002). A second drawback is fraud. A study of 1995 filings found that claims for the EITC exceeded the amount to which filers were actually eligible by 25 percent, though new compliance measures enacted in subsequent years have probably reduced this level of fraud (Hotz and Scholz 2000). For purposes of comparison, data on overall U.S. tax compliance suggest that 15 to 20 percent of total taxes owed are not paid. A third drawback is that, because the level of the credit is based on total household income, it may deter labor market entry for a spouse when her or his partner has a paying job with earnings near the credit ceiling (OECD 2003a, 118–19). This disincentive appears to have relatively little impact in practice, but to the extent that it is a problem it can be remedied through a more gradual phaseout of the credit. In other words, the slope of the lines on the right side of figure 8.1 can be flattened somewhat by moving the income threshold for eligibility further to the right (Wasow 2000).

Because of its overall positive work incentives, its effective targeting of transfers to households most in need, and its administrative efficiency, an employment-conditional negative income tax has a great deal going for it as a policy tool (see also Blank 1997; Blau and Kahn 2002a, ch. 8; Corcoran 2001, 160; Danziger and Gottschalk 1995, 158–65; Greenstein 1991; Hotz and Scholz 2000; Moffitt 2003; Myles and Quadagno 2000; Page and Simmons 2000; Wilson 1996). I would be surprised if some variant of it were not implemented in a number of affluent countries within the next decade or so. An employment-conditional negative income tax holds particular promise for countries in which high wages at the low end of the distribution impede job creation. It makes it possible to allow low-end pay levels to drop a bit without that resulting in excessively low posttax-posttransfer household incomes or in a substantial rise in income inequality.

Gøsta Esping-Andersen (1999, 178–80; 2001) has argued recently that affluent countries should forsake the goal of contemporaneous equality in favor of equality over the life course. He suggests that such nations need high employment in order to fund a generous welfare state and that employment growth requires lower wage levels in low-productivity service jobs than presently exist in the Nordic and perhaps also the continental countries. In his view, high-quality public child care and schooling along with an eradication of child poverty will enable people to move up the occupational ladder over time. An individual may start in a low-productivity and hence relatively low-paying job, but with a strong educational foundation and continued opportunity for training, she or he will be able to advance into a more lucrative and fulfilling position.

I fully endorse the call for intensive early intervention as a means of enhancing work-family balance and reducing inequality of opportunity (see discussion later in this chapter), but I am less optimistic about the possibility of a society characterized by extensive upward intragenerational mobility. In the United States, for example, more than one-quarter of the labor force (approximately 35 million people) work in the following low-productivity, low-paying occupations: retail sales, janitor/cleaner, secretary/administrative assistant, cashier, truck driver, lower-level food preparation worker, office clerk, assembler/fabricator, waiter/waitress, stock clerk/order filler, nursing aide/orderly/attendant, teaching assistant, child care worker, hand packer/packager, receptionist, and bus driver (U.S. Bureau of the Census, various years). Even if cognitive and other skills were substantially equalized, is it realistic to expect that a significant share of individuals who begin their adult lives in these types of occupations will move into higher-skill, higher-paying ones?

In my view, the best mechanism for remedying the effects of lower wages is through an employment-conditional negative income tax targeted to households with low to moderate earnings. Countries that find it necessary to reduce wage levels at the bottom of the distribution may suffer greater earnings inequality among employed individuals, but with an effective negative income tax that need not carry over into greater poverty or income inequality among households.

Supports for Work Interruption

Unemployment, sickness, and disability benefits have been among the central pillars of welfare states in most affluent countries since the 1930s. Along with public pensions, these are the classic social insurance programs: individuals pay into a fund during their working career and draw (earnings-related) benefits if their wage or salary is disrupted by unemployment, illness, or disability. When a working-age household has low income but is not eligible for unemployment, sickness, or disability benefits—for example, because no individual in the household qualifies for such benefits or because the eligibility period has run out—social assistance benefits typically are provided. Social assistance includes cash transfers and near-cash benefits such as housing allowances and food support.

These programs will continue to play a vital role in modern welfare states. The challenge is to keep eligibility requirements, benefits, and duration at levels that provide meaningful income support to those in need without creating excessive adverse work incentives. There is, alas, no magic formula. The only way to do this is through trial and error. In some countries benefits may be too generous. This was almost certainly true of disability benefits in the Netherlands in the early 1980s (Visser and Hemerijck 1997) and of sickness benefits in Sweden in the early 1990s (Agell 1996). In other nations benefits are too stingy. For instance, the United States could reduce income inequality and poverty by increasing the generosity of its social assistance package. Temporary Assistance to Needy Families (TANF) is the principal U.S. cash social assistance program for the working-age population. As of 2001 the average maximum TANF benefit for a three-person family across the fifty states was $4,668, which amounted to only one-third of the poverty line (Children's Defense Fund 2002, 51). Even adding in the value of food stamps, a typical recipient family is left with an income of no more than two-thirds of the poverty line. With the imposition of time limits beginning in 1997, the danger of long-term benefit dependence has been substantially lessened. Thus, TANF benefit levels could be increased with little or no adverse employment effect.

Child Care

High employment requires greater employment of women. As figure 8.3 indicates, employment rates for males are relatively high in all of the affluent countries. The deficit, and the cross-country variation, is mainly (though not exclusively) in female employment. For example, Germany's male employment rate is almost as high as Sweden's, but the female employment rate in the two countries differs by fifteen percentage points. The mean for male employment across the sixteen countries is 76 percent, while for female employment it is 63 percent. The coefficient of variation (standard deviation divided by the mean) for male employment is .07, while for female employment it is .14. As various observers have noted, the male-female contrast is even more pronounced if we focus on full-time employment (Daly 2000; Gornick and Meyers 2003; Orloff 2002). This is shown in figure 8.4. Here the mean for males is 70 percent and the coefficient of variation is .06, compared to 47 percent and .22 for females.

In terms of sustaining a generous welfare state, women's employment appears to be doubly beneficial. Not only does it increase the tax base, but the cross-country evidence from recent decades suggests that it also contributes to a higher level of fertility, which means that it may help to ease the demographic crunch (Castles 2003; Esping-Andersen 1999, 67–68).

A shift toward a full-employment society poses a challenge in terms of care for preschool-age children. There are several possible options.

In the United States 67 percent of working-age women, and 64 per-

Figure 8.3   Male and Female Employment in Sixteen Countries, 2002

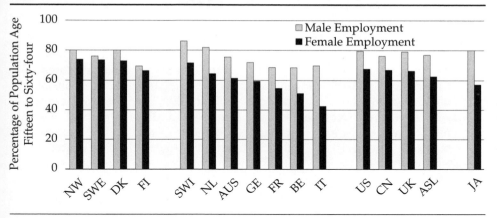

Source: Author's compilation; see appendix.

cent of married mothers with children under age six, are employed. Relatively few working Americans have access to paid parental leave, so children are often put in nonfamily-based child care at a very early age. Indeed, nearly half of children less than one year old are in child care for more than thirty hours per week (Vandell and Wolfe 2000, i). In most states there is little or no publicly provided care prior to age five, when kindergarten begins (CED 2002). Affluent parents and more and more middle-class dual-earner couples pay for private child care and

Figure 8.4   Male and Female Full-Time Employment in Sixteen Countries, 2002

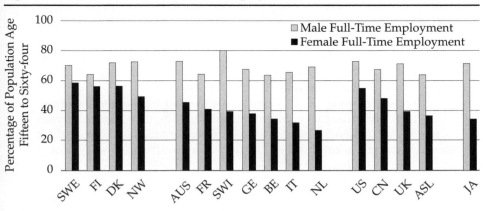

Source: Author's compilation; see appendix.

preschool. Some of this is of high quality. Many low-income dual-earner couples and single parents also pay for private care, but the care they can afford tends to be of much lower quality (Blau 2001; Kamerman and Kahn 1995; Vandell and Wolfe 2000). Since 1990 child care subsidies have been available to low-income parents through the federal Child Care and Development Fund, but the quantity of funds allocated is so small that only 10 percent of families formally eligible to receive a subsidy actually do (Helburn and Bergmann 2002, 23). Most child care is informal and unregulated: more than two-thirds of preschool-age children of employed women are cared for in homes rather than in child care centers (Blau 2001, 13). Even in formal child care centers, two-thirds of the staff have no more than a high school degree and staff turnover is very high (Vandell and Wolfe 2000). The low quality of the child care that is affordable for low-income parents has potentially worrisome effects on economic and social opportunities for such children: there is compelling evidence that child care quality at early ages affects cognitive development (Blau 2001, ch. 7; Buchinal 1999; Vandell and Wolfe 2000).

In Germany institutions and policies are structured around the presumption of a male breadwinner household, with child care performed by the mother in the home (Gornick and Meyers 2003; Gottschall and Bird 2003; Morgan and Zippel 2003). Public preschool is available for children age three to six, and approximately 80 percent of such children attend. But this schooling is half-day, which poses a problem for parents in full-time jobs. Moreover, child care for children under three is grossly undersupplied; there are spaces for only 6 percent of such children (Appelbaum et al. 2001, 30). A three-year parental/child care leave, introduced in 1986, has strengthened the normative idea that young children should be cared for in the family. Those employed prior to taking the leave are guaranteed job security and no drop in pay upon return to work. The leave is paid for the first two years, though the benefit is means-tested after six months. Karin Gottschall and Katherine Bird (2003, 124) find that a three-year "baby break" has become "a virtually universal phenomenon" among employed German women who have a child. Among West German mothers with children under age three, the labor force participation rate fell from 28 percent to 23 percent between 1986, when the leave was first implemented, and 2000. And for mothers who do return to the workforce, the break appears to encourage part-time rather than full-time employment. Half-day schooling through the end of secondary school forces many couples with school-age children to keep one parent home during the heart of the working day. The German pension system further reinforces the male breadwinner model: if a husband qualifies for a pension, the wife automatically does too. The same holds for Germany's joint taxation, under which a second earner's income is subject to steep marginal tax rates (Dingeldey 2001; Sainsbury 1999b, 198). The German approach may or may not be beneficial for young children, but it certainly is not conducive to high levels of female employment.

In contrast, the strategy pursued in the Nordic countries is to make child care largely a public responsibility (Gornick and Meyers 2003; Kamerman and Kahn 1995; OECD 2002a, ch. 3; Sainsbury 1999a). Parents in these countries are granted paid parental leave of up to a year, so having one parent take a considerable period of time off from work is attractive. But after the first year, formal child care tends to be the option of choice. High-quality and relatively inexpensive child care is available in the home and in public centers beginning around six months of age, and a large proportion of parents make use of this option. Denmark is illustrative. Sixty-four percent of Danish children age six months to two years are in formal child care. The high quality stems in part from oversight by both local municipalities and parent boards. It is also a product of the fact that the training requirements and pay levels for child care teachers are on par with those for schoolteachers. Heavy public subsidies help limit the cost to parents to 10 to 20 percent of an average production worker's earnings, or 5 to 10 percent of household earnings if (as is usually the case) both spouses have full-time jobs. In a 2000 survey, Danish respondents gave the formal child care system an average score of 4.4 out of 5 on overall satisfaction.

A fourth approach is to substantially increase the flexibility of employment arrangements, thereby allowing a combination of in-home care by parents and formal child care (Appelbaum et al. 2001; Gornick and Meyers 2003). Collective bargaining or public policy can mandate that employers permit not only a six-month or one-year leave upon the birth of a child but also a switch to part-time employment or a job-sharing arrangement upon return to work. Flexibility is needed in terms of not only the number of hours worked but also when those hours are worked—what time of day, which days of the week, and how many days each month. Parents remain in the workforce, but they are able to spend more time than "normal" full-time workers caring for their children. Gornick and Meyers (2003, 95) describe one possible allocation of paid work and child care for a dual-earner couple:

> During the first year of a child's life, parents in an earner-carer society would share time away from the market symmetrically to allow them to care for children at home. They might choose, for example, to work two half-time jobs at twenty hours a week each. Parents with children aged one and two might reduce their working hours and stagger their sched-

ules so that between them they could cover most of the caregiving time; they would supplement parental care with substitute child care to fit their children's needs. One possibility is that each works for pay twenty-five hours a week and cares for their child for fifteen hours a week. Assuming that parents can arrange some nonoverlapping employment hours, the child would spend about thirty hours in parental care and ten hours in substitute care (of the forty-hour work week).

Of course, salaries and benefits would have to be prorated, but a reduced-hour schedule must not entail complete loss of benefits if it is to be financially viable for low- and middle-income families.

This approach appears to be the current choice in the Netherlands. Despite the surge in female labor force participation during the past two decades, only 48 percent of married or cohabiting couples in the Netherlands are dual-earner couples, compared to 73 percent in the United States and 92 percent in Sweden (Appelbaum et al. 2001, 5). There continues to be a strong preference for care by parents. Paid child care, particularly for very young children, is in short supply and therefore prohibitively expensive for some families. Only 17 percent of Dutch children age zero to three are in formal child care (OECD 2002a, 86). This is part of the reason why job growth in the Netherlands has been so heavily tilted toward part-time employment. Among employed females with children, 85 percent in the Netherlands are in part-time jobs, compared to just 8 percent in Denmark (OECD 2002a, 55, 58). Public policy has attempted to accommodate this trend. In the mid-1990s rights to pensions and other social benefits were extended to part-time (and temporary) employees as part of a "flexicurity" accord. In 2000 the Adjustment of Hours Act was passed: it allows both parents of a newborn child to request a reduction to 80 percent of former working time. According to Eileen Appelbaum and her colleagues (2001, 19):

> The act is expected to alter the balance in "kitchen table politics"—and strengthen the hand of mothers when they negotiate with their partners over shared work and shared care responsibilities. The hope is that parents—fathers as well as mothers—will be encouraged to request a 20% reduction in work time and pro-rated reductions in pay and benefits, and that employers will honor these requests from men as well as women.

If the goal is high employment *coupled with* high-quality care for young children, the Nordic (public child care) and flexible employment routes seem clearly preferable to those of the United States and Germany. Relative to the flexible employment approach, the Nordic strategy has the disadvantage that part of the additional tax revenues generated by higher women's employment is offset by the cost of high-quality public child care facilities. Government spending on child care accounted for 2.1 percent of GDP in Denmark in 2001, compared to just 0.2 percent in the Netherlands (OECD 2002a, 59). Yet the Nordic approach has two advantages over the flexible employment approach. First, it promotes greater gender equality because it better facilitates mothers' employment, in terms of both joining the workforce and limiting the interruption that results from the birth of a child. And second, by mixing children from various class backgrounds during the most formative stage of cognitive development, age zero to three, public provision of high-quality child care may help promote equality of opportunity (Esping-Andersen 2003; Helburn and Bergmann 2002; Vandell and Wolfe 2000).

The Nordic and the flexible employment approaches are not mutually exclusive. In fact, one of the Nordic countries, Sweden, pioneered the flexibilization of employment for parents. Since 1978 Swedish parents have had the right to cut back to six hours per day at work, at prorated pay, until their youngest child reaches age eight. Partly as a result, the total number of hours worked by dual-earner couples with children is lower in Sweden than in most other affluent nations, the ratio of hours worked by employed mothers to those by employed fathers is higher, and the ratio of time spent on in-home child care by employed fathers to that by employed mothers is higher (Gornick and Meyers 2003, ch. 3). Yet, as in Denmark, more than half of one- and two-year-old Swedish children are in formal child care (Gornick and Meyers 2003, table 7.2).

A notable gap in the policy supports of all affluent nations, even the Nordic ones, has to do with the school calendar. Public schools typically are in session for about 180 of the 260 weekdays in a year. Eventually, in my view, countries will decide to lengthen the school year to perhaps 220 days—both to facilitate a better work-family balance for parents and to enhance learning.

Appelbaum and her colleagues (2001, 32) offer a nice summary of solutions to balancing work and family:

> A society that values work will make it possible for working families to provide care for children, the sick, and the elderly. . . . Parents need access to reduced hours on their current jobs and/or access to good-quality part-time jobs or job sharing. They need paid maternity leave, paid breaks to nurse infants, short periods of paid leave to care for sick children and relatives, and unpaid leave plus publicly provided cash benefits to care for seriously ill children or relatives. They need health insurance for themselves and their children, and paid sick leave for themselves. Finally, they need subsidized high-quality child care for infants and young children, and public pre-kindergarten education for 3- and 4-year-olds.

The Nordic countries are ahead of other affluent nations in providing these supports. They can serve as a useful model for the Anglo and continental nations.

That does not, of course, mean that all countries must do it the Nordic way. There are a variety of policies and institutions through which countries can provide these types of supports and services to working parents. In the U.S. context, for instance, the private market for child care is so extensive that it is difficult to imagine it being replaced by public facilities. A more reasonable strategy for the United States might consist of four components. The first would be paid parental leave for the first six months of a child's life. Second would be a voucher to help parents defray the cost of paid child care for children under age three. Suzanne Helburn and Barbara Bergmann (2002) suggest that the cost of child care should be fully subsidized for families with incomes below the poverty line and that for others the subsidy should cover care expenses in excess of 20 percent of family income. To encourage high quality, David Blau (2001, 219) recommends that the value of the voucher vary according to the quality of the child care it is used to purchase: "For example, a low-income family might receive a subsidy of 30 percent of the average cost of unaccredited child care if they use unaccredited care, 60 percent of the average cost of care if they use a provider accredited as of good quality, and 100 percent of the average cost of care if they use care accredited as of excellent quality. This gives families an incentive to seek care of high quality, and it gives providers an incentive to offer high-quality care in order to attract consumers." The third component would be full-day year-round public preschool for three-, four-, and five-year-olds. And finally, all employees, whether full-time year-round, part-time, or temporary, should have access to health insurance and employer pension contributions.

Equal Opportunity

Equal opportunity requires preschools, elementary schools, and secondary schools that compensate for differing family circumstances. It requires full access to health care. It also requires a reduction in the inequality of financial resources stemming from inheritance.

Schooling

Cognitive ability is perhaps the single most important determinant of earnings and occupational status in adulthood. Many factors influence cognitive ability, but among the most central is parents. By definition, then, equalizing opportunity requires reducing the influence of parents on children's cognitive skill. The chief mechanism employed by rich countries to do so is the school system.

Educational systems in many affluent countries fall short of the goal of contributing to equality of opportunity in two respects. One is that they intervene too late. The most important years for cognitive development are ages zero to three, and the next most important are ages four and five (Shonkoff and Phillips 2000). Formal schooling, which typically begins at age six, therefore reaches children after a substantial amount of cognitive development has already occurred (or failed to occur). Formal (pre)schooling should begin at age three, and high-quality, educational child care should be available for one- and two-year-olds (Duncan and Magnuson 2003; Wolfe and Scrivner 2003). A number of affluent countries have been moving in this direction already (Gornick and Meyers 2003; OECD 2001d).

The chief deficit in primary and secondary schooling has to do with funding. In most rich countries school funding is relatively equal across districts. But children in less-advantaged families need *more* assistance from schools than do their counterparts with better-educated and/or more affluent parents. To promote equal opportunity, schools in areas with a high proportion of low-education, low-income parents therefore should receive more funding than those in middle-class or upper-class areas. The situation in the United States is even worse: there is substantial inequality of funding across schools and school districts, with those in less affluent areas typically getting less, rather than more, money (Biddle and Berliner 2002; Kozol 1991).

Health Care

Access to affordable health care for children and adults is essential to equality of opportunity. When health care is costly, people tend to use it only when they most need it instead of in a preventive fashion. This approach typically results in worse health outcomes, which in turn tends to adversely affect performance in school and at work.

Among affluent countries, lack of access to health care is a significant barrier to equal opportunity only in the United States, where approximately 15 percent of the population has no health insurance. Most of those without such insurance are in households with incomes just below or just above the official U.S. poverty line. The findings of a recent study by the Center on Budget and Policy Priorities (Broaddus et al. 2002) are revealing. As of 2000, among households with incomes less than 200 percent of the poverty line (about $27,500 for a single parent with two children), 39 percent of parents and 28 percent of children were covered by employer-provided health insurance. An additional 20 percent of parents and 42 percent of children were covered by Medicaid. Some others purchased health insurance on their own, but 33 percent of parents and 21 percent of children in these households were without health insurance. The Institute of Medicine (2002) has estimated that lack of health insurance results in approximately 18,000 premature deaths in the United States each year.

In 1997 the federal government created the State Children's Health Insurance Program (SCHIP), which offers states matching funds to expand health care coverage for children through Medicaid or a separate state children's health care program. By 2000, thirty-seven of the fifty states were providing coverage to children in all households with incomes up to 200 percent of the poverty line. But most states are much stingier in covering adults. In the median state, a working parent with two children is eligible for coverage only if the household income is less than 70 percent of the poverty line (approximately $10,000). In some states coverage is absurdly low. For instance, in Alabama a working parent with two children qualifies for Medicaid coverage only if the household income is less than $3,050.

The United States is the only affluent country in which health insurance is not treated as a basic right of citizenship. The goal should be universal coverage. There are a variety of models from which to choose, including: a single-payer program such as Canada's; a federal government program for adults modeled on SCHIP, which would encourage states to enroll in Medicaid all adults in households with incomes less than twice the poverty line; a program that would leave the existing private insurance market largely intact but mandate that all individuals purchase health insurance and provide government subsidies to make that possible (Halstead 2003; Miller 2003; Mullahy and Wolfe 2001; Physicians for a National Health Program 2003).

Reducing Financial Inheritance

A key source of unequal opportunity is bequests and inheritance. Some people receive substantial sums of money and/or property from parents, grandparents, or other relatives, whereas many receive nothing. This gives the former a considerable head start in life. In most democratic societies there is unlikely to ever be popular support for completely eliminating inheritance, but support does exist for reducing its impact.

The most direct way to do so is through an annual tax on assets. There is considerable precedent (Wolff 1995/2002). Eight of the affluent countries examined in this book have an annual asset tax: Denmark,

Finland, Norway, Sweden, Austria, Germany, the Netherlands, and Switzerland. The tax is administered in conjunction with the personal income tax; in all of these nations except Germany, a joint tax return is filed for both income and wealth. The tax rate varies from 0.5 percent in Germany to 3 percent in Sweden (for assets above $140,000). The exemption threshold for married couples with two children ranges from $50,000 in the Netherlands to $155,000 in Denmark. Most of these countries have had these taxes in place for more than half a century, without any apparent crippling effect on investment, economic growth, or employment.

Revenues from an asset tax could be used to provide each citizen with a onetime lump-sum cash grant upon reaching adulthood. The most detailed proposal along these lines has been offered by Bruce Ackerman and Anne Alstott (1999), who suggest that a modest wealth tax in the United States would be sufficient to fund an $80,000 grant for each citizen (see also Boshara 2003). In their proposal the grant would be distributed in $20,000 increments over a period of four years beginning at age eighteen. Such a grant would substantially enhance economic opportunity for young adults from lower- and middle-class families—making it possible to finance a college or postgraduate education, start a business, put a down payment on a home, or pursue other options that currently are available mainly to the well-to-do.

A wealth tax and/or lump-sum grant also would help to stem a source of inequality about which I have said little in this book: rising incomes at the very top, which pull this segment further away from the rest of society. For instance, at the end of the 1970s the average CEO in the United States earned 30 times what the average production worker made. By the end of the 1990s the ratio had risen to more than 100 (Mishel, Bernstein, and Boushey 2003, 213). In 1986 the highest-paid American CEO made $20 million; his counterpart in 2001 took home $706 million (*Fortune* 2002). Although the trend has been most dramatic in the United States, it is not alone in this development: rising incomes at the top also increased income inequality between 1995 and 2000 in Sweden and Finland (my calculations from LIS data). This is worrisome not merely in terms of a normative commitment to a reasonable degree of economic equality, but also because excessive inequality might engender adverse social and political consequences. Beyond a certain point, such exorbitant incomes may generate growing frustration, leading to rising crime, withdrawal from civic engagement, and loss of social cohesion. It also may further accentuate the political influence of the wealthy (Krugman 2002; Phillips 2002).

Egalitarian Policies and Institutional Coherence

In offering a list of policies that might help to promote a dynamic, productive, and egalitarian society, I risk conveying the notion that countries can simply pick and choose from a menu of options, implementing whatever combination seems most desirable. This runs against the grain of much recent thinking.

Students of comparative political economy, for example, frequently conclude that the institutions and policies of particular countries or groups of countries tend to cohere, in the sense that the structure of the financial system, the type of relationship between firms and their suppliers, the dominant mode of industrial relations, the system of skill development, and social-welfare policies tend to complement one another. The most explicit formulation of this view is offered by Peter Hall and David Soskice (2001), who suggest that political economies tend to be characterized by "institutional complementarities" (see also Crouch and Streeck 1997). A complementarity exists when the presence of one institution increases the effectiveness of another. For instance, "long-term employment is more feasible where the financial system provides capital on terms that are not sensitive to current profitability. Conversely, fluid labor markets may be more effective at sustaining employment in the presence of financial markets that transfer resources readily among endeavors, thereby maintaining a demand for labor" (Hall and Soskice 2001, 18). Because institutional complementarities generate beneficial returns, Hall and Soskice suggest that "nations with a particular type of coordination in one sphere of the economy should tend to develop complementary practices in other spheres as well" (18). One implication of this view, suggested by Estevez-Abe, Iversen, and Soskice (2001), is that countries in which firms rely heavily on firm- or industry-specific skills—such as Germany, Austria, Sweden, Norway, Belgium, and Japan—may require higher levels of employment protection.

A related view is advanced by some proponents of the "third way" strategy developed by and for the British Labour Party in the late 1990s. After two decades of Conservative Party rule, which led to significant weakening of British unions and reduction in the generosity of social-welfare programs, the Labour government elected in 1997 put into place a number of new programs that are consistent with those I have outlined in this chapter (Clasen 2002; Ferrera and Hemerijck 2003; Hills 2003; Taylor-Gooby, Daguerre, and Larsen 2003). It increased funding for training and job placement programs, tied benefit access to participation in such programs, introduced a statutory minimum wage and an employment-conditional negative income tax, increased paid parental leave, mandated that employers consider requests for flexible work hours due to family constraints, and introduced a tax credit to help defray the cost of child care. Some "third way" proponents suggest that an approach to social-welfare policy centered on high employment and equal opportunity is best combined with a relatively unregulated labor market, free trade, and a balanced government budget (Giddens 2000; Reich 1999).

If certain types of social-welfare programs fit better with particular types of financial systems, industrial relations practices, or other institutions, then the menu of policy choices for any given country may be partially or severely circumscribed. My own view is that to the extent a coupling between policies and institutions is required, it tends to be fairly loose. That is, institutional configurations do render certain policies more or less effective, but they nevertheless tend to allow considerable leeway. It is perhaps no accident that some of the countries that performed relatively successfully during the 1980s and 1990s, such as Denmark and the Netherlands, have institutions and policies that are among the least coherent (Kenworthy 2002b). Policymakers and leaders of organized interest groups in these countries displayed both an interest in combining equality with high employment and a pragmatic willingness to experiment with new strategies.

It also is worth emphasizing that there are multiple ways to achieve a high employment rate, a mobile workforce, decent wages and household incomes, care and stimulation for young children, quality schooling and health care for all, limitations on intergenerational transmission of wealth, and relatively low levels of income inequality. The policy suggestions I have offered in this chapter are not meant to imply that there is one best way.

Politics and Progress

For half a century, from roughly 1930 to 1980, the trend in the world's most affluent nations was unambiguously in the direction of greater equality. In the 1980s and 1990s, however, the tide turned in the opposite direction. In many of these countries pay levels became more dispersed, tax systems less progressive, and social-welfare programs less generous. Will we look back on those two decades as the beginning of a long-term reversal of the egalitarian trend or as merely a temporary interruption of that trend?

Egalitarian capitalism is largely a product of strong unions and social democratic political parties (Esping-Andersen 1985; Hicks 1999; Huber and Stephens 2001; Korpi 1983; Stephens 1979). Sometimes separately but often in concert, these organizations put in place a set of institutions (collective bargaining, coordinated wage setting, corporatist policymaking) and policies (education, social welfare, active labor market, family, fiscal, monetary) that reduce the degree of inequality produced by the market. Once set in place, these institutions and policies generated further public support. Coupled with institutional inertia, this support has helped egalitarian institutions and policies to survive despite recent economic and political challenges (Pierson 1996, 2001).

There are a number of social actors that could potentially coalesce in favor of reducing economic inequality, but in all likelihood organized labor and affiliated political parties will continue to play a central role. Thus, there is good reason to predict that countries in which labor is comparatively strong will, for the foreseeable future, continue to be the most egalitarian.

Does this mean that weak-labor countries such as the United States are forever doomed to domination by market liberalism? Not necessarily. Egalitarian shifts are possible even in circumstances in which institutional forces are relatively inhospitable. Like the United States, Canada is influenced by a frontier culture that prizes liberty and independence, and it too has limited labor strength and a liberal welfare state. Yet Canada has nevertheless managed to construct a set of policies that yield substantially less income inequality than in the United States, with little or no sacrifice in terms of employment or living standards (see figure 7.3). Recent developments in the United Kingdom also offer reason for optimism. The Blair government's policy initiatives will not turn the United Kingdom into Sweden or Denmark, but they represent a substantial shift in the direction of employment-friendly egalitarianism in an otherwise market-liberal context.

Even in the United States there are rays of hope. Public opinion surveys and historical experience indicate that a majority of Americans support relatively generous social-welfare programs if they encourage or reward employment for able-bodied, working-age adults (Gilens 1999; Skocpol 2000).

Though it often hinders passage of progressive legislation by the federal government, the decentralized character of the U.S. political system enables considerable experimentation at the state and local levels. About one-fifth of the states set a minimum wage that is higher than the national minimum, and Alaska, Oregon, and Washington index the state minimum wage to inflation. One-third of the states offer a state Earned Income Tax Credit that supplements the federal EITC. Five states grant paid leave to mothers following the birth of a child, and in 2002 California began offering a six-week paid leave to both mothers and fathers. Georgia provides universal public preschool for four-year-olds, and several other states have moved in this direction. In a growing number of states the majority of funding for public primary and secondary schools now comes from the state government rather than from local property taxes, and the state money is allocated to help equalize per-student expenditures across school districts. Several states have developed innovative strategies for reducing the share of their population that lacks health insurance. For instance, since 1999 Wisconsin has leveraged federal Medicaid and SCHIP money to fund a state program called BadgerCare, which offers free or low-cost health insurance to families with children that have incomes below roughly twice the poverty line (Trubek 2003).

Community organizations, labor unions, and public-private partnerships at the state and local levels have also stepped in to help address needs missed by markets and government programs. Particularly noteworthy have been a variety of job training and placement programs, such as the Wisconsin Regional Training Partnerships in the greater Milwaukee area and Project QUEST in a variety of southwestern cities (Dresser and Rogers 2003; Osterman 2003).

Nor, in my view, is dire pessimism warranted when it comes to federal government policy. The U.S. Earned Income Tax Credit has gradually been expanded from a minor benefit in the mid-1970s into a significant antipoverty program. Although it is severely underfunded, a federal program offering subsidies to help low-income parents pay for child care was instituted in 1990. Legislation was passed in 1993 requiring employers to provide twelve weeks of leave, albeit unpaid, to parents with a new child or a sick relative. Funds were allocated beginning in 1998 to extend government health coverage to all children in low-income households. Indeed, a plan to provide health insurance to all Americans was given serious consideration in the early 1990s. Though business opposition eventually blocked the plan, that outcome was by no means predetermined.

Are an aggressive active labor market policy, a higher minimum wage, a more generous Earned Income Tax Credit, higher unemployment and social assistance benefits, affordable high-quality child care, universal health care, pension benefits for part-time and temporary employees, equalization of school funding, an asset tax, and a lump-sum grant impossible in the United States? They certainly do not appear to be imminent. But despite their substantial cost, there is no reason to think they are impossible. Martin Luther King Jr. once remarked: "The moral arc of the universe is long, but it bends toward justice." Developments in the twentieth century certainly bore this out. There is good reason to suspect that in the twenty-first century the United States will continue to move closer—perhaps slowly but nonetheless steadily—toward the kind of high-employment, not-too-unequal society in which many Americans would prefer to live.

= Appendix: Variables =

All of the data used in the analyses in this book are available, in Excel format, on my webpage: www.emory.edu/SOC/lkenworthy.

Comparative Country Data

10th percentile household income: Posttax-posttransfer household income per equivalent person at the 10th percentile of the distribution. Households with heads age twenty-five to fifty-nine only. Converted into U.S. dollars using purchasing power parities and adjusted for inflation using the U.S. consumer price index (CPI-U-RS). Incomes adjusted for household size using the square root of the number of persons in the household as the equivalence scale. Incomes top-coded at ten times the unequivalized median and bottom-coded at 1 percent of the equivalized mean. *Source*: My calculations from Luxembourg Income Study data (variable: DPI).

Absolute poverty level: Poverty rate (share of persons in households with incomes below the poverty line) multiplied by the poverty gap (poverty line minus the average income among the poor, divided by the poverty line). Poverty line set at $12,763 per equivalent person, in 2000 U.S. dollars. Households with heads age twenty-five to fifty-nine only. Incomes converted into U.S. dollars using purchasing power parities and adjusted for inflation using the U.S. consumer price index. Incomes adjusted for household size using the square root of the number of persons in the household as the equivalence scale. Incomes top-coded at ten times the unequivalized median and bottom-coded at 1 percent of the equivalized mean. *Source*: My calculations from Luxembourg Income Study data (variables: MI for pretax-pretransfer income, DPI for posttax-posttransfer income).

Active labor market policy: Expenditures on active labor market policy as a share of GDP. *Source*: OECD (2001c).

Agricultural and manufacturing employment: As a share of total employment. *Source*: My calculations from data in OECD (various years[b]).

175

Business concentration: Index with three categories: 0 = fragmentation among business confederations and/or central confederation with little authority over members. 0.5 = central confederation with moderate authority and/or moderately contested by competitors. 1 = central confederation with substantial authority over members and weakly contested by competing confederations. *Source*: Hicks and Kenworthy (1998, 1642).

Decommodification: Scale that taps the degree to which individuals "can uphold a socially acceptable standard of living independently of market participation" (Esping-Andersen 1990, 37). Takes into account the rules governing access to pension, sickness, and unemployment benefits, the degree of income replacement provided by those benefits, and the range of entitlements they encompass. *Source*: Esping-Andersen (1990, 52).

Earnings inequality among full-time, year-round employed individuals (pay inequality): Ratio of annual earnings of a person at the 90th or 50th percentile of the earnings distribution to a person at the 10th percentile. I have adjusted the figures for Canada; see the discussion in chapter 5, note 2. *Source*: OECD (n.d.[b]).

Earnings inequality among households: Gini coefficient for household earnings. Households with heads age twenty-five to fifty-nine only. Earnings adjusted for household size using the square root of the number of persons in the household as the equivalence scale. Earnings top-coded at ten times the unequivalized median and bottom-coded at 1 percent of the equivalized mean. *Source*: My calculations from Luxembourg Income Study data (variable: EARNING).

Educational attainment: Share of persons age twenty-five to sixty-four with a tertiary education. *Source*: OECD (2001b, table A2.1b, tertiary-type A and advanced research programs).

Employment: As a share of the population age fifteen to sixty-four. *Source*: OECD (various years[a, b]).

Employment in private-sector consumer services: Employment in private-sector consumer-oriented services—wholesale and retail trade, restaurants and hotels, and community, social, and personal services (ISIC 6 and 9; ISIC revision 3 50–52, 55, 90–93)—as a percentage of the population age fifteen to sixty-four. Unfortunately, private- and public-sector employment in these industries can be distinguished only through 1995, so the time series for this variable ends in that year. *Source*: Calculated from OECD data by Torben Iversen, Department of Government, Harvard University; for discussion, see Iversen and Wren (1998).

Employment: male and female: As a share of the male or female population age fifteen to sixty-four (for figure 8.3). *Source*: OECD (2003a, 301–2).

Employment: male and female full-time: As a share of the male or female population age fifteen to sixty-four (for figure 8.4). *Source*: My calculations from data in OECD (2003a, 301–2, 320).

Employment regulations: Index ranging from zero to ten, with each country scored from zero (lax or no legislation) to two (strict legislation) on each of five types of employment regulations: working time, fixed-term contracts, employment protection, minimum wages, and employees' representation rights (on works councils, company boards, and so on). *Source*: CEP (n.d.); for discussion, see Nickell (1997).

Female labor force participation: Female labor force participants as a share of the female population age fifteen to sixty-four. *Source*: OECD (various years[b]).

Firm-level economic cooperation: Index of four types of cooperation between and within firms: strategic alliances among competing firms; long-term partnerships among companies and their suppliers; cooperation among workers in the form of participatory work teams; and cooperation among functional divisions within firms in the form of multidivisional project teams. *Source*: Hicks and Kenworthy (1998, 1642).

Functional literacy among adults: Based on the OECD's 1994–95 International Adult Literacy Survey. Scores range from one (functionally illiterate) to five (high functional literacy). *Source*: OECD (1998a, 54).

Government cash social expenditures on the working-age population: Sum of family benefits and benefits for unemployment, disability, occupational injury and disease, sickness, and "other contingencies" (mainly low income) as a share of GDP. *Source*: My calculations from data in OECD (2001c).

Government tax revenues: Current receipts of government as a share of GDP. *Source*: OECD (various years[b]).

Government transfers: Government transfers as a share of GDP. *Source*: OECD (various years[b]).

Growth of real GDP: Average annual rate of change of real gross domestic product. *Source*: OECD (various years[b]).

Growth of real GDP per capita: Average annual rate of change of real gross domestic product per capita. *Source*: OECD (various years[b]).

Hours worked: Average annual hours worked per employed person. *Source*: OECD (2003a, 322).

Income inequality among households: Gini coefficient for household income. In chapters 3, 5, and 7: households with heads age twenty-five to fifty-nine only. In chapter 4: all households. Incomes adjusted for household size using the square root of the number of persons in the household as the equivalence scale. Incomes top-coded at ten times the unequivalized median and bottom-coded at 1 percent of the equivalized mean. *Source*: My calculations from Luxembourg Income Study data (variables: MI for pretax-pretransfer income; DPI for posttax-posttransfer income).

Inflation: Percentage change in the consumer price index. *Source*: OECD (various years[b]).

Institutional coherence: Factor scores, adjusted to vary between zero and one, from a factor analysis of six indicators, each measured as of the early or mid-1990s: (1) shareholder power (legal protection and likely influence over firms of ordinary shareholders relative to managers or dominant shareholders); (2) dispersion of control (how many firms in the country are widely held relative to the number with controlling shareholders); (3) size of the stock market (market valuation of equities on the stock exchanges of a nation as a percentage of its gross domestic product); (4) level of wage-setting coordination; (5) degree of wage-setting coordination; and (6) labor turnover (number of employees who had held their jobs for less than one year as a percentage of all employees). High and low scores on this index indicate institutional coherence; intermediate scores indicate incoherence. I have rescaled the index by subtracting scores below .50 from 1.00. This allows the variable to range linearly from low to high institutional coherence. *Source*: Hall and Gingerich (2001, table 2).

Investment: Gross fixed capital formation as a share of GDP. *Source*: OECD (various years[b]).

Labor force participation: Labor force participants as a share of the population age fifteen to sixty-four. *Source*: OECD (various years[b]).

Left government: Left party cabinet portfolios as a share of total cabinet portfolios, cumulative from 1946 forward. *Source*: My calculations from data in Huber, Ragin, and Stephens (1997/2001, variable: LEFTCABCUM).

Marital homogamy: Pearson correlation between earnings of household "heads" and earnings of household "spouses." Households with heads age twenty-five to fifty-nine only. *Source*: My calculations from Luxembourg Income Study data (variables: V39, V41).

Median household income: Posttax-posttransfer household income per equivalent person at the 50th percentile of the distribution. Households with heads age twenty-five to fifty-nine only. Converted into U.S. dollars using purchasing power parities and adjusted for inflation using the U.S. consumer price index (CPI-U-RS). Incomes adjusted for household size using the square root of the number of persons in the household as the equivalence scale. Incomes top-coded at ten times the unequivalized median and bottom-coded at 1 percent of the equivalized mean. *Source*: My calculations from Luxembourg Income Study data (variable: DPI).

Net government transfers to the poor: Average transfers (cash and near-cash) minus taxes to working-age households with pretax-pretransfer incomes below the poverty line. *Source*: My calculations from Luxembourg Income Study data.

Nonworking-age population: Share of the population under age fifteen or over age sixty-four. *Source*: My calculations from data in OECD (various years[b]).

Outward direct foreign investment: Outward direct foreign investment as a share of GDP. *Source*: Duane Swank, Department of Political Science, Marquette University.

Paid maternity leave: Weeks of mandated paid maternity leave. *Source*: Gornick and Meyers (2003, table 5.2).

Part-time employment: As a share of total employment. Defined as usually working less than thirty hours per week. *Source*: OECD (various years[a, b]).

Public child care: Government child care expenditures as a share of gross domestic product. *Source*: OECD (2001c, variable: FORMAL DAY CARE).

Public employment: Government employment as a percentage of the population age fifteen to sixty-four. *Source*: My calculations from data in OECD (various years[b]).

Real GDP per capita: *Source*: My calculations from data in OECD (2003b).

Real long-term interest rates: *Source*: My calculations from data in OECD (2003b).

Redistribution: Gini coefficient for household earnings minus Gini coefficient for posttax-posttransfer household income. Households with heads age twenty-five to fifty-nine only. Incomes adjusted for household size using the square root of the number of persons in the household as the equivalence scale. Incomes top-coded at ten times the unequivalized median and bottom-coded at 1 percent of the equivalized mean. *Source*: My calculations from Luxembourg Income Study data (variables: EARNING, DPI).

Relative poverty rate: Share of persons in households with posttax-posttransfer incomes below the poverty line. Poverty line set at 50 percent of the median within each country. Households with heads age twenty-five to fifty-nine only. Incomes adjusted for household size using the square root of the number of persons in the household as the equivalence scale. Incomes top-coded at ten times the unequivalized median and bottom-coded at 1 percent of the equivalized mean. *Source*: My calculations from Luxembourg Income Study data (variable: DPI).

Single-earner households: Single-earner households as a share of households that have at least one earner. Households with heads age twenty-five to fifty-nine only. *Source*: My calculations from Luxembourg Income Study data (variable: D6).

Social capital: Percentage responding, "Most people can be trusted," to the question: "Generally speaking, would you say that most people can be trusted, or that you can't be too careful in dealing with people?" Measured in 1981 only. *Source*: Knack and Keefer (1997, data appendix, using World Values Survey data).

Tax rate on a typical worker: Sum of the average payroll, income, and consumption tax rates for a typical worker. *Source*: Nickell et al. (2001, 32, table 8).

Terms of trade: Ratio of export prices to import prices. *Source*: My calculations from data in OECD (2003b).

Trade: Exports plus imports as a share of gross domestic product. *Source*: My calculations from data in OECD (2003b).

Unemployment: Standardized unemployment rates. Owing to data limitations, unstandardized rates are used for Austria (prior to 1993), Denmark (prior to 1983), Ireland (prior to 1983), and Switzerland (prior to 1991). *Source*: OECD (various years[b]). Data for Italy are from U.S. Department of Labor (n.d.[a]) for reasons discussed in Nickell and Layard (1999, 3033).

Unemployment benefit duration: Calculated as: [(.06 multiplied by replacement rate in second and third years of an unemployment spell) plus (.04 multiplied by replacement rate in fourth and fifth years of a spell)] divided by (replacement rate in first year of a spell). *Source*: Nickell et al. (2001, 27, table 3).

Unemployment benefit replacement rate: Percentage of a worker's former earnings (pretax) that is replaced by unemployment compensation and related benefits—for a worker with earnings at two-thirds of the national median (the 33rd percentile) in the first year after losing his or her job. *Source*: OECD (n.d.[a]); for discussion, see Martin (1996).

Union concentration: Average of standardized values for two measures of concentration: (1) Herfindahl index of union concentration across union confederations. This indicates the extent to which union members belong to a single confederation rather than being divided among multiple confederations. (2) Approximate Herfindahl index of union concentration for affiliates of the largest union confederation, using the membership of the three largest affiliates and the total number of affiliates. This indicates the extent to which the membership of the largest union confederation is concentrated within a small number of affiliates rather than being spread out across a large number of affiliates. *Source*: Golden, Lange, and Wallerstein (1997, variables: HERF, APPHRF1).

Unionization: Employed union membership as a share of the labor force. *Source*: Ebbinghaus and Visser (2000); Golden, Lange, and Wallerstein (1997).

Wage-setting coordination: Index with five categories. Larger numbers indicate greater coordination. *Source*: Kenworthy (2001a; 2001b).

Comparative U.S. States Data

Business concentration: Coded one if there is a single business peak association in the state and zero otherwise. *Source*: Leicht and Jenkins (1998, table 1).

Earnings inequality among households: Gini coefficient for household earnings. Households with heads age twenty-five to fifty-nine only. Earnings adjusted for household size using the square root of the number of persons in the household as the equivalence scale. Earnings top-coded at ten times the unequivalized median and bottom-coded at 1 percent of the equivalized mean. *Source*: My calculations from Luxembourg Income Study data (variable: EARNING).

Economic development policies: Number of state government programs (out of thirty-seven for which data are available) providing financial assistance, tax incentives, or special services to firms and industry. *Source*: My calculations from data in IAMC (various years).

Educational attainment: Share of persons age twenty-five and over with a four-year college degree. *Source*: U.S. Bureau of the Census (various years).

Employment: Employment as a share of the population age eighteen to sixty-four. *Source*: My calculations from data in U.S. Department of Labor (n.d.[b]); U.S. Bureau of the Census (various years).

Government tax revenues: Government tax revenues as a share of gross state product. *Source*: My calculations from data in U.S. Bureau of the Census (various years); U.S. Department of Commerce (n.d.[a]).

Growth of real GSP per capita: Average annual rate of change in real gross state product per capita. *Source*: My calculations from data in U.S. Department of Commerce (n.d.[a]).

Income inequality among households: Gini coefficient for pretax-post-transfer household income. *Source*: U.S. Bureau of the Census (n.d.[a], "Table S4: Gini Ratios by State: 1969, 1979, 1989").

Labor force participation: Labor force participants as a share of the population age sixteen and over. *Source*: My calculations from unpublished U.S. Department of Labor, Bureau of Labor Statistics data; U.S. Bureau of the Census (various years).

Left government: Share of years in which the Democratic Party controlled both houses of the state legislature and the governorship simultaneously. *Source*: My calculations from data in U.S. Bureau of the Census (various years).

Military expenditures: Federal military contracts plus payroll expenditures as a share of gross state product. *Source*: My calculations from data in U.S. Bureau of the Census (various years).

Nonworking-age population: Share of the population under age sixteen or over age sixty-four. *Source*: My calculations from data in U.S. Bureau of the Census (various years).

Poverty: Share of persons in households with (size-adjusted) pretax-posttransfer incomes below the official U.S. government poverty line. Does not include capital gains or near-cash transfers. *Source*: U.S. Bureau of the Census (n.d.[b], table 2).

Social capital: Index of fourteen indicators, such as attitudes toward trust, participation in groups and community activities, and voter turnout. *Source*: Putnam (2000); see www.bowlingalone.com.

Sunbelt: Dummy variable coded one for seventeen "sunbelt" states (Alabama, Arizona, Arkansas, California, Colorado, Florida, Georgia, Louisiana, Mississippi, Nevada, New Mexico, North Carolina, South Carolina, Tennessee, Texas, Utah, and Virginia) and zero for others.

Unionization: Union members as a share of the employed labor force. *Source*: Hirsch and Macpherson (various years).

Over-Time Data for the United States

Educational attainment: Share of the population age twenty-five and over with a four-year college degree. *Source*: U.S. Bureau of the Census (various years).

Family income: Real pretax-posttransfer family income at various percentiles of the distribution (20th, 40th, 60th, 80th, and 95th). Does not include capital gains or near-cash transfers. *Source*: U.S. Bureau of the Census (n.d.[a], "Table F-1: Income Limits for Each Fifth and Top 5 Percent of Families (All Races): 1947 to 2001").

Income inequality among families: Gini coefficient for pretax-posttransfer family income. Does not include capital gains or near-cash transfers. *Source*: U.S. Bureau of the Census (n.d.[a], "Table F-4: Gini Ratios for Families, by Race and Hispanic Origin of Householder: 1947 to 2001").

Income share of the top 10 percent: Income share of the top 10 percent of tax units. Includes capital gains and corporate income and employer payroll taxes, but not individual income and employee payroll taxes. *Source*: Picketty and Saez (2001, table A3, column 1).

Investment: Net private fixed investment as a share of gross domestic product. *Source*: U.S. Department of Commerce (n.d.[b]).

Labor force participation: Labor force participants as a share of persons age sixteen to sixty-four. *Source*: U.S. Department of Labor (n.d.[c]).

Poverty (official income definition): Share of persons in households with (size-adjusted) pretax-posttransfer incomes below the official U.S. government poverty line. Does not include capital gains or near-cash transfers. *Source*: U.S. Bureau of the Census (n.d.[b], "Table 2: Poverty Status of People by Family Relationship, Race, and Hispanic Origin 1959 to 2002").

Poverty (alternative income definition): Share of persons in households with (size-adjusted) incomes below the official U.S. government poverty line. Includes sources of income counted in the official income definition plus capital gains, taxes, near-cash government transfers, and near-cash employer benefits. *Source*: U.S. Bureau of the Census (n.d.[b], "Table RDP-6: Percent of People in Poverty, by Definition of Income: 1979 to 2002," definition 14).

Productivity: Real gross domestic product per hour worked. Business sector only (excludes government and nonprofits). *Source*: U.S. Department of Labor (n.d.[d]).

Savings: Personal savings as a share of personal disposable income. *Source*: U.S. Department of Commerce (2003).

═ Notes ═

Chapter 2

1. This is especially germane here because it is common in small-N quantitative analyses for coefficients to be substantively significant but not, according to conventional criteria, statistically significant (whereas the reverse is more likely when the number of cases is very large).

Chapter 3

1. In almost all countries the difference between the Gini coefficient for household earnings and the Gini for pretax-pretransfer household income is less than .005. Across the thirteen countries analyzed in this chapter, the correlation between the Gini for household earnings and the Gini for pretax-pretransfer household income is .99 for the mid-1980s and .98 for the mid-1990s. For change over time (mid-1990s Ginis minus mid-1980s Ginis), the correlation is .99.

2. Some of these studies are pooled time-series cross-section analyses that include information about both levels and trends, but the data tend to be dominated by the cross-sectional variation in levels.

3. Data are available for Belgium, but they are inconsistent over time. The mid-1990s household earnings data for Belgium are based on gross (that is, pretax) earnings, but the data for the mid-1980s are based on net (after-tax) earnings. This inconsistency renders a measure of change over time problematic.

4. In the best available data source on earnings inequality among employed individuals (OECD, n.d.[b]), it is not possible to calculate a Gini coefficient.

5. Switzerland is omitted in calculating this correlation. The relatively small number of observations in the 1992 Swiss dataset yields an unreliable Gini coefficient for earnings inequality among households in the bottom half of the distribution.

6. In a study of developments in the four Nordic countries, Rolf Aaberge and his colleagues (2000) reach a similar conclusion. Their findings are more mixed for Finland, but that may be due in part to the slightly more restricted range of years they cover—1989 to 1994—whereas the analysis here covers 1987 to 1995.

7. It is more plausible to assert that high *levels* of redistribution (at the beginning of the period) may have caused declines in employment, which then led to increases in redistribution. I examine this issue in chapter 6.

8. The replacement rate is for a worker with earnings at the 33rd percentile in the first year after losing her or his job. The net replacement rate would be a more useful measure, since it incorporates taxes. Unfortunately, data on net replacement rates are available only for the late 1990s. Figures for 1999 net replacement rates (from OECD 2002b, 40) correlate at .71 with the mid-1980s to mid-1990s gross replacement rate figures I use here, and the regression results are similar if the former are used instead of the latter.

9. This does not contradict the findings of prior studies on the causes of cross-country variation in welfare state effort. Such studies have aimed to explain variation in intended redistribution, which is included here as an explanatory factor.

Chapter 4

1. For five countries the earliest available observation is in the mid-1980s: Austria 1987, Belgium 1985, Denmark 1987, Finland 1987, and Italy 1986. Given the stability of cross-country differences over time, this does not seem likely to be unduly problematic.

Chapter 5

1. "Western Europe" here refers to Austria, Belgium, Denmark, Finland, France, Germany, Italy, the Netherlands, Norway, Sweden, Switzerland, and the United Kingdom.

2. The OECD data for Canada from 1980 to 1994 suggest that Canada's 50th percentile/10th percentile ratio is the highest (most unequal) among the countries analyzed here. However, data from the Luxembourg Income Study suggest that Canada's earnings ratio is slightly lower than that of the United States (my calculations). (I do not use the LIS data in the analyses for this chapter because with the LIS database it is possible to generate a comparable measure of earnings inequality among full-time employed individuals for only a small group of countries.) A new labor force survey was introduced in Canada in the late 1990s, and the data from that survey also indicate a slightly lower level of earnings inequality than in the United States. I therefore use an adjusted 50th percentile/10th percentile ratio for Canada for 1980 to 1994—in these figures and in the analyses throughout this chapter. In terms of assessing the impact of earnings inequality on employment growth, this has the effect of biasing the analyses toward finding support for the trade-off view—namely, a positive effect of inequality on job growth. If the OECD's 1980 to 1994 data for Canada's earnings inequality are used, the findings regarding the impact of earnings inequality are weaker than those I present here.

3. Another source of data on earnings inequality is the International Adult Literacy Survey (IALS) conducted by the OECD. Francine Blau and Lawrence Kahn (2002b, figs. 1 and 2) have calculated earnings ratios for seven countries based on the wage data in the IALS. These figures correlate at .85 with the figures I use here.

4. Elsewhere (Kenworthy 2003) I have conducted a pooled time-series cross-section analysis, using annual observations, that yields results similar to those here regarding the effect of earnings inequality.

5. It would be helpful to also control for the strictness of the criteria used to decide who is eligible to receive unemployment compensation, but no comparative measures exist (see Grubb 2000–2001).

Chapter 6

1. The strong inverse association could conceivably be due to the fact that countries with generous welfare states also tend to have lower pretax-pretransfer relative poverty, but these studies find that the association between welfare state generosity and low posttax-posttransfer relative poverty is even stronger when controlling for pretax-pretransfer poverty.

2. A related but separate assertion by welfare state critics focuses on static rather than dynamic effects. It holds that government benefits encourage some (or many) people to not work (or to work less than they otherwise would) and thereby increase the poverty rate immediately, not just over time. I do not address this assertion here because it is less compelling on both theoretical and empirical grounds. In most countries, very few people in the situation of choosing between welfare and work would escape poverty immediately if they chose work. And contemporaneous measures of social-welfare program generosity and absolute poverty are negatively, rather than positively, correlated (Smeeding and Rainwater 2002).

3. This poverty line is absolute not only across countries but also over time, which strikes me as sensible given that the period covered is only twenty-five years. Over a very long period, it seems more appropriate to adjust the poverty line for changes in living standards. For instance, few would argue that we should use the same poverty line for the year 2000 as for 1900.

4. The poverty line used by the U.S. government was $17,500 for a family of four in 2000.

5. Robert DeFina and Kishor Thanawala (2002, 24) find that the measured reduction in relative poverty achieved by government taxes and transfers tends to be greater when the poverty measure incorporates the poverty gap than when it is based solely on the headcount. An additional aspect of the depth of poverty is the degree of inequality among the poor. However, several studies have found that, for affluent countries, including the degree of inequality among the poor makes little difference and thus adds unneeded complexity (see Brady 2003).

6. Note that posttax-posttransfer poverty is not always substantially lower than pretax-pretransfer poverty. On the surface this is surprising. But these figures include only working-age households. Public pension programs are the largest category of social-welfare expenditures (along with health insurance) in each of these countries, and they are funded on a pay-as-you-go basis—earnings are taxed from the working-age population and transferred directly to the retired. These transfers pull many elderly households out of poverty, but the tax payments reduce the incomes of working-age households. While some low-income working-age households receive government benefits that more than offset the tax payments, not all do.

7. The low cost of such services in countries such as Sweden and Germany is incorporated to some degree into the income calculations used here, because currency adjustments are made using purchasing power parities. But this is true to only a limited extent, since PPPs represent the prices of *all* goods and services for a household with an *average* income. For example, the average U.S. household has employer-provided health insurance, so its estimated cost for health care in PPP calculations is relatively low— higher than for its Swedish counterpart, but not much higher. Yet many low-income households in the United States (mainly those just below and just above the poverty line) do not have employer-provided or government-provided health insurance. Hence, the real difference between the two countries in the cost of health care *for low-income households* is underestimated in the PPP adjustment.

Chapter 7

1. The maximum length of eligibility was reduced from seven years to five, and a requirement that benefit recipients participate in a labor market program after the second year was introduced. In 1999 the maximum length was further reduced to four years, with participation required after one year.

2. Several years ago, in their assessment of employment and welfare outcomes among the rich countries, Anton Hemerijck and Martin Schludi (2000, 187) concluded similarly that "while Sweden is unlikely to reduce unemployment to the extremely low levels it used to have in the 1980s, the country seems to have found a new equilibrium combining macroeconomic stability and high levels of employment with a still very generous welfare state." See also Krugman (2003, 400–2).

3. Indeed, welfare state typologies frequently include it in the social-democratic group together with the Nordic countries (Esping-Andersen 1990, 1999; Goodin et al. 1999). One of the most noteworthy successes of the Dutch welfare state is its effectiveness in reducing poverty among single mothers (Casper, McLanahan, and Garfinkel 1994; Sainsbury and Morissens 2002, 317).

═ References ═

Aaberge, Rolf, Anders Björklund, Markus Jänti, Mårten Palme, Peder J. Pedersen, Nina Smith, and Tom Wennemo. 2002. "Income Inequality and Income Mobility in the Scandinavian Countries Compared to the United States." *Review of Income and Wealth* 48(4, December): 443–69.

Aaberge, Rolf, Anders Björklund, Markus Jänti, Peder J. Pedersen, Nina Smith, and Tom Wennemo. 2000. "Unemployment Shocks and Income Distribution: How Did the Nordic Countries Fare During Their Crises?" *Scandinavian Journal of Economics* 102(1): 77–99.

Åberg, Rune. 2003. "Unemployment Persistency, Over-education, and the Employment Chances of the Less Educated." *European Sociological Review* 19(2, April): 199–216.

Acemoglu, Daron. 2002. "Technical Change, Inequality, and the Labor Market." *Journal of Economic Literature* 40(1, March): 7–72.

Ackerman, Bruce, and Anne Alstott. 1999. *The Stakeholder Society*. New Haven, Conn.: Yale University Press.

Adams, J. Stacy. 1965. "Inequity in Social Exchange." In *Advances in Experimental Social Psychology*, vol. 2, edited by Leonard Berkowitz. New York: Academic Press.

Adsera, Alicia, and Carles Boix. 2000. "Must We Choose? European Unemployment, American Inequality, and the Impact of Education and Labor Market Institutions." *European Journal of Political Economy* 16(4, November): 611–38.

Agell, Jonas. 1996. "Why Sweden's Welfare State Needed Reform." *Economic Journal* 106(439): 1760–71.

Aghion, Philippe, Eve Caroli, and Cecilia García-Peñalosa. 1999. "Inequality and Economic Growth: The Perspective of the New Growth Theories." *Journal of Economic Literature* 37(4): 1615–60.

Akerlof, George, and Janet Yellen, eds. 1986. *Efficiency Wage Models of the Labor Market*. Cambridge: Cambridge University Press.

———. 1990. "The Fair Wage-Effort Hypothesis and Unemployment." *Quarterly Journal of Economics* 105(2, May): 255–83.

Albert, Michel. 1993. *Capitalism Against Capitalism*. London: Whurr Publishers.

Alderson, Arthur S., and François Nielsen. 2002. "Globalization and the Great U-Turn: Income Inequality Trends in Sixteen OECD Countries." *American Journal of Sociology* 107(5): 1244–99.

Alesina, Alberto, and Dani Rodrik. 1994. "Distributive Politics and Economic Growth." *Quarterly Journal of Economics* 109(2): 465–90.

Appelbaum, Eileen. 2000. "What Explains Employment Developments in the United States?" Briefing paper 100. Washington, D.C.: Economic Policy Institute (November). Available at: www.epinet.org.

Appelbaum, Eileen, Thomas Bailey, Peter Berg, and Arne L. Kalleberg. 2001. *Shared Work, Valued Care.* Washington, D.C.: Economic Policy Institute.

Arrow, Kenneth J. 1979. "The Trade-off Between Growth and Equity." In *Theory for Economic Efficiency: Essays in Honor of Abba P. Lerner,* edited by Harry I. Greenfield, Albert M. Levenson, and William Hamovitch. Cambridge, Mass.: MIT Press.

Atkinson, Anthony B. 1995. "The Welfare State and Economic Performance." *National Tax Journal* 48(2): 171–98.

Atkinson, Anthony B., and Andrea Brandolini. 2001. "Promise and Pitfalls in the Use of `Secondary' Datasets: Income Inequality in OECD Countries as a Case Study." *Journal of Economic Literature* 39(3): 771–99.

Atkinson, Anthony B., Lee Rainwater, and Timothy M. Smeeding. 1995. *Income Distribution in OECD Countries.* Paris: Organization for Economic Cooperation and Development.

Auer, Peter. 2000. *Employment Revival in Europe: Labor Market Success in Austria, Denmark, Ireland, and the Netherlands.* Geneva: International Labor Organization.

Australian Bureau of Statistics. 2003. *Revised Household Income Distribution Statistics.* Available at: www.abs.gov.au/Ausstats.

Bane, Mary Jo, and David T. Ellwood. 1994. *Welfare Realities: From Rhetoric to Reform.* Cambridge, Mass.: Harvard University Press.

Barro, Robert J. 2000. "Inequality and Growth in a Panel of Countries." *Journal of Economic Growth* 5(1): 5–32.

Bartik, Timothy J. 2001. *Jobs for the Poor: Can Labor Demand Policies Help?* New York: Russell Sage Foundation; Kalamazoo, Mich.: Upjohn Institute.

Baumol, William J., Richard R. Nelson, and Edward N. Wolff, eds. 1994. *Convergence of Productivity.* Oxford: Oxford University Press.

Bazen, Stephen. 2000. "The Impact of the Regulation of Low Wages on Inequality and Labor-Market Adjustment: A Comparative Analysis." *Oxford Review of Economic Policy* 16(1): 57–69.

Beck, Nathaniel, and Jonathan N. Katz. 2001. "Throwing Out the Baby with the Bath Water: A Comment on Green, Kim, and Yoon." *International Organization* 55(2): 487–95.

Becker, Gary S. 1996. "Why Europe Is Drowning in Joblessness." *Business Week,* April 8, 22.

Becker, Uwe. 2001. "A `Dutch Model': Employment Growth by Corporatist Consensus and Wage Restraint? A Critical Assessment of an Idyllic View." *New Political Economy* 6(1): 19–43.

Bénabou, Roland. 1996. "Inequality and Growth." In *National Bureau of Economic Research Macroeconomics Annual 1996,* edited by Ben S. Bernanke and Julio J. Rotemberg. Cambridge, Mass.: MIT Press.

Benner, Mats, and Torben Bundgaard Vad. 2000. "Sweden and Denmark: Defending the Welfare State." In *Welfare and Work in the Open Economy,* vol. 2, *Diverse Responses to Common Challenges,* edited by Fritz W. Scharpf and Vivien A. Schmidt. Oxford: Oxford University Press.

Beramendi, Pablo. 2001. "The Politics of Income Inequality in the OECD: The Role of Second Order Effects." Working paper 284. Luxembourg Income Study (September). Available at: www.lisproject.org/publications.htm.

Berk, Richard A., Bruce Western, and Robert E. Weiss. 1995. "Statistical Inference for Apparent Populations." *Sociological Methodology* 25: 421–58.

Bernhardt, Annette, Martina Morris, Mark S. Handcock, and Marc A. Scott. 2001. *Divergent Paths: Economic Mobility in the New American Labor Market.* New York: Russell Sage Foundation.

Bernstein, Jared, Chauna Brocht, and Maggie Spade-Aguilar. 2000. *How Much Is Enough? Basic Family Budgets for Working Families.* Washington, D.C.: Economic Policy Institute.

Bernstein, Jared, and John Schmitt. 1998. *Making Work Pay: The Impact of the 1996– 1997 Minimum Wage Increase.* Washington, D.C.: Economic Policy Institute.

Bertola, Giuseppe, and Andrea Ichino. 1995. "Wage Inequality and Unemployment: United States Versus Europe." In *National Bureau of Economic Research Macroeconomics Annual 1995,* edited by Ben S. Bernanke and Julio J. Rotemberg. Cambridge, Mass.: MIT Press.

Biddle, Bruce J., and David C. Berliner. 2002. "What Research Says About Unequal Funding for Schools in America." Unpublished paper. Education Policy Studies Laboratory, Arizona State University. Available at: www.asu.edu/educ/epsl/eprp.htm.

Birdsall, Nancy, David Ross, and Richard Sabot. 1995. "Inequality and Growth Reconsidered." *World Bank Economic Review* 9(3): 477–508.

Björklund, Anders. 2000. "Going Different Ways: Labor Market Policy in Denmark and Sweden." In *Why Deregulate Labor Markets?* edited by Gøsta Esping-Andersen and Marino Regini. Oxford: Oxford University Press.

Blanchard, Olivier, and Justin Wolfers. 2000. "Shocks and Institutions and the Rise of European Unemployment: The Aggregate Evidence." *Economic Journal* 110(462): 1–33.

Blank, Rebecca M. 1997. *It Takes a Nation: A New Agenda for Fighting Poverty.* New York and Princeton, N.J.: Russell Sage Foundation and Princeton University Press.

———. 2000. "Fighting Poverty: Lessons from Recent U.S. History." *Journal of Economic Perspectives* 14(2): 3–19.

Blank, Rebecca M., and Alan S. Blinder. 1986. "Macroeconomics, Income Distribution, and Poverty." In *Fighting Poverty: What Works and What Doesn't,* edited by Sheldon Danziger and Daniel H. Weinberg. New York and Cambridge, Mass.: Russell Sage Foundation and Harvard University Press.

Blank, Rebecca M., David Card, and Philip K. Robins. 2000. "Financial Incentives for Increasing Work and Income Among Low-income Families." In *Finding Jobs: Work and Welfare Reform,* edited by David Card and Rebecca M. Blank. New York: Russell Sage Foundation.

Blau, David M. 2001. *The Child Care Problem: An Economic Analysis.* New York: Russell Sage Foundation.

Blau, Francine D., and Lawrence M. Kahn. 2002a. *At Home and Abroad: U.S. Labor Market Performance in International Perspective.* New York: Russell Sage Foundation.

————. 2002b. "Do Cognitive Test Scores Explain Higher U.S. Wage Inequality?" Unpublished paper. Department of Economics, Cornell University, Ithaca, N.Y.

Boggess, Scott, and Camille Ryan. 2002. *Financing the Future: Postsecondary Students, Costs, and Financial Aid, 1996–1997.* Current Population Reports P70–83. Washington: U.S. Bureau of the Census (October). Available at: www.census.gov/prod/2002pubs/p70–83.pdf.

Boix, Carles. 1998. *Political Parties, Growth, and Equality.* Cambridge: Cambridge University Press.

Bollen, Kenneth A. 1995. "Apparent and Nonapparent Significance Tests." *Sociological Methodology* 25: 459–68.

Boshara, Ray. 2003. "The $6,000 Solution." *Atlantic Monthly* (January–February): 91, 94–95.

Boushey, Heather, Chauna Brocht, Bethney Gundersen, and Jared Bernstein. 2001. *Hardships in America: The Real Story of Working Families.* Washington, D.C.: Economic Policy Institute.

Bowles, Samuel, and Herbert Gintis. 1995. "Escaping the Efficiency-Equity Trade-off: Productivity-Enhancing Asset Redistributions." In *Macroeconomic Policy After the Conservative Era*, edited by Gerald A. Epstein and Herbert Gintis. Cambridge: Cambridge University Press.

Brace, Paul. 1993. *State Government and Economic Performance.* Baltimore: Johns Hopkins University Press.

Bradbury, Katharine, and Jane Katz. 2002. "Are Lifetime Incomes Growing More Unequal? Looking at New Evidence on Family Income Mobility." *Federal Reserve Bank of Boston Regional Review*, qtr. 4: 3–5.

Bradley, David. 2002. "The Political Economy of Employment Performance: Testing the Deregulation Thesis." Ph.D. diss. Department of Political Science, University of North Carolina.

Bradley, David, Evelyne Huber, Stephanie Moller, François Nielsen, and John Stephens. 2003. "Distribution and Redistribution in Postindustrial Democracies." *World Politics* 55(2): 193–228.

Brady, David. 2001. "Could We Win a War on Poverty? The Welfare State and Poverty in Western Nations, 1967–1997." Unpublished paper. Department of Sociology, Duke University, Durham, N.C.

————. 2003. "Rethinking the Sociological Measurement of Poverty." *Social Forces* 81(3): 715–52.

Brandolini, Andrea, and Nicola Rossi. 1998. "Income Distribution and Growth in Industrial Countries." In *Income Distribution and High-Quality Growth*, edited by Vito Tanzi and Ke-young Chu. Cambridge, Mass.: MIT Press.

Broaddus, Matthew, Shannon Blaney, Annie Dude, Jocelyn Guyer, Leighton Ku, and Jaia Peterson. 2002. "Expanding Family Coverage: States' Medicaid Eligibility Policies for Working Families in the Year 2000." Washington, D.C.: Center on Budget and Policy Priorities. Available at: www.cbpp.org.

Browning, Edgar K., and William R. Johnson. 1984. "The Trade-off Between Equality and Efficiency." *Journal of Political Economy* 92(2, April): 175–203.

Buchinal, Margaret. 1999. "Child Care Experiences and Developmental Outcomes." *Annals of the American Academy of Political and Social Science* 563: 73–97.

Burtless, Gary. 1998. "Technological Change and International Trade: How Well Do They Explain the Rise in U.S. Income Inequality?" In *The Inequality Paradox*, edited by James A. Auerbach and Richard S. Belous. Washington, D.C.: National Policy Association.

———. 1999. "Effects of Growing Wage Disparities and Changing Family Composition on the U.S. Income Distribution." *European Economic Review* 43(4/6): 853–65.

———. 2001. "Has Widening Inequality Promoted or Retarded U.S. Growth?" Paper presented to the Conference on Linkages Between Economic Growth and Inequality. Institute for Research on Public Policy—Centre for the Study of Living Standards, Ottawa (January 26–27, 2001). Available at: www.irpp.org/events/index.htm.

Burtless, Gary, and Christopher Jencks. 2003. "American Inequality and Its Consequences." In *Agenda for the Nation*, edited by Henry J. Aaron, James M. Lindsay, and Pietro Nivola. Washington, D.C.: Brookings Institution.

Canberra Group (Canberra International Expert Group on Household Income Statistics). 2001. *Final Report and Recommendations.* Ottawa: Canberra Group.

Card, David, and Alan B. Krueger. 1995. *Myth and Measurement: The New Economics of the Minimum Wage.* Princeton, N.J.: Princeton University Press.

Carlin, Wendy, and David Soskice. 1990. *Macroeconomics and the Wage Bargain.* Oxford: Oxford University Press.

Casper, Lynne M., Sara S. McLanahan, and Irwin Garfinkel. 1994. "The Gender Poverty Gap: What We Can Learn from Other Countries." *American Sociological Review* 59(4): 594–605.

Castles, Francis G., ed. 1993. *Families of Nations: Patterns of Public Policy in Western Democracies.* Aldershot, Eng.: Dartmouth.

———. 2003. "The World Turned Upside Down: Below Replacement Fertility, Changing Preferences, and Family-Friendly Public Policy in Twenty-one OECD Countries." *Journal of European Social Policy* 13(3): 209–27.

CBPP (Center on Budget and Policy Priorities). 2002. "Facts About the Earned Income Credit." Available at: www.cbpp.org.

CED (Committee for Economic Development). 2002. *Preschool for All.* New York: CED.

CEP (Centre for Economic Performance). n.d. "Centre for Economic Performance OECD Dataset." London: CEP.

Chevan, Albert, and Randall Stokes. 2000. "Growth in Family Income Inequality, 1970–1990: Industrial Restructuring and Demographic Change." *Demography* 37(3): 365–80.

Children's Defense Fund. 2002. *The State of Children in America's Union.* Washington, D.C.: Children's Defense Fund.

Citro, Constance F., and Robert T. Michael, eds. 1995. *Measuring Poverty: A New Approach.* Washington, D.C.: National Academy Press.

Clarke, George R. G. 1995. "More Evidence on Income Distribution and Growth." *Journal of Development Economics* 47(2): 403–27.

Clasen, Jochen. 2002. "Unemployment and Unemployment Policy in the United Kingdom: Increasing Employability and Redefining Citizenship." In *Europe's New State of Welfare: Unemployment, Employment Policies, and Citizenship*, edited by Jørgen Goul Andersen, Jochen Clasen, Wim van Oorschot, and Knut Halvorsen. Bristol, Eng.: Policy Press.

Clayton, Richard, and Jonas Pontusson. 1998. "Welfare-State Retrenchment Revisited: Entitlement Cuts, Public-Sector Restructuring, and Inegalitarian Trends in Advanced Capitalist Societies." *World Politics* 51(1, October): 67–98.

Cook, Karen S., and Karen A. Hegtvedt. 1983. "Distributive Justice, Equity, and Equality." *Annual Review of Sociology* 9: 217–41.

Corcoran, Mary. 2001. "Mobility, Persistence, and the Consequences of Poverty for Children: Child and Adult Outcomes." In *Understanding Poverty*, edited by Sheldon H. Danziger and Robert H. Haveman. New York and Cambridge, Mass.: Russell Sage Foundation and Harvard University Press.

Crouch, Colin, and Wolfgang Streeck, eds. 1997. *Political Economy of Modern Capitalism*. London: Sage Publications.

Daly, Mary. 2000. "A Fine Balance: Women's Labor Market Participation in International Competition." In *Welfare and Work in the Open Economy*, vol. 2, *Diverse Responses to Common Challenges*, edited by Fritz W. Scharpf and Vivien A. Schmidt. Oxford: Oxford University Press.

Danziger, Sheldon H., and Peter Gottschalk. 1995. *America Unequal*. New York and Cambridge, Mass.: Russell Sage Foundation and Harvard University Press.

Danziger, Sheldon H., and Daniel H. Weinberg. 1994. "The Historical Record: Trends in Family Income, Inequality, and Poverty." In *Confronting Poverty*, edited by Sheldon H. Danziger, Gary D. Sandefur, and Daniel H. Weinberg. New York and Cambridge, Mass.: Russell Sage Foundation and Harvard University Press.

DeFina, Robert H. and Kishor Thanawala. 2002. "International Evidence on the Impact of Transfers and Taxes on Alternative Poverty Indexes." Working Paper 325. Luxembourg Income Study. Available at: www.lisproject.org.

Deininger, Klaus, and Lyn Squire. 1996. "A New Dataset Measuring Income Inequality." *World Bank Economic Review* 10(3): 565–91.

———. N.d. "Deininger and Squire Dataset: A New Dataset Measuring Income Inequality." World Bank Group Economic Growth Research Dataset. Available at: www.worldbank.org/research/growth/dddeisqu.htm.

Dickert-Conlin, Stacy, and Douglas Holtz-Eakin. 2000. "Employee-Based Versus Employer-Based Subsidies to Low-wage Workers: A Public Finance Perspective." In *Finding Jobs: Work and Welfare Reform*, edited by David Card and Rebecca M. Blank. New York: Russell Sage Foundation.

Dingeldey, Irene. 2001. "European Tax Systems and Their Impact on Family Employment Patterns." *Journal of Social Policy* 30(4): 653–72.

Dresser, Laura, and Joel Rogers. 2003. "Part of the Solution: Emerging Workforce Intermediaries in the United States." In *Governing Work and Welfare in a New Economy*, edited by Jonathan Zeitlin and David M. Trubek. Oxford: Oxford University Press.

Duncan, Greg J., and Katherine Magnuson. 2003. "Promoting the Healthy Development of Young Children." In *One Percent for the Kids*, edited by Isabel V. Sawhill. Washington, D.C.: Brookings Institution.

Ebbinghaus, Bernhard, and Jelle Visser. 2000. *Trade Unions in Western Europe Since 1945*. London: Macmillan.

Economic Policy Institute. 2003. "Minimum Wage Facts at a Glance." Available at: www.epinet.org.

The Economist. 1997. "Europe Hits a Brick Wall." April 5, 21–23.

Edin, Kathryn, and Christopher Jencks. 1995. "Do Poor Women Have the Right to Bear Children?" *The American Prospect* (Winter): 43–62.

Edin, Kathryn, and Laura Lein. 1997. *Making Ends Meet: How Single Mothers Survive Welfare and Low-wage Work*. New York: Russell Sage Foundation.

Ellwood, David. 1996. "Welfare Reform as I Knew It." *The American Prospect* (May–June): 26.

———. 2000. "Antipoverty Policy for Families in the Next Century." *Journal of Economic Perspectives* 14(1): 187–98.

Esping-Andersen, Gøsta. 1985. *Politics Against Markets*. Princeton, N.J.: Princeton University Press.

———. 1990. *The Three Worlds of Welfare Capitalism*. Princeton, N.J.: Princeton University Press.

———. 1994. "Welfare States and the Economy." In *The Handbook of Economic Sociology*, edited by Neil J. Smelser and Richard Swedberg. New York and Princeton, N.J.: Russell Sage Foundation and Princeton University Press.

———. 1999. *Social Foundations of Postindustrial Economies*. Oxford: Oxford University Press.

———. 2000a. "Regulation and Context: Reconsidering the Correlates of Unemployment." In *Why Deregulate Labor Markets?*, edited by Gøsta Esping-Andersen and Marino Regini. Oxford: Oxford University Press.

———. 2000b. "Who Is Harmed by Labor Market Regulations? Quantitative Evidence." In *Why Deregulate Labor Markets?*, edited by Gøsta Esping-Andersen and Marino Regini. Oxford: Oxford University Press.

———. 2001. "A Welfare State for the Twenty-first Century." In *The Global Third Way Debate*, edited by Anthony Giddens. Cambridge: Polity Press.

———. 2003. "Money, Culture, and Mobility." Unpublished paper. Department of Political and Social Sciences, Universitat Pompeu Fabra, Barcelona, Spain.

Esping-Andersen, Gøsta, with Duncan Gallie, Anton Hemerijck, and John Myles. 2002. *Why We Need a New Welfare State*. Oxford: Oxford University Press.

Esping-Andersen, Gøsta, and Marino Regini, eds. 2000. *Why Deregulate Labor Markets?* Oxford: Oxford University Press.

Estevez-Abe, Margarita, Torben Iversen, and David Soskice. 2001. "Social Protection and the Formation of Skills: A Reinterpretation of the Welfare State." In *Varieties of Capitalism*, edited by Peter A. Hall and David Soskice. Oxford: Oxford University Press.

Ferrera, Maurizio, and Anton Hemerijck. 2003. "Recalibrating Europe's Welfare Regimes." In *Governing Work and Welfare in a New Economy*, edited by Jonathan Zeitlin and David M. Trubek. Oxford: Oxford University Press.

Ferrera, Maurizio, Anton Hemerijck, and Martin Rhodes. 2000. "The Future of

Social Europe: Recasting Work and Welfare in the New Economy." Report prepared for the Portuguese Presidency of the European Union.

Firebaugh, Glenn, and Frank D. Beck. 1994. "Does Economic Growth Benefit the Masses? Growth, Dependence, and Welfare in the Third World." *American Sociological Review* 59(5): 631–53.

Forbes, Kristin J. 2000. "A Reassessment of the Relationship Between Inequality and Growth." *American Economic Review* 90(4): 869–87.

Förster, Michael, and Mark Pearson. 2002. "Income Distribution and Poverty in the OECD Area: Trends and Driving Forces." *OECD Economic Studies* 34: 7–39.

Fortune. 2002. "System Failure." June 24.

Franzese, Robert J. 2001. *Macroeconomic Policies of Developed Democracies.* Cambridge: Cambridge University Press.

Freeman, Richard B. 1995. "The Limits of Wage Flexibility to Curing Unemployment." *Oxford Review of Economic Policy* 11(1): 63–72.

———. 2001. "The Rising Tide Lifts . . . ?" In *Understanding Poverty*, edited by Sheldon H. Danziger and Robert H. Haveman. New York and Cambridge, Mass.: Russell Sage Foundation and Harvard University Press.

Freeman, Richard B., and Ronald Schettkat. 2000. "Low-wage Services: Interpreting the U.S.-German Difference." In *Labor Market Inequalities*, edited by Mary Gregory, Wiemer Salverda, and Stephen Bazen. Oxford: Oxford University Press.

Friedman, Milton. 1962. *Capitalism and Freedom.* Chicago: University of Chicago Press.

Friedman, Milton, and Rose Friedman. 1979. *Free to Choose.* San Diego: Harcourt Brace Jovanovich.

Furåker, Bengt. 2002. "Is High Unemployment Due to Welfare State Protection? Lessons from the Swedish Experience." In *Europe's New State of Welfare: Unemployment, Employment Policies, and Citizenship*, edited by Jørgen Goul Andersen, Jochen Clasen, Wim van Oorschot, and Knut Halvorsen. Bristol, Eng.: Policy Press.

Galbraith, James K. 1998. *Created Unequal: The Crisis in American Pay.* New York: Free Press.

Galbraith, James K., Pedro Conceição, and Pedro Ferreira. 1999. "Inequality and Unemployment in Europe: The American Cure." *New Left Review* 237: 28–51.

Ganghof, Steffen. 2000. "Adjusting National Tax Policy to Economic Internationalization: Strategies and Outcomes." In *Welfare and Work in the Open Economy*, vol. 2, *Diverse Responses to Common Challenges*, edited by Fritz W. Scharpf and Vivien A. Schmidt. Oxford: Oxford University Press.

Garibaldi, Pietro, and Paolo Mauro. 2002. "Employment Growth: Accounting for the Facts." *Economic Policy* 34: 67–113.

Garrett, Geoffrey. 1995. "Capital Mobility, Trade, and the Domestic Politics of Economic Policy." *International Organization* 49(4): 657–87.

———. 1998. *Partisan Politics in the Global Economy.* Cambridge: Cambridge University Press.

Gemmell, Norman. 1996. "Evaluating the Impacts of Human Capital Stocks and Accumulation on Economic Growth: Some New Evidence." *Oxford Bulletin of Economics and Statistics* 58(1): 9–28.

Genschel, Philipp. 2001. "Globalization, Tax Competition, and the Fiscal Viability of the Welfare State." Working paper 01/1. Köln: Max Planck Institute for the Study of Societies. Available at: www.mpi-fg-koeln.mpg.de.

Giddens, Anthony. 2000. *The Third Way and Its Critics*. Cambridge: Polity Press.

Gilbert, Neil. 2002. *Transformation of the Welfare State: The Silent Surrender of Public Responsibility*. Oxford: Oxford University Press.

Gilens, Martin. 1999. *Why Americans Hate Welfare*. Chicago: University of Chicago Press.

Ginsburg, Helen. 1983. *Full Employment and Public Policy: The United States and Sweden*. Lexington, Mass.: D. C. Heath.

Glyn, Andrew, and Wiemer Salverda. 2000. "Employment Inequalities." In *Labor Market Inequalities*, edited by Mary Gregory, Wiemer Salverda, and Stephen Bazen. Oxford: Oxford University Press.

Golden, Miriam, Peter Lange, and Michael Wallerstein. 1997. "Union Centralization Among Advanced Industrial Societies: An Empirical Study." Dataset (November 2, 1998 version). Available at: www.shelley.polisci.ucla.edu/data.

Gomez, Rafael, and Noah Meltz. 2001. "The Zero Sum Illusion: Industrial Relations and Modern Economic Approaches to Growth and Income Distribution." Paper presented to the Conference on Linkages between Economic Growth and Inequality. Institute for Research on Public Policy—Centre for the Study of Living Standards, Ottawa (January 26–27, 2001). Available at: www.irpp.org/events/index.htm.

Goodin, Robert E. 2001. "Work and Welfare: Towards a Post-productivist Welfare Regime." *British Journal of Political Science* 31(1): 13–39.

Goodin, Robert E., Bruce Headey, Ruud Muffels, and Henk-Jan Dirven. 1999. *The Real Worlds of Welfare Capitalism*. Cambridge: Cambridge University Press.

Gornick, Janet C., and Marcia K. Meyers. 2003. *Families That Work: Policies for Reconciling Parenthood and Employment*. New York: Russell Sage Foundation.

Gorter, Cees. 2000. "The Dutch Miracle?" In *Why Deregulate Labor Markets?* edited by Gøsta Esping-Andersen and Marino Regini. Oxford: Oxford University Press.

Gottschalk, Peter. 1998. "The Impact of Changes in Public Employment on Low-wage Labor Markets." In *Generating Jobs: How to Increase Demand for Less-Skilled Workers*, edited by Richard B. Freeman and Peter Gottschalk. New York: Russell Sage Foundation.

Gottschalk, Peter, and Sheldon Danziger. 1998. "Family Income Mobility: How Much Is There and Has It Changed?" In *The Inequality Paradox: Growth of Income Disparity*, edited by James A. Auerbach and Richard S. Belous. Washington, D.C.: National Academy Press.

———. 2003. "Wage Inequality, Earnings Inequality, and Poverty in the United States over the Last Quarter of the Twentieth Century." Unpublished paper. Boston College and University of Michigan, Ann Arbor.

Gottschall, Karin, and Katherine Bird. 2003. "Family Leave Policies and Labor Market Segregation in Germany: Reinvention or Reform of the Male Breadwinner?" *Review of Policy Research* 20(1): 115–34.

Gough, Ian. 1996. "Social Welfare and Competitiveness." *New Political Economy* 1: 209–32.

Goul Andersen, Jørgen. 2002. "Denmark: From the Edge of the Abyss to a Sustainable Welfare State." In *Europe's New State of Welfare: Unemployment, Employment Policies, and Citizenship*, edited by Jørgen Goul Andersen, Jochen Clasen, Wim van Oorschot, and Knut Halvorsen. Bristol, Eng.: Policy Press.

Goul Andersen, Jørgen, and Jan Bendix Jensen. 2002. "Employment and Unemployment in Europe: Overview and New Trends." In *Europe's New State of Welfare: Unemployment, Employment Policies, and Citizenship*, edited by Jørgen Goul Andersen, Jochen Clasen, Wim van Oorschot, and Knut Halvorsen. Bristol, Eng.: Policy Press.

Goul Andersen, Jørgen, Per Arnt Pettersen, Stefan Svallfors, and Hannu Uusitalo. 1999. "The Legitimacy of the Nordic Welfare States: Trends, Variations, and Cleavages." In *Nordic Social Policy*, edited by Mikko Kautto, Matti Heikkilä, Bjørn Hvinden, Staffan Marklund, and Niels Ploug. London: Routledge.

Gray, Virginia, and David Lowery. 1988. "Interest Group Politics and Economic Growth in the U.S. States." *American Political Science Review* 82(1, March): 109–31.

Greenstein, Robert. 1991. "Universal and Targeted Approaches to Relieving Poverty: An Alternative View." In *The Urban Underclass*, edited by Christopher Jencks and Paul E. Peterson. Washington, D.C.: Brookings Institution.

Gregg, Paul. 1996. "It Takes Two: Employment Polarization in the OECD." Discussion paper 304. London: Centre for Economic Performance. Available at: cep.lse.ac.uk/pubs.

Grubb, David. 2000–2001. "Eligibility Criteria for Unemployment Benefits." *OECD Economic Studies* 31: 147–84.

Gustafsson, Bjorn, and Mats Johansson. 1999. "In Search of Smoking Guns: What Makes Income Inequality Vary over Time in Different Countries?" *American Sociological Review* 64(4, August): 585–605.

Hall, Peter A., and Daniel Gingerich. 2001. "Varieties of Capitalism and Institutional Complementarities in the Macroeconomy: An Empirical Analysis." Unpublished paper. Department of Government, Harvard University, Cambridge, Mass.

Hall, Peter A., and David Soskice. 2001. "An Introduction to Varieties of Capitalism." In *Varieties of Capitalism*, edited by Peter A. Hall and David Soskice. Oxford: Oxford University Press.

Halstead, Ted. 2003. "To Guarantee Universal Coverage, Require It." *New York Times*, January 31.

Hanratty, Maria J., and Rebecca M. Blank. 1992. "Down and Out in North America: Recent Trends in Poverty Rates in the United States and Canada." *Quarterly Journal of Economics* 107(1, February): 233–54.

Hartog, Joop. 1999. "The Netherlands: So What's So Special About the Dutch Model?" Employment and Training Paper 54. International Labor Organization. Available at: www.ilo.org.

Haveman, Robert H. 1997. "Equity with Employment." *Boston Review* (Summer). Available at: bostonreview.net/BR22.3/haveman.html.

Hayek, Friedrich A. 1960. *The Constitution of Liberty*. Chicago: University of Chicago Press.

Helburn, Suzanne, and Barbara R. Bergmann. 2002. *America's Child Care Problem: The Way Out*. New York: Palgrave.

Helliwell, John F. 1998. *How Much Do National Borders Matter?* Washington, D.C.: Brookings Institution.

Hemerijck, Anton, and Martin Schludi. 2000. "Sequences of Policy Failures and Effective Policy Responses." In *Welfare and Work in the Open Economy*, vol. 1, *From Vulnerability to Competitiveness*, edited by Fritz W. Scharpf and Vivien A. Schmidt. Oxford: Oxford University Press.

Hewitt, Christopher. 1977. "The Effect of Political Democracy and Social Democracy on Equality in Industrial Societies: A Cross-national Comparison." *American Sociological Review* 42(3, June): 450–64.

Hicks, Alexander. 1999. *Social Democracy and Welfare Capitalism*. Ithaca, N.Y.: Cornell University Press.

Hicks, Alexander, and Lane Kenworthy. 1998. "Cooperation and Political Economic Performance in Affluent Democratic Capitalism." *American Journal of Sociology* 103(6, May): 1631–72.

———. 2003. "Varieties of Welfare Capitalism." *Socioeconomic Review* 1: 27–61.

Hicks, Alexander, and Duane Swank. 1984. "Governmental Redistribution in Rich Capitalist Democracies." *Policy Studies Journal* 13: 265–86.

Hills, John. 2003. "The Blair Government and Child Poverty: An Extra One Percent for Children in the United Kingdom." In *One Percent for the Kids*, edited by Isabel V. Sawhill. Washington, D.C.: Brookings Institution.

Hirsch, Barry T., and David A. Macpherson. Various years. *Union Membership and Earnings Data Book*. Washington, D.C.: Bureau of National Affairs.

Hoffman, Saul D., and Laurence S. Seidman. 2003. *Helping Working Families: The Earned Income Tax Credit*. Kalamazoo, Mich.: Upjohn Institute for Employment Research.

Hotz, V. Joseph, and John Karl Scholz. 2000. "Not Perfect, but Still Pretty Good: The EITC and Other Policies to Support the U.S. Low-wage Labor Market." *OECD Economic Studies* 31: 25–42.

Houseman, Susan N. 1998. "The Effects of Employer Mandates." In *Generating Jobs: How to Increase Demand for Less-Skilled Workers*, edited by Richard B. Freeman and Peter Gottschalk. New York: Russell Sage Foundation.

Howell, David R. 2002. "Increasing Earnings Inequality and Unemployment in Developed Countries: Markets, Institutions, and the `Unified Theory.'" *Politics and Society* 30(2): 193–243.

Huber, Evelyne, Charles Ragin, and John D. Stephens. 1997. "Comparative Welfare States Dataset." Updated April 2001 by David Brady and Jason Beckfield. Northwestern University and University of North Carolina.

Huber, Evelyne, and John D. Stephens. 2001. *Development and Crisis of the Welfare State*. Chicago: University of Chicago Press.

Iceland, John. 2003. *Poverty in America*. Berkeley: University of California Press.

IAMC (Industrial Asset Management Council). Various years. *Industrial Devel-*

opment and Site Selection Handbook (known as *Site Selection Handbook* prior to 1985). Atlanta: Conway Data.

Institute of Medicine. 2002. *Care Without Coverage: Too Little, Too Late.* Washington, D.C.: National Academy Press.

ISSP (International Social Survey Program). 1992. *International Social Survey Program: Social Inequality, 1992.* Available at: www.icpsr.umich.edu.

———. 1999. *International Social Survey Program: Social Inequality III, 1999.* Available at Inter-university Consortium for Political and Social Research, www.icpsr.umich.edu.

Iversen, Torben. 1999. *Contested Economic Institutions.* Cambridge: Cambridge University Press.

Iversen, Torben, and Thomas R. Cusack. 2000. "The Causes of Welfare State Expansion: Deindustrialization or Globalization?" *World Politics* 52(3, April): 313–49.

Iversen, Torben, and Anne Wren. 1998. "Equality, Employment, and Budgetary Restraint: The Trilemma of the Service Economy." *World Politics* 50(4): 507–46.

Jackman, Robert W. 1985. "Cross-national Statistical Research and the Study of Politics." *American Journal of Political Science* 29(1, February): 161–82.

Jencks, Christopher. 2002. "Does Inequality Matter?" *Daedalus* (Winter): 49–65.

Jencks, Christopher, and Kathryn Edin. 1995. "Do Poor Women Have the Right To Bear Children?" *The American Prospect* (20, Spring): 31–50.

Johnson, Nicholas, Joseph Llobrera, and Bob Zahradnik. 2003. "A Hand Up: How State Earned Income Tax Credits Help Working Families Escape Poverty in 2003." Washington, D.C.: Center on Budget and Policy Priorities. Available at: www.cbpp.org.

Kahneman, Daniel, Jack L. Knetsch, and Richard H. Thaler. 1991. "Fairness and the Assumptions of Economics." In *Quasi Rational Economics,* edited by Richard H. Thaler. New York: Russell Sage Foundation.

Kaldor, Nicholas. 1956. "Alternative Theories of Distribution." *Review of Economic Studies* 23(2): 83–100.

———. 1957. "A Model of Economic Growth." *Economic Journal* 67(268, December): 591–624.

Kamerman, Sheila B., and Alfred J. Kahn. 1995. *Starting Right: How America Neglects Its Youngest Children and What We Can Do About It.* New York: Oxford University Press.

Kane, Thomas J. 2001. "College-Going and Inequality: A Literature Review." Working paper. Russell Sage Foundation. Available at: www.russellsage.org/special_interest/socialinequality/revkane01.pdf.

Katz, Claudio J., Vincent A. Mahler, and Michael G. Franz. 1983. "The Impact of Taxes on Growth and Distribution in Developed Capitalist Countries: A Cross-national Study." *American Political Science Review* 77(4, December): 871–86.

Katz, Lawrence F. 1998. "Wage Subsidies for the Disadvantaged." In *Generating Jobs: How to Increase Demand for Less-Skilled Workers,* edited by Richard B. Freeman and Peter Gottschalk. New York: Russell Sage Foundation.

Kaus, Mickey. 1992. *The End of Equality.* New York: Basic Books.

Kautto, Mikko, Matti Heikkilä, Bjørn Hvinden, Staffan Marklund, and Niels Ploug, eds. 1999. *Nordic Social Policy*. London: Routledge.

Keil, Manfred, Donald Robertson, and James Symons. 2001. "Minimum Wages and Employment." Discussion paper 497. London: Centre for Economic Performance. Available at: www.cep.lse.ac.uk/pubs.

Kelley, Jonathan, and M. D. R. Evans. 1993. "The Legitimation of Inequality: Occupational Earnings in Nine Nations." *American Journal of Sociology* 99(1, July): 75–125.

Keman, Hans. 2003. "Explaining Miracles: Third Ways and Work and Welfare." *West European Politics* 26(2): 115–35.

Kenworthy, Lane. 1995. *In Search of National Economic Success: Balancing Competition and Cooperation*. Thousand Oaks, Calif.: Sage Publications.

———. 1999a. "Do Social Welfare Policies Reduce Poverty? A Cross-national Assessment." *Social Forces* 77(3): 1119–39.

———. 1999b. "Economic Integration and Convergence: A Look at the U.S. States." *Social Science Quarterly* 80(4): 858–69.

———. 2001a. "Wage-Setting Coordination Scores." Dataset (version dated June 17, 2001). Available at: www.emory.edu/SOC/lkenworthy.

———. 2001b. "Wage-Setting Measures: A Survey and Assessment." *World Politics* 54(1): 57–98.

———. 2002a. "Corporatism and Unemployment in the 1980s and 1990s." *American Sociological Review* 67(3): 367–88.

———. 2002b. "Institutional Coherence and Macroeconomic Performance: A Comment." Unpublished paper. Available at: www.emory.edu/SOC/lkenworthy.

———. 2003. "Do Affluent Countries Face an Incomes-Jobs Trade-off?" *Comparative Political Studies* 36(10): 1180–1209.

———. Forthcoming. "Is Rising Inequality Due to a Surge in Incomes at the Top?" *Indicators: The Journal of Social Health*.

Kenworthy, Lane, and Jonas Pontusson. 2004. "Inegalitarian Market Trends and the Politics of Compensatory Redistribution in OECD Countries." Unpublished paper. Department of Sociology, Emory University; Department of Government, Cornell University.

Kim, Hwanjoon. 2000. "Antipoverty Effectiveness of Taxes and Income Transfers in Welfare States." *International Social Security Review* 53(4): 105–29.

Kittel, Bernhard. 1999. "Sense and Sensitivity in Pooled Analysis of Political Data." *European Journal of Political Research* 35(2): 225–53.

Kittel, Bernhard, and Herbert Obinger. 2001. "Political Parties, Institutions, and Welfare State Dynamics in Times of Austerity." Discussion paper 02/1. Köln: Max Planck Institute for the Study of Societies. Available at: www.mpi-fg-koeln.mpg.de.

Knack, Stephen, and Philip Keefer. 1997. "Does Social Capital Have an Economic Payoff? A Cross-country Investigation." *Quarterly Journal of Economics* 112: 1251–88.

Korpi, Walter. 1983. *The Democratic Class Struggle*. London: Routledge.

———. 1991. "Political and Economic Explanations for Unemployment: A

Cross-national and Long-term Analysis." *British Journal of Political Science* 21(3, July): 315–48.

Korpi, Walter, and Joakim Palme. 1998. "The Paradox of Redistribution and Strategies of Equality: Welfare State Institutions, Inequality, and Poverty in the Western Countries." *American Sociological Review* 63(5, October): 661–87.

Kozol, Jonathan. 1991. *Savage Inequalities: Children in America's Schools.* New York: Crown.

Krugman, Paul. 1996. "The Causes of High Unemployment." *Policy Options* (July–August): 20–24.

———. 2002. "For Richer." *New York Times Magazine*, October 20.

———. 2003. *The Great Unraveling: Losing Our Way in the New Century.* New York: W. W. Norton.

Kuhnle, Stein. 2000. "The Scandinavian Welfare State in the 1990s: Challenged but Viable." *West European Politics* 23(2): 209–28.

Kuznets, Simon. 1955. "Economic Growth and Income Inequality." *American Economic Review* 45(1, March): 1–28.

Kvist, Jon, and Niels Ploug. 2003. "Active Labor Market Policies: When Do They Work? And Where Do They Fail?" Paper presented to the annual meeting of Research Committee 19 of the International Sociological Association, Toronto (August).

Lansbury, Russell, and John Niland. 1995. "Managed Decentralization? Recent Trends in Australian Industrial Relations and Human Resource Policies." In *Employment Relations in a Changing World Economy*, edited by Richard Locke, Thomas Kochan, and Michael Piore. Cambridge, Mass.: MIT Press.

Lazear, Edward P. 1989. "Pay Equality and Industrial Politics." *Journal of Political Economy* 97(3, June): 561–80.

Leamer, Edward E. 1983. "Let's Take the Con out of Econometrics." *American Economic Review* 73(1, March): 31–43.

———. 1985. "Sensitivity Analyses Would Help." *American Economic Review* 75(3, June): 308–13.

Leicht, Kevin T., and J. Craig Jenkins. 1998. "Political Resources and Direct State Intervention: The Adoption of Public Venture Capital Programs in the American States, 1974–1990." *Social Forces* 76(4): 1323–45.

Leisering, Lutz, and Stephan Leibfried. 1999. *Time and Poverty in Western Welfare States.* Cambridge: Cambridge University Press.

Letwin, William. 1983. "The Case Against Equality." In *Against Equality*, edited by William Letwin. London: Macmillan.

Levine, David I. 1991. "Cohesiveness, Productivity, and Wage Dispersion." *Journal of Economic Behavior and Organization* 15(2): 237–55.

Levine, Ross, and David Renelt. 1992. "A Sensitivity Analysis of Cross-country Growth Regressions." *American Economic Review* 82(4, September): 942–63.

Levy, Frank. 1998. *The New Dollars and Dreams.* New York: Russell Sage Foundation.

Lindbeck, Assar. 1995. "Hazardous Welfare State Dynamics." *American Economic Review* 85(2, May): 9–15.

———. 1997. "The Swedish Experiment." *Journal of Economic Literature* 35(3, September): 1273–1319.

Lindert, Peter. 2003. "Why the Welfare State Looks Like a Free Lunch." Working paper 9869. Cambridge, Mass.: National Bureau of Economic Research. Available at www.nber.org.

Madsen, Per Kongshøj. 1999. "Denmark: Flexibility, Security, and Labor Market Success." Employment and Training Paper 53. International Labor Organization. Available at: www.ilo.org.

Manow, Philip, and Eric Seils. 2000a. "Adjusting Badly: The German Welfare State, Structural Change, and the Open Economy." In *Welfare and Work in the Open Economy*, vol. 2: *Diverse Responses to Common Challenges*, edited by Fritz W. Scharpf and Vivien A. Schmidt. Oxford: Oxford University Press.

———. 2000b. "The Employment Crisis of the German Welfare State." *West European Politics* 23(2): 137–60.

Marklund, Staffan, and Anders Nordlund. 1999. "Economic Problems, Welfare Convergence, and Political Instability." In *Nordic Social Policy*, edited by Mikko Kautto, Matti Heikkilä, Bjørn Hvinden, Staffan Marklund, and Niels Ploug. London: Routledge.

Martin, John P. 1996. "Measures of Replacement Rates for the Purpose of International Comparisons: A Note." *OECD Economic Studies* 26: 99–115.

———. 2000–2001. "What Works Among Active Labor Market Policies: Evidence from OECD Countries' Experiences." *OECD Economic Studies* 30: 79–113.

Mayer, Susan E. 1995. "A Comparison of Poverty and Living Conditions in the United States, Canada, Sweden, and Germany." In *Poverty, Inequality, and the Future of Social Policy*, edited by Katherine McFate, Roger Lawson, and William Julius Wilson. New York: Russell Sage Foundation.

———. 2001. "How Did the Increase in Economic Inequality Between 1970 and 1990 Affect Children's Educational Attainment?" *American Journal of Sociology* 107: 1–32.

Mayer, Susan E., and Christopher Jencks. 1989. "Poverty and the Distribution of Material Hardship." *Journal of Human Resources* 24: 88–114.

McCloskey, Deirdre N., and Stephen T. Ziliak. 1996. "The Standard Error of Regressions." *Journal of Economic Literature* 34(1, March): 97–114.

McMurrer, Daniel P., and Isabel V. Sawhill. 1998. *Getting Ahead: Economic and Social Mobility in America*. Washington, D.C.: Urban Institute.

Meyer, Bruce D., and Douglas Holtz-Eakin. 2002. "Introduction." In *Making Work Pay: The Earned Income Tax Credit and Its Impact on America's Families*, edited by Bruce D. Meyer and Douglas Holtz-Eakin. New York: Russell Sage Foundation.

Meyer, Bruce D., and Dan T. Rosenbaum. 2002. "Making Single Mothers Work: Recent Tax and Welfare Policy and Its Effects." In *Making Work Pay: The Earned Income Tax Credit and Its Impact on America's Families*, edited by Bruce D. Meyer and Douglas Holtz-Eakin. New York: Russell Sage Foundation.

Miller, Matthew. 2003. *The Two Percent Solution*. New York: Public Affairs.

Mirrlees, J. A. 1971. "An Exploration into the Theory of Optimum Income Taxation." *Review of Economic Studies* 38(2, April): 175–208.

Mishel, Lawrence, Jared Bernstein, and Heather Boushey. 2003. *The State of*

Working America, 2002–2003. Ithaca, N.Y.: ILR Press/Economic Policy Institute.

Mishel, Lawrence, Jared Bernstein, and John Schmitt. 2001. *The State of Working America, 2000–2001*. Ithaca, N.Y.: ILR Press/Economic Policy Institute.

Mitchell, Deborah. 1991. *Income Transfers in Ten Welfare States*. Brookfield, Mass.: Avebury.

Moffitt, Robert A. 2003. "The Negative Income Tax and the Evolution of U.S. Welfare Policy." *Journal of Economic Perspectives* 17(3): 119–40.

Moller, Stephanie, David Bradley, Evelyne Huber, François Nielsen, and John D. Stephens. 2003. "Determinants of Relative Poverty in Advanced Capitalist Democracies." *American Sociological Review* 68(1): 22–51.

Morgan, Kimberly, and Kathrin Zippel. 2003. "Paid to Care: The Origins and Effects of Care Leave Policies in Western Europe." *Social Politics* 10(1): 49–85.

Morris, Martina, and Bruce Western. 1999. "Inequality in Earnings at the Close of the Twentieth Century." *Annual Review of Sociology* 25: 623–57.

Mosher, Jim. 2002. "Testing Political and Neoclassical Economic Explanations of Wage Inequality." Ch. 5 of Ph.D. diss., Department of Political Science, University of Wisconsin, Madison.

Mullahy, John, and Barbara L. Wolfe. 2001. "Health Policies for the Non-Elderly Poor." In *Understanding Poverty*, edited by Sheldon H. Danziger and Robert H. Haveman. New York: Russell Sage Foundation; Cambridge, Mass.: Harvard University Press.

Muller, Edward N. 1989. "Distribution of Income in Advanced Capitalist States: Political Parties, Labor Unions, and the International Economy." *European Journal of Political Research* 17: 367–400.

Murray, Charles. 1984. *Losing Ground: American Social Policy, 1950–1980*. New York: Basic Books.

Musco, Thomas D., and Thomas F. Wildsmith. 2002. "Individual Health Insurance: Access and Affordability." Briefing paper. Health Insurance Association of America. Available at: www.hiaa.org/research/research_studies.cfm.

Myles, John. 1996. "When Markets Fail: Social Welfare in Canada and the United States." In *Welfare States in Transition*, edited by Gøsta Esping-Andersen. London: Sage Publications.

Myles, John, and Jill Quadagno. 2000. "Envisioning a Third Way: The Welfare State in the Twenty-first Century." *Contemporary Sociology* 29(1, January): 156–67.

Neumark, David. 2002. *How Living Wage Laws Affect Low-wage Workers and Low-income Families*. San Francisco: Public Policy Institute of California (March).

Neumark, David, and William Wascher. 2000. "Minimum Wages and Employment: A Case Study of the Fast-food Industry in New Jersey and Pennsylvania: Comment." *American Economic Review* 90(5, December): 1362–96.

Nickell, Stephen. 1997. "Unemployment and Labor Market Rigidities: Europe Versus North America." *Journal of Economic Perspectives* 11(3): 55–74.

Nickell, Stephen, and Brian Bell. 1996. "Changes in the Distribution of Wages and Unemployment in OECD Countries." *American Economic Review* (AEA Papers and Proceedings) 86: 302–8.

Nickell, Stephen, and Richard Layard. 1999. "Labor Market Institutions and

Economic Performance." In *Handbook of Labor Economics*, vol. 3C, edited by Orley Ashenfelter and David Card. Amsterdam: Elsevier.

Nickell, Stephen, Luca Nunziata, Wolfgang Ochel, and Glenda Quintini. 2001. "The Beveridge Curve, Unemployment, and Wages in the OECD from the 1960s to the 1990s." Discussion paper 502. London: Centre for Economic Performance. Available at: cep.lse.ac.uk/pubs.

Nielsen, François, and Arthur S. Alderson. 2001. "Trends in Income Inequality in the United States." In *Sourcebook of Labor Markets*, edited by Ivar Berg and Arne L. Kalleberg. New York: Plenum.

OECD (Organization for Economic Cooperation and Development). 1994. *The OECD Jobs Study: Evidence and Explanations*. Paris: OECD.

———. 1996a. "Earnings Inequality, Low-paid Employment, and Earnings Mobility." In *OECD Employment Outlook*. Paris: OECD.

———. 1996b. "Making Work Pay." In *OECD Employment Outlook*. Paris: OECD.

———. 1998a. *OECD Education at a Glance: 1998*. Paris: OECD.

———. 1998b. "Recent Labor Market Developments and Prospects." In *OECD Employment Outlook*. Paris: OECD.

———. 1999a. *Education Policy Analysis*. Paris: OECD.

———. 1999b. "Recent Labor Market Developments and Prospects: Special Focus on the Quality of Part-time Jobs." In *OECD Employment Outlook*. Paris: OECD.

———. 2000. "Employment in the Service Economy: A Reassessment." In *OECD Employment Outlook*. Paris: OECD.

———. 2001a. "The Characteristics and Quality of Service-Sector Jobs." In *OECD Employment Outlook*. Paris: OECD.

———. 2001b. *OECD Education at a Glance: 2001*. Paris: OECD.

———. 2001c. *OECD Social Expenditure Database: 1980–1998*. Paris: OECD.

———. 2001d. *Starting Strong: Early Childhood Education and Care*. Paris: OECD. Available at: www1.oecd.org/publications/e-book/9101011e/pdf.

———. 2001e. "When Money Is Tight: Poverty Dynamics in OECD Countries." In *OECD Employment Outlook*. Paris: OECD.

———. 2002a. *Babies and Bosses: Reconciling Work and Family Life*, vol. 1, *Australia, Denmark, and the Netherlands*. Paris: OECD.

———. 2002b. *Benefits and Wages: OECD Indicators*. Paris: OECD.

———. 2002c. "Recent Labor Market Developments and Prospects." In *OECD Employment Outlook*. Paris: OECD.

———. 2003a. *OECD Employment Outlook: Towards More and Better Jobs*. Paris: OECD.

———. 2003b. *OECD Statistical Compendium*. Paris: OECD.

———. Various years[a]. *OECD Employment Outlook*. Paris: OECD.

———. Various years[b]. *OECD Historical Statistics*. Paris: OECD.

———. Various years[c]. *Labor Force Statistics*. Paris: OECD.

———. N.d.[a]. "OECD Database on Benefit Entitlements and Replacement Rates." Dataset. Paris: OECD.

———. N.d.[b]. "OECD Database on Trends in Earnings Dispersion." Dataset. Paris: OECD.

———. N.d.[c]. "Purchasing Power Parities for GDP: Historical Series." Dataset. Paris: OECD.

Okun, Arthur M. 1975. *Equality and Efficiency: The Big Trade-off.* Washington, D.C.: Brookings Institution.

Olsen, Gregg M. 2002. *The Politics of the Welfare State: Canada, Sweden, and the United States.* Oxford: Oxford University Press.

Olson, Mancur. 1982. *The Rise and Decline of Nations.* New Haven, Conn.: Yale University Press.

Orloff, Ann Shola. 2002. "Women's Employment and Welfare Regimes." Social Policy and Development Paper 12. New York: United Nations Research Institute for Social Development.

Osberg, Lars. 1984. *Economic Inequality in the United States.* Armonk, N.Y.: M. E. Sharpe.

Osterman, Paul. 1988. *Employment Futures.* Oxford: Oxford University Press.

———. 1999. *Securing Prosperity.* Princeton, N.J.: Princeton University Press.

———. 2003. "Organizing the U.S. Labor Market: National Problems, Community Strategies." In *Governing Work and Welfare in a New Economy,* edited by Jonathan Zeitlin and David M. Trubek. Oxford: Oxford University Press.

Page, Benjamin I., and James R. Simmons. 2000. *What Government Can Do: Dealing with Poverty and Inequality.* Chicago: University of Chicago Press.

Palier, Bruno. 2000. "'Defrosting' the French Welfare State." *West European Politics* 23(2): 113–36.

Palley, Thomas I. 2001. "The Role of Institutions and Policies in Creating High European Unemployment." Working paper 336. New York: Jerome Levy Institute. Available at: http://www.levy.org/2/index.asp?interface=standard& screen=publications_preview&datasrc=f73a204134 (accessed February 12, 2004).

Palme, Joakim, Åke Bergmark, Olof Bäckman, Felipe Estrada, Johan Fritzell, Olle Lundberg, Ola Sjöberg, Lena Sommestad, and Marta Szebehely. 2002. *Welfare in Sweden: The Balance Sheet for the 1990s.* Stockholm: Ministry of Health and Social Affairs.

Perotti, Roberto. 1996. "Growth, Income Distribution, and Democracy: What the Data Say." *Journal of Economic Growth* 1: 149–87.

Persson, Torsten, and Guido Tabellini. 1994. "Is Inequality Harmful for Growth?" *American Economic Review* 84(3, June): 600–21.

Pfaller, Alfred, Ian Gough, and Goran Therborn, eds. 1991. *Can the Welfare State Compete?* London: Macmillan.

Phelps, Edmund S. 1996. *Rewarding Work.* Cambridge, Mass.: Harvard University Press.

Phillips, Kevin. 2002. *Wealth and Democracy: A Political History of the American Rich.* New York: Broadway Books.

Physicians for a National Health Program. 2003. "Proposal of the Physicians' Working Group for Single-Payer National Health Insurance." Chicago: Physicians for a National Health Program (August 13). Available at: www.pnhp.org/publications.

Picketty, Thomas, and Emmanuel Saez. 2001. "Income Inequality in the United States, 1913–1998." Working paper 8467. Cambridge, Mass.: National Bureau of Economic Research (September). Available at www.nber.org/papers/w8467.

Pierson, Paul. 1996. "The New Politics of the Welfare State." *World Politics* 48(2, January): 143–79.

———, ed. 2001. *The New Politics of the Welfare State.* Oxford: Oxford University Press.

Ploug, Niels. 1999. "Cuts in and Reform of the Nordic Cash Benefit Systems." In *Nordic Social Policy*, edited by Mikko Kautto, Matti Heikkilä, Bjørn Hvinden, Staffan Marklund, and Niels Ploug. London: Routledge.

Plümper, Thomas, Vera Troeger, and Philip Manow. Forthcoming. "Panel Data Analysis in Comparative Politics: Linking Method to Theory." *European Journal of Political Research.*

Pontusson, Jonas. Forthcoming. *Social Europe Versus Liberal America.* New York: Century Foundation.

Porter, Michael. 1990. *The Competitive Advantage of Nations.* New York: Free Press.

Prais, Sigmund J., Valerie Jarvis, and Karin Wagner. 1989. "Productivity and Vocational Skills in Services in Britain and Germany: Hotels." *National Institute Economic Review* (November): 52–74.

Putnam, Robert D. 2000. *Bowling Alone: The Collapse and Revival of American Community.* New York: Simon & Schuster.

Rawls, John. 1971. *A Theory of Justice.* Cambridge, Mass.: Harvard University Press.

Rehn, Gøsta. 1985. "Swedish Active Labor Market Policy: Retrospect and Prospect." *Industrial Relations* 24: 62–89.

Reich, Robert. 1999. "We Are All Third Wayers Now." *The American Prospect* (March–April). Available at: www.prospect.org/print/V10/43/reich-r.html.

Rhodes, Martin. 1996. "Globalization and West European Welfare States: A Critical Review of Recent Debates." *Journal of European Social Policy* 6: 305–27.

———. 2000. "Restructuring the British Welfare State: Between Domestic Constraints and Global Imperatives." In *Welfare and Work in the Open Economy*, vol. 2, *Diverse Responses to Common Challenges*, edited by Fritz W. Scharpf and Vivien A. Schmidt. Oxford: Oxford University Press.

Roemer, John E. 1997. *Equality of Opportunity.* Cambridge, Mass.: Harvard University Press.

Rothstein, Bo. 1998. *Just Institutions Matter: The Moral and Political Logic of the Universal Welfare State.* Cambridge: Cambridge University Press.

Rueda, David, and Jonas Pontusson. 2000. "Wage Inequality and Varieties of Capitalism." *World Politics* 52(3, April): 350–83.

Sainsbury, Diane. 1999a. "Gender and Social-Democratic Welfare States." In *Gender and Welfare State Regimes*, edited by Diane Sainsbury. Oxford: Oxford University Press.

———. 1999b. "Taxation, Family Responsibilities, and Employment." In *Gender and Welfare State Regimes*, edited by Diane Sainsbury. Oxford: Oxford University Press.

Sainsbury, Diane, and Ann Morissens. 2002. "Poverty in Europe in the Mid-1990s: The Effectiveness of Means-Tested Benefits." *Journal of European Social Policy* 12(4): 307–27.

Sala-i-Martin, Xavier. 1997. "I Just Ran Four Million Regressions." Working paper 6252. Cambridge, Mass.: National Bureau of Economic Research (November). Available at www.nber.org/papers/w6252.

Salverda, Wiemer. 1998. "Incidence and Evolution of Low-wage Employment in the Netherlands and the United States, 1979–1989." In *Low-wage Employment in Europe*, edited by Stephen Bazen, Mary Gregory, and Wiemer Salverda. Northampton, Mass.: Edward Elger.

Salverda, Wiemer, Stephen Bazen, and Mary Gregory. 2001. *The European-American Employment Gap, Wage Inequality, Earnings Mobility, and Skill: A Study for France, Germany, the Netherlands, the United Kingdom, and the United States*. European Low-wage Employment Research Network. Available at: www.uva-aias.net/lower.asp.

Samuelson, Robert J. 1996. "Why America Creates Jobs." *Newsweek*, July 29, 49.

Saunders, Peter. 2002. *The Ends and Means of Welfare: Coping with Economic and Social Change in Australia*. Cambridge: Cambridge University Press.

Sawhill, Isabel V. 1988. "Poverty in the United States: Why Is It So Persistent?" *Journal of Economic Literature* 26(3, September): 1073–1119.

Scarpetta, Stefano. 1996. "Assessing the Role of Labor Market Policies and Institutional Settings on Unemployment: A Cross-country Study." *OECD Economic Studies* 26: 43–98.

Scharpf, Fritz W. 1997. "Employment and the Welfare State: A Continental Dilemma." Working paper 97/7. Köln: Max Planck Institute for the Study of Societies. Available at: www.mpi-fg-koeln.mpg.de.

———. 2000. "Economic Changes, Vulnerabilities, and Institutional Capabilities." In *Welfare and Work in the Open Economy*, vol. 1, *From Vulnerability to Competitiveness*, edited by Fritz W. Scharpf and Vivien A. Schmidt. Oxford: Oxford University Press.

Scharpf, Fritz W., and Vivien A. Schmidt. 2000. "Conclusions." In *Welfare and Work in the Open Economy*, vol. 1, *From Vulnerability to Competitiveness*, edited by Fritz W. Scharpf and Vivien A. Schmidt. Oxford: Oxford University Press.

Schiller, Bradley R. 2001. *The Economics of Poverty and Discrimination*. 8th ed. Upper Saddle River, N.J.: Prentice-Hall.

Schmid, Günther. 1993. "Equality and Efficiency in the Labor Market: Towards a Socioeconomic Theory of Cooperation in the Globalizing Economy." *Journal of Socioeconomics* 22(1): 31–67.

Schor, Juliet B. 1999. *The Overspent American: Why We Want What We Don't Need*. New York: HarperCollins.

Schwartz, Herman M. 2000. "Internationalization and Two Liberal Welfare States: Australia and New Zealand." In *Welfare and Work in the Open Economy*, vol. 2, *Diverse Responses to Common Challenges*, edited by Fritz W. Scharpf and Vivien A. Schmidt. New York: Oxford University Press.

———. 2002. "Internationalization and Two Liberal Welfare States: Australia and New Zealand." In *Welfare and Work in the Open Economy*, vol. 2: *Diverse Responses to Common Challenges*, edited by Fritz W. Scharpf and Vivien A. Schmidt. Oxford: Oxford University Press.

Schwarz, John E., and Thomas J. Volgy. 1992. *The Forgotten Americans*. New York: W. W. Norton.

Sen, Amartya. 1976. "Poverty: An Ordinal Approach to Measurement." *Econometrica* 44(2, March): 219–31.

Shonkoff, Jack P., and Deborah A. Phillips, eds. 2000. *From Neurons to Neighborhoods: The Science of Early Childhood Development.* Washington, D.C.: National Academy Press.

Siebert, Horst. 1997. "Labor Market Rigidities: At the Root of Unemployment in Europe." *Journal of Economic Perspectives* 11(3): 37–54.

Skocpol, Theda. 2000. *The Missing Middle: Working Families and the Future of American Social Policy.* New York: W. W. Norton.

Slemrod, Joel. 2003. "The Truth About Taxes and Economic Growth." *Challenge* (January–February): 5–14.

Smeeding, Timothy M. 1992. "Why the U.S. Antipoverty System Doesn't Work Very Well." *Challenge* (January–February): 30–35.

———. 1998. "U.S. Income Inequality in a Cross-national Perspective: Why Are We So Different?" In *The Inequality Paradox*, edited by James A. Auerbach and Richard S. Belous. Washington, D.C.: National Policy Association.

Smeeding, Timothy M., and Lee Rainwater. 2002. "Comparing Living Standards Across Nations: Real Incomes at the Top, the Bottom, and the Middle." Working paper 266. Luxembourg Income Study (February). Available at: www.lisproject.org/publications.htm.

Smeeding, Timothy M., Lee Rainwater, and Gary Burtless. 2001. "U.S. Poverty in a Cross-national Context." In *Understanding Poverty*, edited by Sheldon H. Danziger and Robert H. Haveman. New York and Cambridge, Mass.: Russell Sage Foundation and Harvard University Press.

Smith, Kristin. 2002. "Who's Minding the Kids? Child Care Arrangements, Fall 1997." Current Population Reports P70–86. Washington: U.S. Bureau of the Census (Spring). Available at: www.census.gov/prod/2002pubs/p70-86.pdf.

Smith, Michael R. 1999. "Doing Well by Doing Good? What Happened to Corporatist Countries in the 1990s, and Why?" Paper presented to the annual meeting of the Society for the Advancement of Socioeconomics, Madison, Wisc. (June 1999).

———. 2002. "Income Inequality and Economic Growth in Rich Countries: A Reconsideration of the Evidence." *Current Sociology* 50(4, July): 573–93.

Solow, Robert M. 1990. *The Labor Market as a Social Institution.* Cambridge, Mass.: Basil Blackwell.

Steinmo, Sven. 2002. "Globalization and Taxation: Challenges to the Swedish Welfare State." *Comparative Political Studies* 35(7, September): 839–62.

Stephens, John D. 1979. *The Transition from Capitalism to Socialism.* London: Macmillan.

Stiglitz, Joseph. 1969. "The Distribution of Income and Wealth Among Individuals." *Econometrica* 37(3, August): 382–97.

Streeck, Wolfgang. 1997. "German Capitalism: Does It Exist? Can It Survive?" *New Political Economy* 2(2): 237–56.

———. 2001. "High Equality, Low Activity: The Contribution of the Social Welfare System to the Stability of the German Collective Bargaining Regime." *Industrial and Labor Relations Review* 54: 698–705.

————. Forthcoming. "From State Weakness as Strength to State Weakness as Weakness." In *Semisovereignty Revisited: Governance, Institutions, and Policies in United Germany*, edited by Simon Green and Willie Paterson.

Swank, Duane. 2002. *Global Capital, Political Institutions, and Policy Change in Developed Welfare States*. Cambridge: Cambridge University Press.

Swenson, Peter. 1989. *Fair Shares: Unions, Pay, and Politics in Sweden and West Germany*. Ithaca, N.Y.: Cornell University Press.

Taylor-Gooby, Peter, Anne Daguerre, and Trine Larsen. 2003. "The Genuinely Liberal Genuine Welfare State." Unpublished paper. Department of Social Policy, University of Kent.

Thurow, Lester C. 1981. "Equity, Efficiency, Social Justice, and Redistribution." In *The Welfare State in Crisis*. Paris: OECD.

Traxler, Franz, Sabine Blaschke, and Bernhard Kittel. 2001. *National Labor Relations in Internationalized Markets*. Oxford: Oxford University Press.

Trubek, Louise G. 2003. "Health Care and Low-wage Work in the United States: Linking Local Action for Expanded Coverage." In *Governing Work and Welfare in a New Economy*, edited by Jonathan Zeitlin and David M. Trubek. Oxford: Oxford University Press.

Tullock, Gordon. 1997. "The Reality of Redistribution." In *Poverty and Inequality*, edited by Jon Neill. Kalamazoo, Mich.: Upjohn Institute for Employment Research.

U.S. Bureau of the Census. Various years. *Statistical Abstract of the United States*. Washington: U.S. Government Printing Office. Available at: www.census. gov/statab/www.

————. N.d.[a]. *Historical Income Tables*. Washington: U.S. Government Printing Office. Available at: www.census.gov/hhes/income/histinc.

————. N.d.[b]. *Historical Poverty Tables*. Washington: U.S. Government Printing Office. Available at: www.census.gov/hhes/poverty/histpov.

U.S. Congress. Office of Technology Assessment. 1990. *Making Things Better: Competing in Manufacturing*. Washington: U.S. Government Printing Office.

U.S. Department of Agriculture. Food and Nutrition Service. 2003. *Food Stamp Program Annual Summary*. Available at: www.fns.usda.gov/pd/fssummar. htm.

U.S. Department of Commerce. Bureau of Economic Analysis. 2003. *2003 Comprehensive Revision of the National Income and Product Accounts*. www.bea. doc.gov/bea/dn1.htm.

————. N.d.[a]. *Regional Economic Accounts*. Available at: www.bea.doc.gov/ bea/regional/data.htm.

————. N.d.[b]. *National Economic Accounts*. Available at: www.bea.doc.gov/ bea/dn/nipaweb/Index.asp.

U.S. Department of Health and Human Services. Administration for Children and Families. N.d. *ACF Data and Statistics*. Available at: www.acf.hhs. gov/news/stats/3697.htm.

U.S. Department of Labor. Bureau of Labor Statistics. N.d.[a]. "Comparative Civilian Labor Force Statistics, Ten Countries, 1959–2000." Available at: stats.bls.gov.

———. N.d.[b]. *Current Employment Survey.* Available at: stats.bls.gov/sae/home.htm.

———. N.d.[c]. *U.S. Bureau of Labor Statistics Data.* Available at: www.bls.gov/data.

———. N.d.[d]. *Productivity and Costs.* Available at: www.bls.gov/lpc/home.htm#data.

U.S. National Center for Health Statistics. N.d. *Health Care Coverage and Utilization.* Available at: www.cdc.gov/nchs/SSBR/024para.htm.

Van Arnhem, J. Cornia M., and Geurt J. Schotsman. 1982. "Do Parties Affect the Distribution of Incomes? The Case of Advanced Capitalist Democracies." In *The Impact of Parties,* edited by Francis G. Castles. Beverly Hills, Calif.: Sage Publications.

Vandell, Deborah Lowe, and Barbara Wolfe. 2000. *Child Care Quality: Does It Matter and Does It Need to Be Improved?* Special Report 78. Institute for Research on Poverty, University of Wisconsin, Madison. Available at: www.ssc.wisc.edu/irp/sr/sr78execsumm.pdf.

Van Oorschot, Wim. 2002. "Labor Market Participation in the Netherlands: Trends, Policies, and Outcomes." In *Europe's New State of Welfare: Unemployment, Employment Policies, and Citizenship,* edited by Jørgen Goul Andersen, Jochen Clasen, Wim van Oorschot, and Knut Halvorsen. Bristol, Eng.: Policy Press.

Visser, Jelle. 2002. "The First Part-Time Economy in the World: A Model To Be Followed?" *Journal of European Social Policy* 12(1, February): 23–42.

Visser, Jelle, and Anton Hemerijck. 1997. *"A Dutch Miracle": Job Growth, Welfare Reform, and Corporatism in the Netherlands.* Amsterdam: Amsterdam University Press.

Wallerstein, Michael. 1999. "Wage-setting Institutions and Pay Inequality in Advanced Industrial Societies." *American Journal of Political Science* 43(3): 649–80.

Wasow, Bernard. 2000. "Expanding the Earned Income Tax Credit for Working Families." Idea Brief 11. New York: The Century Foundation. Available at: www.tcf.org.

Welch, Finis. 1999. "In Defense of Inequality." *American Economic Review (Papers and Proceedings)* 89(2): 1–17.

Wessel, David, and Daniel Benjamin. 1994. "Looking for Work: In Employment Policy, America and Europe Make a Sharp Contrast." *Wall Street Journal,* March 14, A1, A6.

Western, Bruce. 1997. *Between Class and Market: Postwar Unionization in the Capitalist Democracies.* Princeton, N.J.: Princeton University Press.

Western, Bruce, and Kieren Healy. 1999. "Explaining the OECD Wage Slowdown: Recession or Labor Decline?" *European Sociological Review* 15: 233–49.

Wilensky, Harold L. 2002. *Rich Democracies.* Berkeley: University of California Press.

Wilson, William Julius. 1996. *When Work Disappears.* New York: Vintage.

Wolfe, Barbara, and Scott Scrivner. 2003. "Providing Universal Preschool for Four-Year-Olds." In *One Percent for the Kids,* edited by Isabel V. Sawhill. Washington, D.C.: Brookings Institution.

Wolff, Edward N. 2002. *Top Heavy: A Study of the Increasing Inequality of Wealth in America and What Can Be Done About It*. New York: New Press. (Orig. pub. in 1995.)

Wright, Erik Olin, and Rachel Dwyer. 2003. "The Patterns of Job Expansions in the USA: A Comparison of the 1960s and 1990s." *Socioeconomic Review* 1(3, September): 289–325.

Wright, Gavin. 1987. "The Economic Revolution in the American South." *Journal of Economic Perspectives* 1(1, Summer): 161–78.

Zuberi, Dan. 2001. "Transfers Matter Most." Working paper 271. Luxembourg Income Study (May). Available at: www.lisproject.org/publications.htm.

$=$ Index $=$

Boldface numbers refer to figures and tables.